Rudolf Dick

JAPANESE BLACKSMITHING

Traditional Forging Methods for Tools, Knives, and Swords

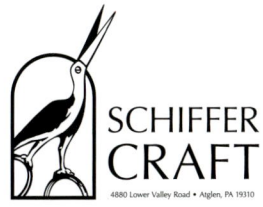

SCHIFFER
CRAFT

4880 Lower Valley Road • Atglen, PA 19310

Other Schiffer Books on Related Subjects:
Japanese Knife Sharpening: With Traditional Waterstones, Rudolf Dick, ISBN 978-0-7643-4680-4

Blacksmithing Techniques: The Basics Explained Step by Step, Complete with 10 Projects, José Antonio Ares, ISBN 978-0-7643-4935-5

From Fire to Form: Sculpture from the Modern Blacksmith and Metalsmith, Mathew S. Clarke, ISBN 978-0-7643-3247-0

Translated from the German by David Johnston. Originally published as *Japanische Schmiedekunst*, © 2018, Wieland Verlag GmbH, Bad Aibling

Library of Congress Control Number: 2024932190

Cover design by Ashley Millhouse
Type set in Caecilia LT Std/Melior LT Std

ISBN: 978-0-7643-6851-6
978-1-5073-0417-4 (Epub)
Printed in India

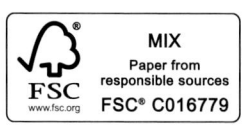

MIX
Paper from
responsible sources
FSC® C016779
FSC
www.fsc.org

Published by Schiffer Publishing, Ltd.
4880 Lower Valley Road
Atglen, PA 19310
Phone: (610) 593-1777; Fax: (610) 593-2002
Email: info@schifferbooks.com
Web: www.schifferbooks.com

For our complete selection of fine books on this and related subjects, please visit our website at www.schifferbooks.com. You may also write for a free catalog.

Schiffer Publishing's titles are available at special discounts for bulk purchases for sales promotions or premiums. Special editions, including personalized covers, corporate imprints, and excerpts, can be created in large quantities for special needs. For more information, contact the publisher.

I dedicate this book to my wife,
Angelika, who shares my love of Japan
and its wonderful people.

Notes on spelling:

Since the translation from Japanese is possible only by a transcription of the original expressions, there may be inconsistencies in the spelling of names and terms, depending on the source.

CONTENTS

ABOUT THE AUTHOR

Dr. Ing. Rudolf Dick, born in 1956, studied mechanical engineering at the Technical University of Munich and received his doctorate in forming technology. As long-standing managing director of Dick GmbH, Fine Tools, he always had a great interest in the creative interaction of tools, people, and materials. The foundation for this was probably laid by his childhood in the workshop of his father, who provided tools and materials for musical instrument making. The spark was finally ignited during an internship in the tool shop of the former Deggendorf shipyard, where forging and sharpening were carried out under the guidance of a master craftsman of the "old school."

After working for several years in technical management consulting, in the early 1990's he joined his parents' company, which he and his brother Heinrich together developed into one of the world's leading suppliers of high-quality hand tools. Primarily through his contact with the toolsmiths and craftsmen of Japan, he came to the awareness that a cutting tool could be more than just a mechanical device that obeys function. Rudolf Dick is convinced that chisels, planes, carving chisels, and knives that are individually made and used have a soul. This is the fourth book in which the author has dedicated himself to the subject of "Handwork and Tools" since his retirement from active business life and the company in 2007.

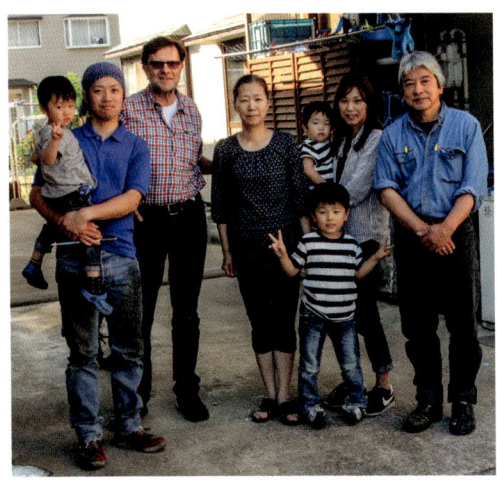

The author surrounded by the Hinoura "Blacksmith family."

ACKNOWLEDGMENTS

The contents of this book are based on the practical experiences of a large number of Japanese smiths, who opened their workshops to me and willingly shared with me the knowledge they had acquired over decades. In this connection, my special thanks are due to Makato Aida, Sadatoshi and Sadanobu Gassan, Haruo Hasegawa, Tsukasa and Mutsumi Hinoura, Shigeyoshi Iwasaki, Tokifusa and Yoshihide Iizuka, Tetsuo Kuribayahi, Hisao and Hirofumi Mizuno, Ryouchi Mizuochi, Mitsuo Nagao, Katsayuki Sekiyama, Motoyuki Tamagawa, Hiroyuki Tanaka, Akio and Michio Tasai, Osamu Tomita, Koichi Tsurumaki, and Dr. Koshi and Noboru Yamamura. In addition to the featured businesses, numerous other craftsmen and tooling experts not mentioned here have contributed to this knowledge pool. I thank them all from the bottom of my heart for their hospitality and generosity.

The workshop visits would not have been possible without the logistical, linguistic, and technical support provided by the companies Kakuri Co., represented by Mutsuhiro and Katsuhiro Kato, and Gyokucho Co., represented by Akihiro Tomosada and Hiroshi Onishi. I owe them a great debt of gratitude for paying so much attention to my project and opening doors for me. Not only linguistic but also cultural bridges were built by Shinako Tomosada and Yuka Komatsu from the Gyokucho Co., and Shoko Fujita as translator, making an important contribution to the success of this work.

Dr. Rudolf Dick

FOREWORD

It was not until a millennium later than in the Western world that the art of extracting and processing iron reached Japan via the Asian mainland. It is, therefore, all the more surprising that an advanced culture of the blacksmith's craft developed on the islands of the Japanese archipelago within just a few centuries that continues to amaze us to this day. It reached its peak in the Kamakura period (thirteenth century), when even the *Tenno Go-Toba*—according to Japanese mythology, a descendant of the sun goddess—helped forge samurai swords. He thus freed this craft from its profane status and elevated it to quasi-divine spheres.

No less amazing is that the art of blade forging, whether knives or other cutting tools, has remained at a very high level until the present day. While similar products in the Western world and China are manufactured almost exclusively on an industrial scale, in Japan this is still dominated by small, family-run craft businesses. They not only maintain the traditional methods of shaping and finishing steel but are also characterized by a high level of identification with their products. This is expressed not least by the fact that each individual piece is signed with the certificate of origin and often with the name of the smith who produced it.

The products, which are predominantly handmade, prove that technical effort is not always synonymous with quality. Rather, the workshops with the least mechanization often produce the finest devices. What is remarkable about the Japanese smiths, however, is not only their "primitive" manufacturing methods, but also their outmoded work ethic. Instead of maximizing profits, their focus is on the well-being of the customer. The goal is not to make the product as good as it needs to be, but as good as it can be.

For the technically interested, a look into the workshops and over the shoulders of the master craftsmen provides technical know-how. But beyond that, it opens up access to a sometimes strange but always fascinating cultural sphere.

How did this book come about? The fact that craftsmen opened the doors of their workshops to outsiders and revealed the knowledge preserved over generations is anything but a matter of course. But engineers are naturally curious people. And so it was for me in the 1980s, when our trading company started importing Japanese tools to Germany. It was a matter of concern to me, to understand not only its function but also the underlying manufacturing processes.

At the same time, getting to know the smiths and their techniques also opened up to me the inner values of the tools. Only through this understanding was it possible to explain to customers the qualitative differences between handmade and industrially produced forged products and the associated price differences. During my regular visits over more than twenty years, the demonstrations by the saw, knife, chisel, and plane blacksmiths have been the most exciting parts of the program. If one wishes to produce something or other, whether as a hobbyist or professional blacksmith, a technical documentation with tricks and tips will help shorten the process considerably by eliminating errors. It was only the free time that became available after I left my active economic career that enabled me to compile my many experiences with the Japanese forging craft into a book. May it go beyond the technical transfer of knowledge to the understanding of a culture of craftsmanship that is, I hope, not dying out.

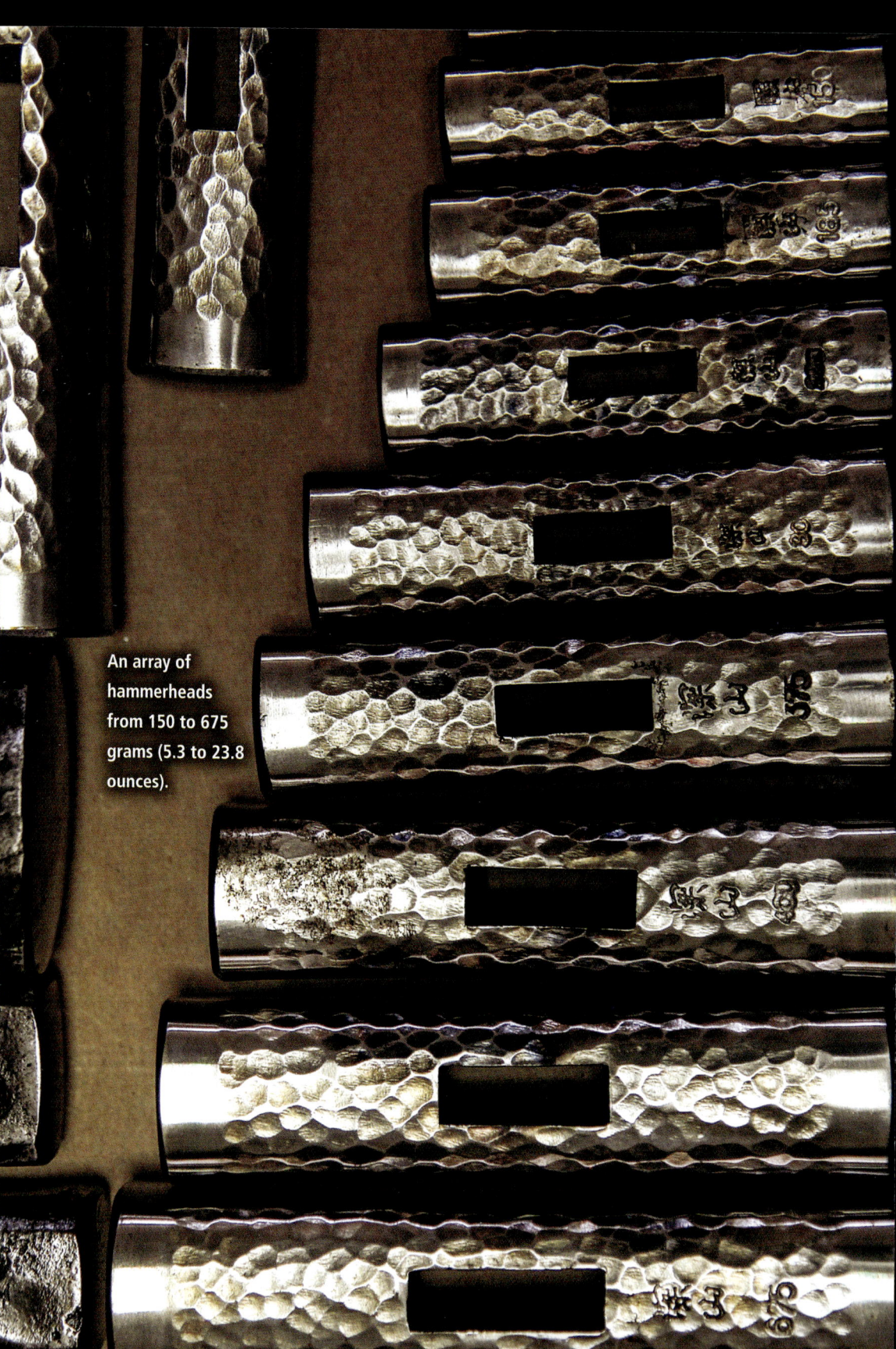

An array of hammerheads from 150 to 675 grams (5.3 to 23.8 ounces).

The Hammer (Genno)

What distinguishes a good hammer? Essentially two things: it must be well balanced and must not bounce. Nothing is more tiring than the energy thrown back into the wrist with every blow.

Traditionally, the iron hammer, probably the most widely used tool of all, has an even greater place in Japan than in the Western world. For there it's also very often used in carpentry, joinery, and sculpture, for example, to drive chisels. The blacksmiths who specialized in the production of hammers were therefore widespread throughout the country.

Today, there are only a handful of them left in the whole of Japan. Cheap imports and mass-produced industrial products, though they differ little externally, are vastly different from the authentic Japanese genno in their inner qualities and have rendered the profession almost extinct. One of the few companies that is still active and specializes in the production of hammerheads is the Aisho company located near Miki. Just a generation ago, thirteen blacksmiths worked there, but today owner Makato Aida, born in 1944, works alone.

The handheld hammer traditionally favored by Japanese blacksmiths has an asymmetric head with a long "nose." The neck and striking face component is usually round and slightly spherical, and its cross-section area is less than that of the rest of the head. This improves the impact effect. The neck and striking face are hardened to a depth of only a few millimeters, so that the rest of the hammer head acts as a damping mass, which suppresses bounce. The relatively long handle also contributes to the hammer's effectiveness.

The Japanese universal hammer is characterized by its long handle and the slender, symmetrical shape of its head.

The Japanese forging hammer
(kozuchi).

The two striking faces are shaped differently: the flat striking face is usually used for hammering, while the crowned one is used mainly for driving nails flush without damaging the surface of the wood.

All hammerheads have a soft core to minimize the rebound effect, and only the necks are hardened. This can be achieved by using a laminate construction, in which steel is wrapped around an iron core; a simpler version is achieved by selective tempering of carbon steel. The latter method is described below.

In order to make a living from hammer forging, maximum efficiency in production is a prerequisite. Makato Aida's workplace demonstrates this in impressive fashion. The entire forging process, including formation of the handle hole (usually called the eye), is done by pneumatic hammer, the forging heated just once, with cycle times of just three to five minutes per hammerhead. No forming die is used in the process. Only for the purpose of forming the handle hole are the anvil saddles repeatedly changed.

HEAD GEOMETRY

A *genno* has one crowned face and one flat face.

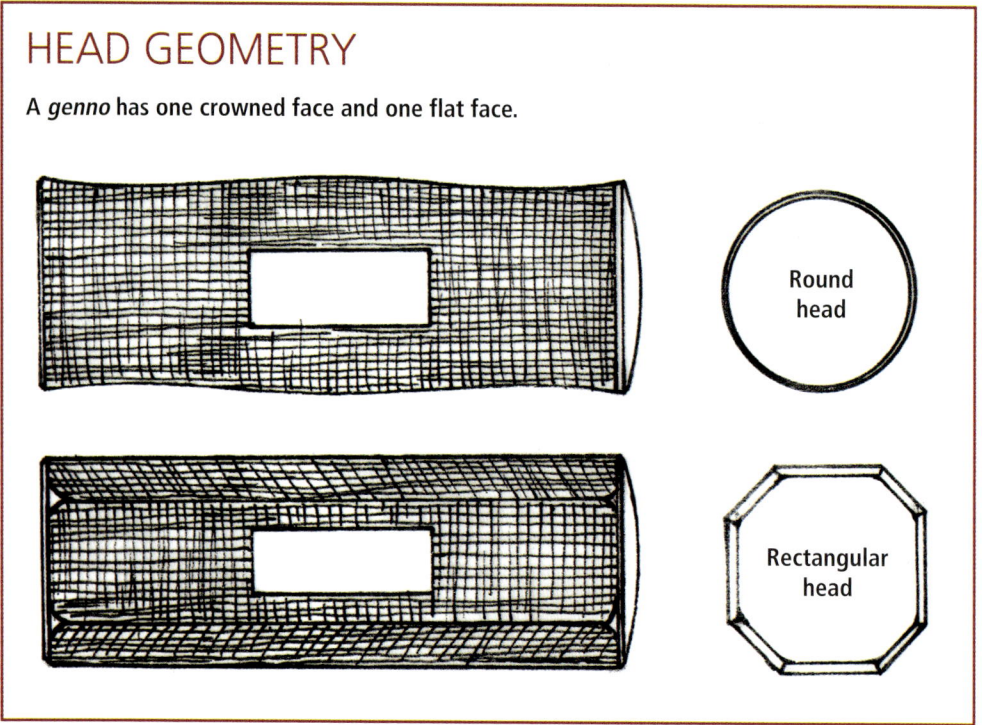

Round head

Rectangular head

Makato also starts from round material for forging rectangular-head hammers, in this case Japanese SK 7 carbon steel (C 0.7%, Mn 0.3%). The rounds, cut to length according to the nominal head weight plus burn-off and grinding loss, are heated in a gas furnace to yellow heat, about 1,000°C (1,832°F). First, with the forging in a vertical position, the end faces are compressed with light blows to achieve a dense microstructure on the head faces. Then the side faces are shaped by means of strong setting strokes, creating a roughly square cross-section with rounded edges. In the next step, the edges are flattened into chamfers about 5 mm (0.2 in.) in width.

Then follows the most demanding step, formation of the handle hole. The hole is first prepunched with a flat slotted chisel. For placement, the blanks are marked with cold-hammered notches in the center of both sides. After inserting a hole saddle, the conical chisel is driven in until it breaks through. For the subsequent accurate enlargement of the hole, three increasingly large arbor chisels and matching hole saddles are used in succession.

The bits are clamped in a holding tool consisting of two steel slats, called tagane. By drilling from both sides, a slightly tapered hole is created in the center, which ensures a reliable stem. Before each start-up, the enlargement tools are briefly cooled in water and lubricated with graphite. Prior to the final enlargement to nominal size, the head is also briefly cooled in water to achieve an exact nominal size.

The lateral bulge that results from the enlargement process can either be left in place or forged back to such an extent that the hammer cheeks are flat again. This means that the resulting side faces of the hammer can also be used for light, flat tapping tasks. During the lateral bulging, it is essential to keep the fitting mandrel in the hole to prevent deformation. Calibrated and precisely aligned rectangular holes made using this free-form technique are an unmistakable sign of mastery.

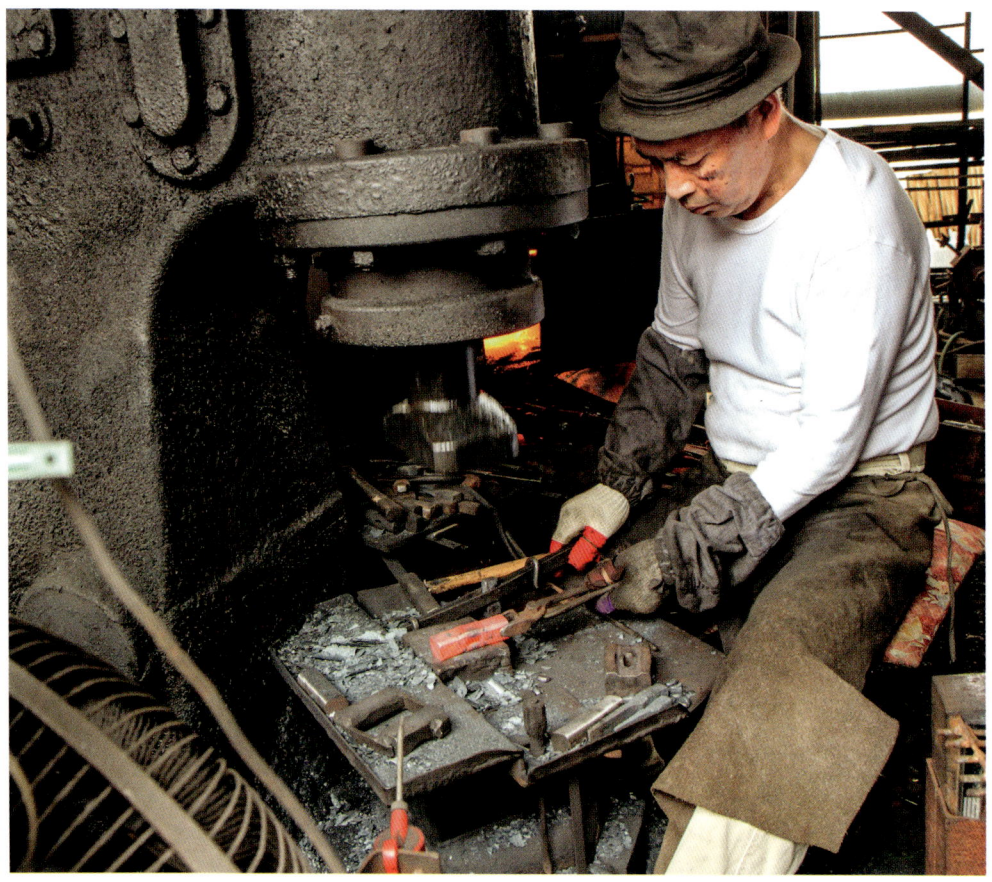

Thanks to more than fifty years of professional experience, Makato Aida is able to forge a *genno* head free-form (without shaping dies) on the air hammer in three to five minutes.

The head, which has cooled below the recrystallization temperature, is then forged again on the face side, whereby the crowned shape of the face can already be predefined by slight inclination. After a final dimensional check, the forging process is completed.

The effort required for subsequent grinding depends on the model. Some types are ground blank over the entire surface, while others are left with the forged skin and only the head faces are ground.

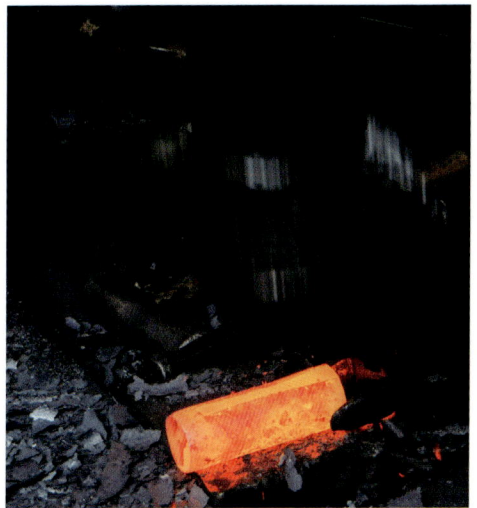

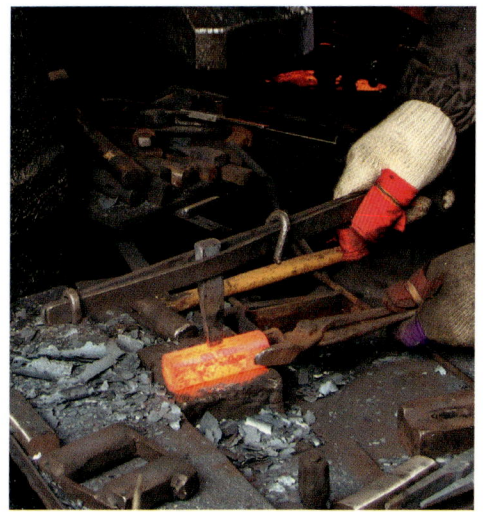

Round steel is also used as the starting material for a rectangular hammerhead. It's subsequently reshaped into a square cross section with chamfered edges.

Punching the handle hole is the decisive operation. The head is pierced from both sides without predrilling, first with a slotted chisel and then with a suitable rectangular tool. The chisels are held in a special quick-clamping tool *(tagane)*.

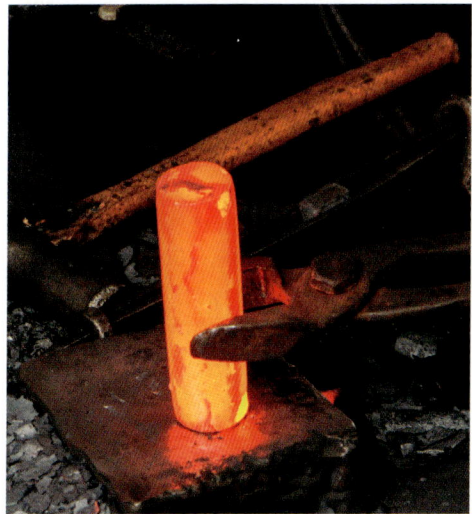

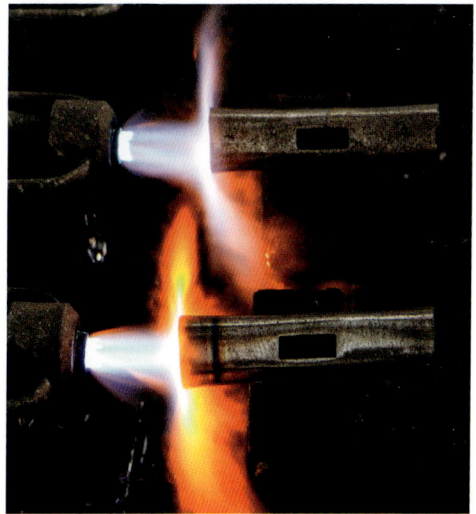

The head faces must also be forged to achieve a fine microstructure.

For hardening, the head faces are heated to 850°C (1,562°F) in the gas flame with a semi-automatic device.

For hardening, Aida-san (san is the Japanese honorific suffix, similar to Mr. in English) has built a semi-automatic device in which the faces of the hammer-heads are heated to 850°C (1,562°F) in the gas flame. As soon as the bright red annealing color has reached a depth of about 10 mm (0.4 in.), the workpiece is quenched with a jet of water sprayed directly onto the face. The quenching process is designed in such a way that the residual heat from the core causes a tempering effect during subsequent storage in the sand bed.

With this trick, an experienced blacksmith can gain two advantages: on the one hand, there is no need to reheat to tempering temperature, and on the other hand, the desired hardness gradient is automatically set. A hardness value of 55 HRC (Rockwell C-scale hardness value) on the faces, dropping to 45 HRC at a depth of 10 mm (0.4 in.), is optimal for a universal hammer so that it pulls well and does not bounce.

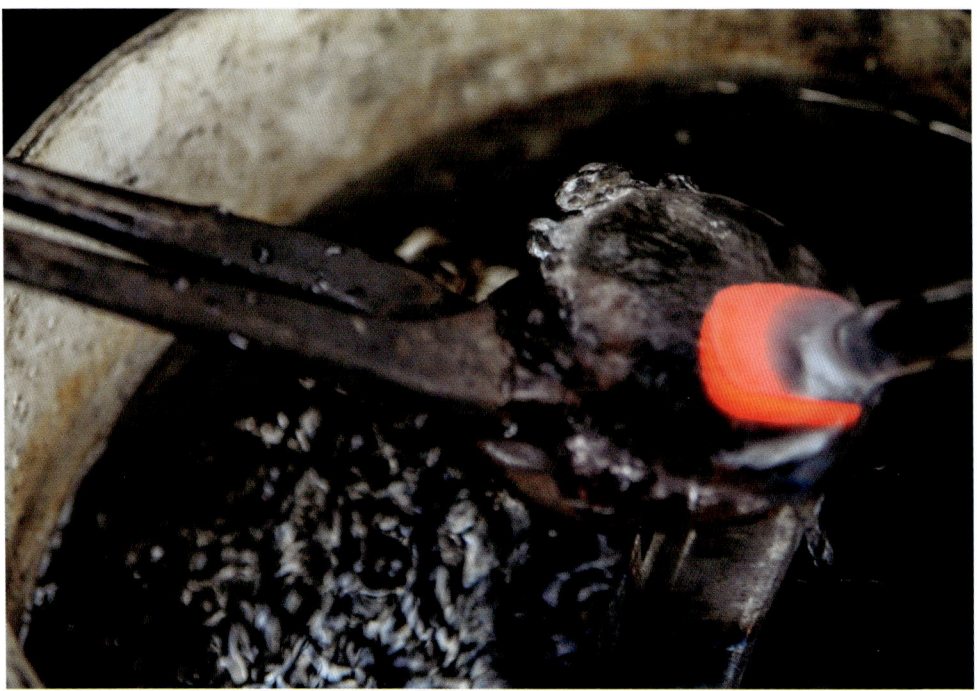

The glowing faces are quenched only briefly under running water. Due to the heat emanating from the core, an experienced blacksmith can thus save himself from reheating for hardening.

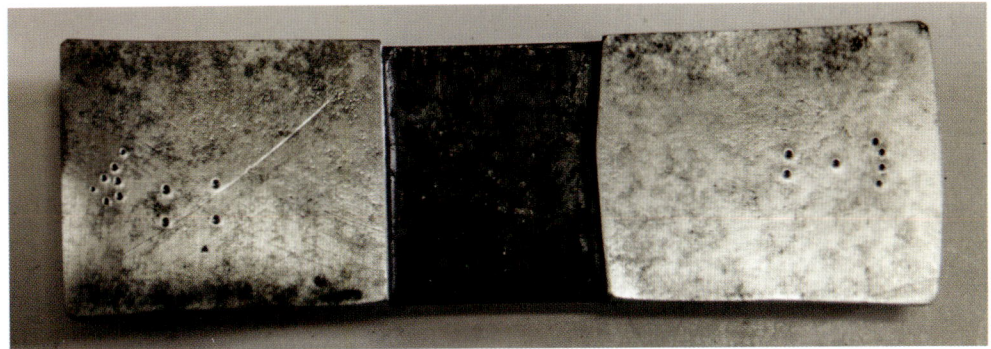

Hardness values of HRC 55 on the head faces, decreasing inward to HRC 45, are optimal. The falling hardness gradient is indicated by the increasing size of the hardness test points on this hammerhead, which has been cut open lengthwise.

Other possible work steps are mainly of an optical nature. For example, a beautiful decoration can be punched into the head or mythological symbols engraved in it to protect the owner from evil spirits.

By the way, making and installing the handle is not the task of the blacksmith. In Japan, it is traditionally left to a craftsman who specializes in this or the user himself. Master Aida's recommendation: use fine-grained white oak and make the handle as long as your forearm.

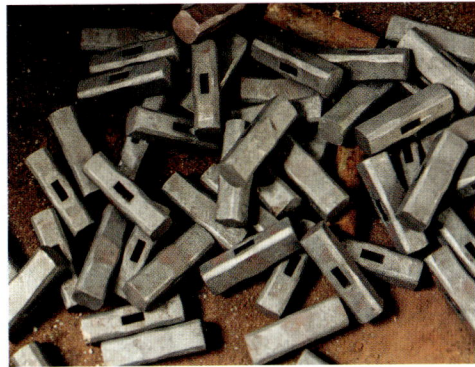

The picture shows approximately one day's production of universal hammerheads.

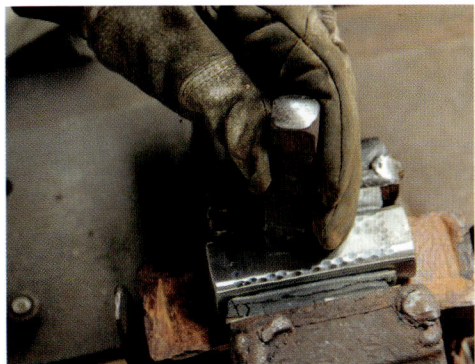

If desired, the heads can be given a decorative finish with a hallmarking iron.

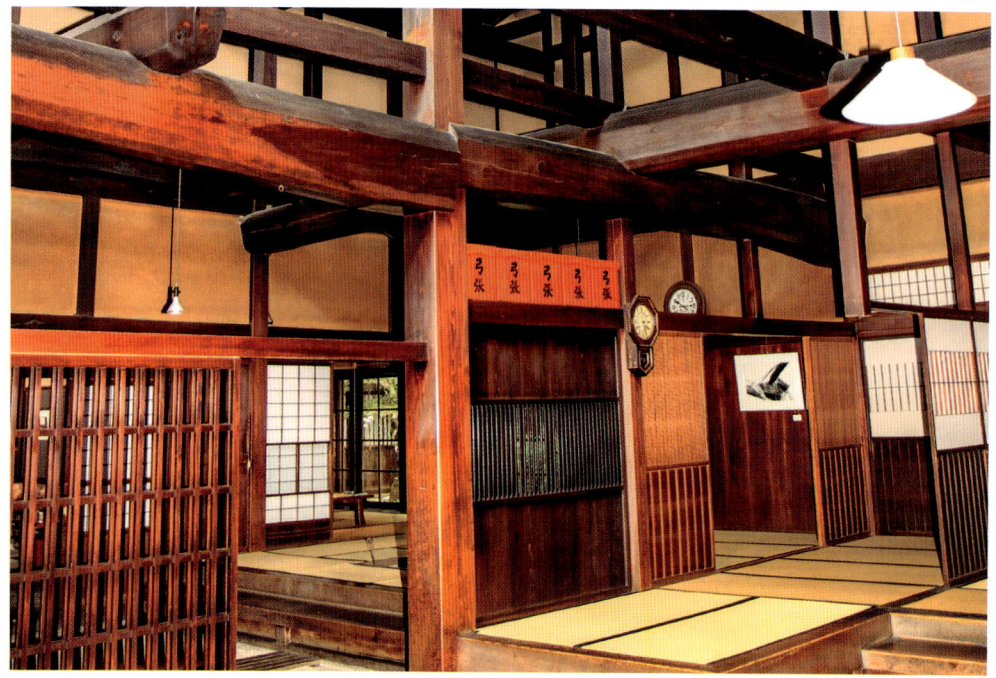

Breathtaking wooden constructions demand excellent tools: the Yoshijima House in Takayama.

The Chisel (*Nomi*)

Alongside the saw and the plane, the chisel *(nomi)* is one of the most important tools of the Japanese carpenter, the *daiku*. It is used to make the elaborate wooden structures that characterize traditional Japanese architecture. Compared to the European chisel, the nomi has some special features that are also reflected in the forging technique used to make the tool.

The nomi is driven with an iron hammer. Therefore, the body must not only be very solid but also suppress bounce. The two-layer construction, in which a hard cutting-edge steel is laminated with a soft and thus dampening iron body, is very conducive to this. It also enables a high degree of hardness and thus long cutting-edge life. The precision with which the interlocking wood joints are made must naturally also be reflected in the tool. From his chisels, the dai-ku expects dimensional accuracy, freedom from distortion, and an ergonomic design with a pleasant balance.

Only a few workshops in Japan still produce nomi of this quality in an artisanal manner. One of these is Akio Tasai's forge, located in the tool metropolis of Sanjo in Niigata Prefecture. Alongside the senior boss, who was born in 1940, his son Michio is now mainly responsible for production. He is no less ambi-tious than his widely respected father and has even acquired a license to forge swords *(katana)*. He has thus ascended to the royal class of the smith's craft.

Using the example of a carpenter's chisel, a *tataki nomi* with a width of 30 mm (1.18 in.), he demonstrates the typical production steps. With a blade length of 90 mm (3.5 in.), this type of chisel is longer than common carpenter's chisels *(oire nomi)* and, with its stronger neck, is designed in particular for wooden joints on beams. Like most Japanese cutting tools, the *tataki nomi* has a two-layer design.

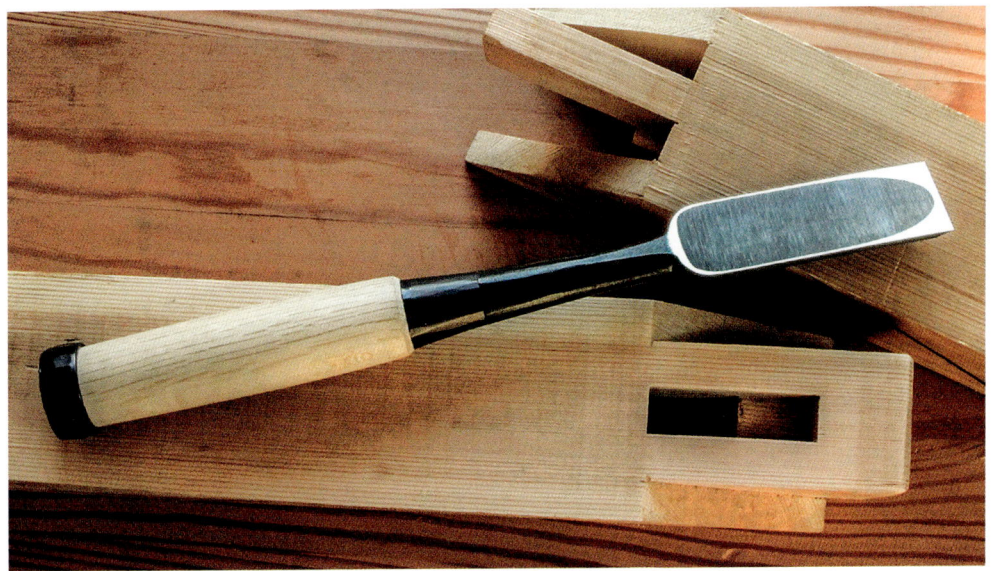

Indispensable for beam joints: the *tataki nomi* from Tasai.

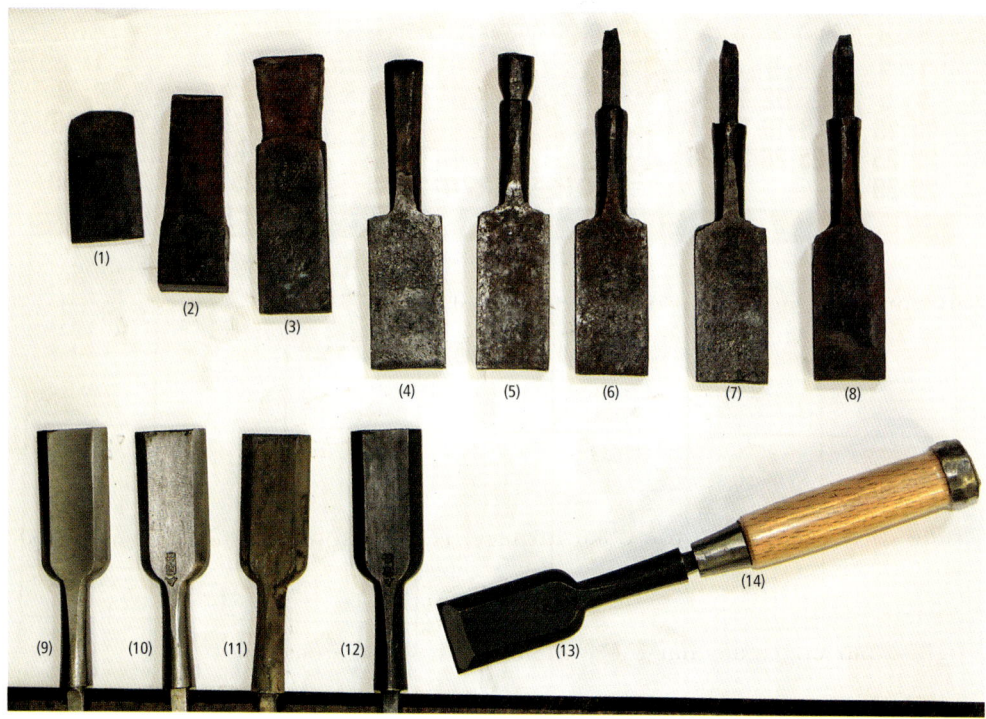

Steps in production of the Japanese chisel:

(1) Forging and beveling jacket steel to desired thickness.

(2) Dimension base body from soft iron.

(3) Forge-welding of cutting-edge steel and base body.

(4) Shaping the neck.

(5) Recess for forming the tang.

(6) Shaping the tang.

(7) Forming the crown.

(8) Fine forging and recrystallization.

(9) Rough grinding.

(10) Finishing touches and signature.

(11) Coating with clay slurry.

(12) Hardening and tempering.

(13) Planing and grinding the bevel.

(14) Handle installation.

Michio uses Blue Paper Steel No. 2 (C 1.1%, Mn 0.25%, W 1.25%) produced by Hitachi as the cutting-edge steel *(kawagane)*. To eliminate the longitudinal alignment of the microstructure produced by rolling, the 5 mm thick (0.2 in.) starting material is first forged through on the spring hammer at about 850°C (1,562°F). The steel is then cut to the desired thickness. The side and rear edges are chamfered—a process Michio calls *kaisaki*.

Non-hardening iron *(shigane)* with 0.04% carbon content is used for the *nomi* body. The bar is forged to a cross section of 20 × 12 mm (0.8 × 0.5 in.). Since the cut steel is also partially drawn over the side edges, the plate prepared for lamination should be about 10 mm (0.4 in.) wider than the base material, here 30 × 56 × 4 mm (1.18 × 2.2 × 0.14 in.).

Father Akio makes the welding flux powder *(hōsan)* himself according to a traditional recipe. The mixture, details of which are kept secret, consists of borax, iron powder, and scale. For this purpose, the ingredients are crushed and mixed in a boat-shaped iron pan with a grinding disk.

For the weld, a generous amount of flux powder is sprinkled on the glowing yellow rod, the plate is placed precisely centered, and the composite is then heated to white heat in the coke furnace. A light spray of star-shaped sparks signals the moment when Michio removes the package and, with light hammer blows, performs the weld. Then, in a second pass, the weld is made along the longitudinal edges so that the platelet encloses the base body in a U shape. The workpiece is now roughly dimensioned in length and width on the spring hammer.

Welding Flux Powder *(hōsan, tansetsu-zai)*

Welding powder has the function of a flux in the case of forge welding. On the one hand, it eliminates the oxide layer by its reduction effect, and on the other hand, it prevents re-oxidation by covering and thus enables a better bond between the two joining surfaces. While in this country borax is used almost exclusively, Japanese smiths usually use their own mixtures, which are often kept as trade secrets. According to the author's knowledge, they usually consist mainly of boron or boron compounds (borax or boric acid), with admixtures of 10% to 20% of finely ground iron granules and/or pulverized iron oxide (rust or scale). Japanese welding flux powder is also available as a ready mix.

TATAGI NOMI DESIGNATIONS

The blade is tapered by 0.5 mm (0.019 in.).

Hollow-ground surface (*ura*)   Shoulder   Neck   Ferrule   Handle   Head ferrule

29.5   29.0

Smooth surface (flat)

NOMI BLADE CROSS SECTION

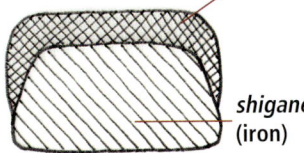

kawagane (cutting steel)

shigane (iron)

After forge-welding: The layer of *kawagane* is wrapped around the main body in a U shape.

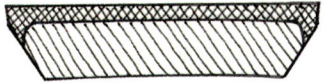

In completed condition: The plating should be of the same thickness across the entire width. The edges are beveled slightly (5°) in the upper area and more sharply (35°) in the lower.

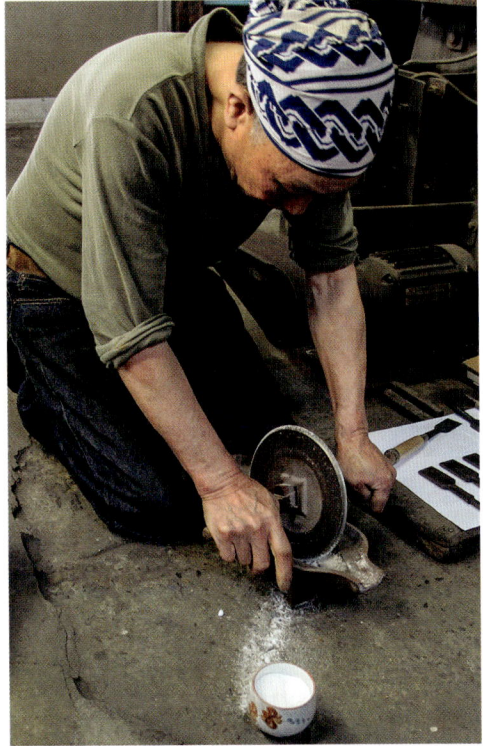

Flux welding powder of the right consistency is a key to success: Akio Tasai makes his own based on an old family recipe.

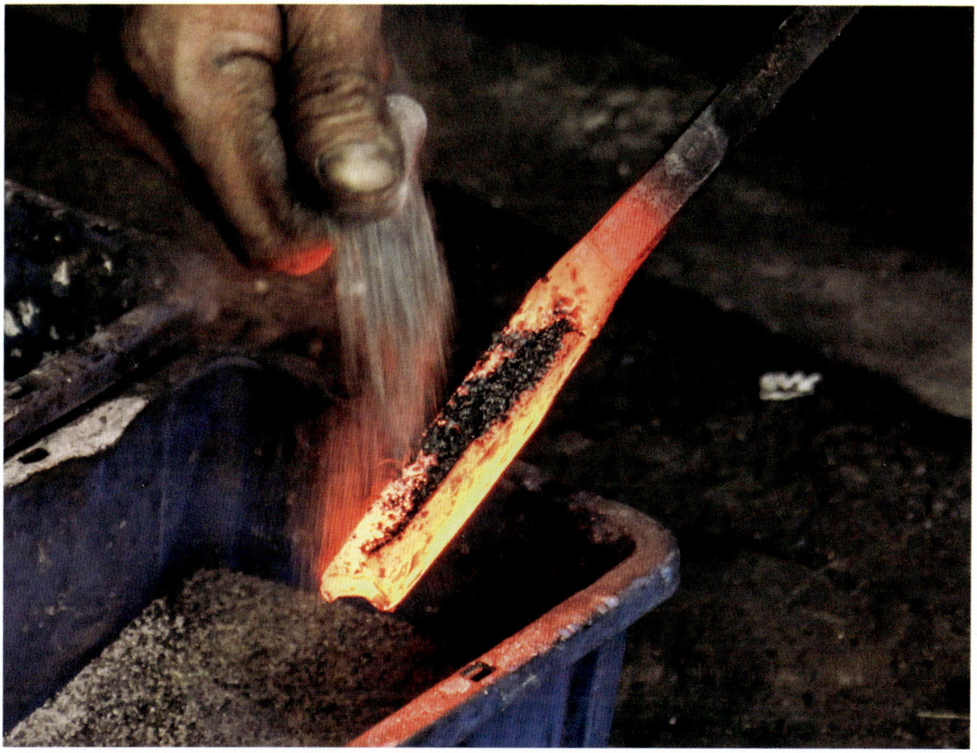

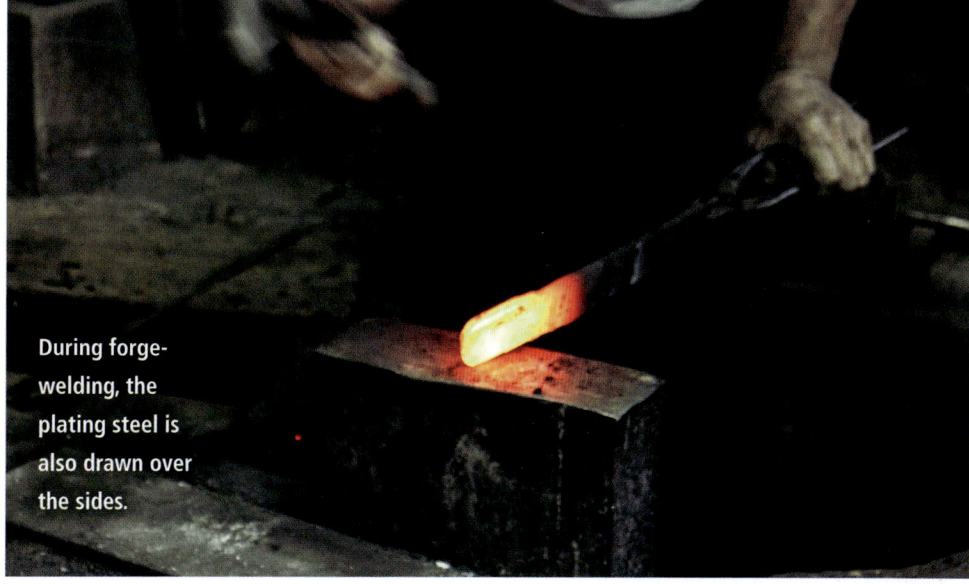

Plenty of flux welding powder is added prior to forge-welding.

During forge-welding, the plating steel is also drawn over the sides.

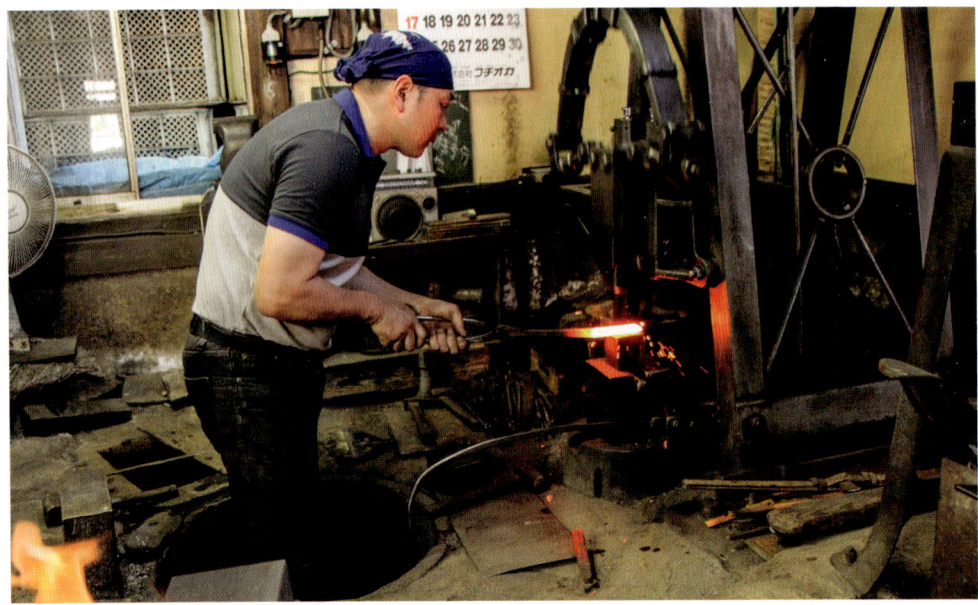

The rough shaping is done on the spring hammer. Contrary to tradition, Michio does not forge sitting down, but standing up in a trough that allows him to work at the correct height on the anvils, which are in fact designed for seated work.

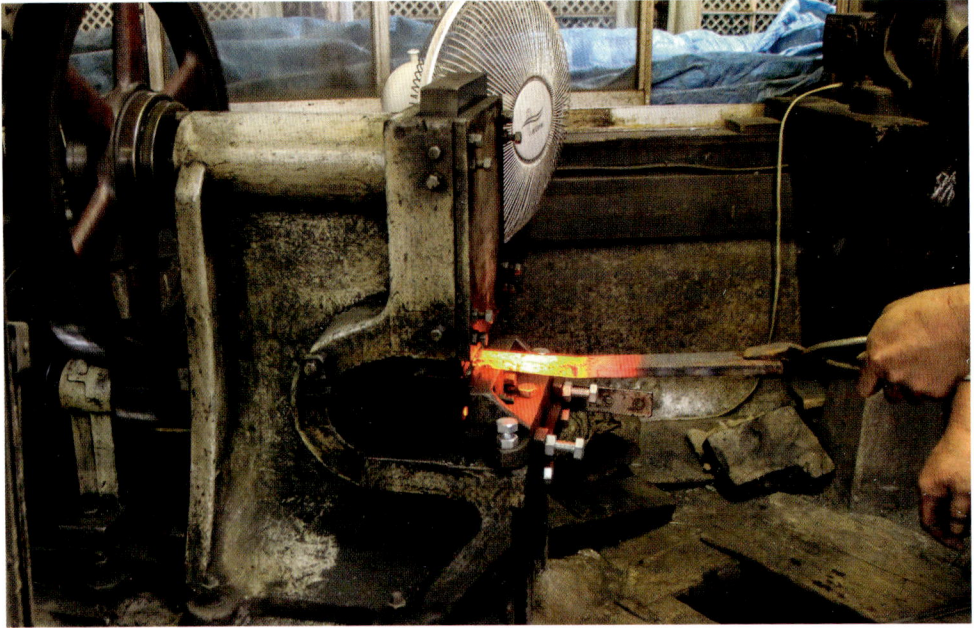

The metallurgically impure end is sheared off.

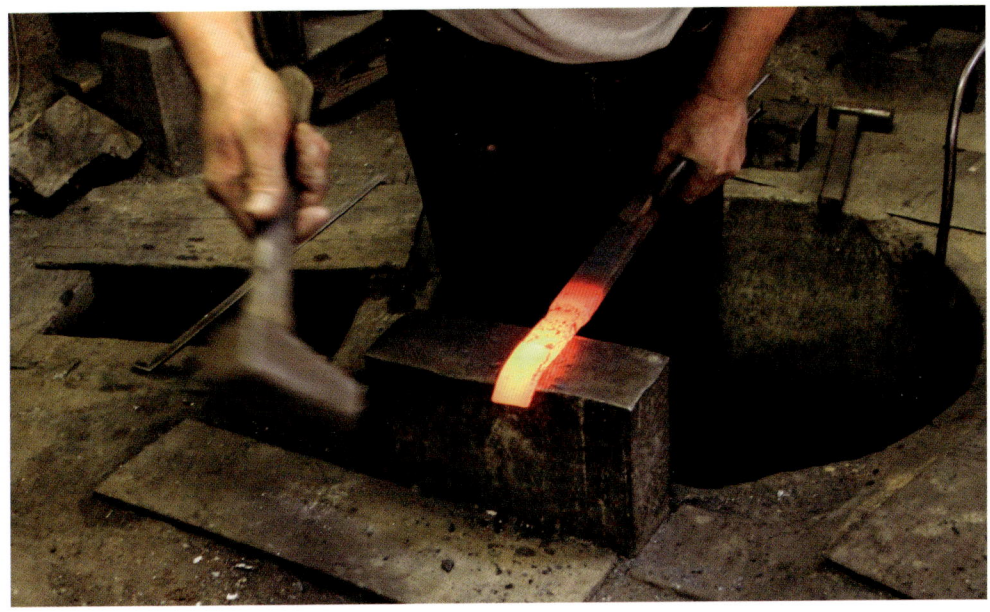

The blade is given a slight curvature to make it easier to grip during subsequent processing.

About 5 mm (0.2 in.) is now sheared off the front end to check the bond and produce a clean front edge. The workpiece is then cut to length from the bar about 5 cm (2 in.) behind the laminate. To make it easier to grip while shaping the neck, the blade is given a slight curvature. When shaping the neck, the smith must make sure that the plating overlaps slightly. This gives the blade greater stability.

Toward the rear, the neck is tapered on the spring hammer to a thickness of 18 mm (0.7 in.), using a simple die. The neck is angled slightly relative to the blade surface so that it does not collide with the workpiece during deep grooving. The shoulder for the tang is then notched with the hand hammer, and the tang is forged out square to a length of about 50 mm (2 in.) in the shape of a bar. The tapered cross section of the blade from 6 mm (0.2 in.) at the tip to 12 mm (0.4 in.) at the end of the blade as well as the beveled rear side are produced during fine forging.

In addition, the blade is given a slight upward curvature. This is intended to compensate for the distortion caused by the expansion of the plating layer (martensite formation) during hardening. The soft back of the blade in particular is worked in the temperature range from 600°C to 800°C (1,112°F to 1,472°F). In order to eliminate the microstructural inhomogeneities created during forging, the blade is subjected to a normalizing anneal at 820°C (1,508°F). The blade is then placed in a bed of rice straw ash to cool and rest for at least eight hours.

Dry grinding on the corundum wheel and processing with the file are limited to smoothing the back of the blade and setting the exact width. For functional reasons, the chisels have a slight undersize. The width at the cutting edge is 0.5 mm (0.02 in.) below the nominal dimension of 30 mm (1.2 in.), and it tapers by a further 0.5 mm (0.02 in.) toward the end of the blade. At this stage of production, the blade is stamped with the smith's signature on the back.

Before hardening, the blade is coated with a carbonaceous clay slurry *(tonoko)*. This is intended to prevent surface decarburization and improve wetting with the quenching water.

For hardening, Michio loads the forge with fine-grained pine charcoal (*matsu sumi*). In it, the blade is evenly heated to about 780°C (1,436°F) after the clay layer has dried and then quenched in the water basin. The water should be at room temperature and not fresh, but low in oxygen.

In order to remove the residual stresses and brittleness from the extremely hard martensite structure, the smith again briefly holds the blade over the embers. Michio judges the correct tempering temperature of 180°C (356°F) for setting the desired service hardness of about 63 HRC by bubbling off some sprayed-on water. After cooling, the blade is straightened by careful hammer blows on the anvil so that the mirror surface is completely flat.

Then the mirror surface is smoothed on the water-cooled cup wheel, and a cutting bevel of 30° is ground. The final sharpening is the responsibility of the user, according to Japanese tradition. Finally, the hollow or *ura* typical of Japanese chisels is ground into the top of the blade on a wheel. It should gradually

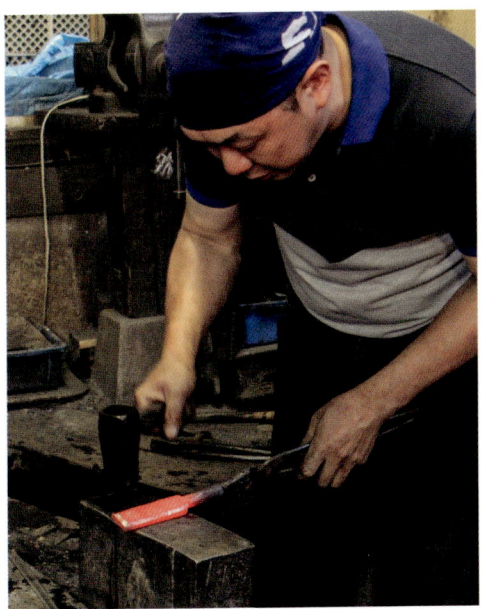

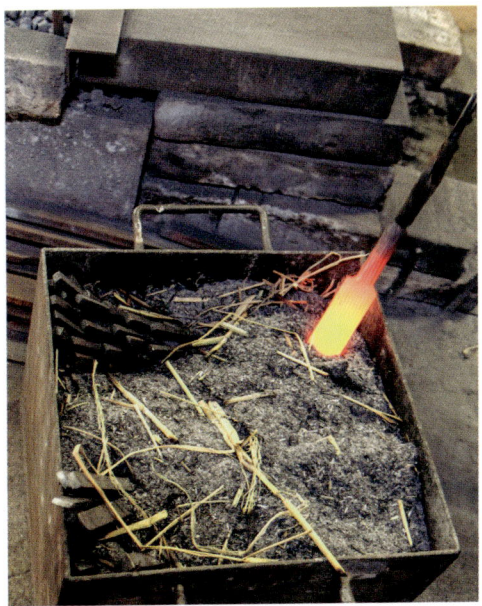

The workpiece is finely forged by hand at reduced temperature. During this process, the workpiece is thinned from the back to the front and beveled on the sides.

For slow cooling, the glowing chisel is stored in a bed of rice straw.

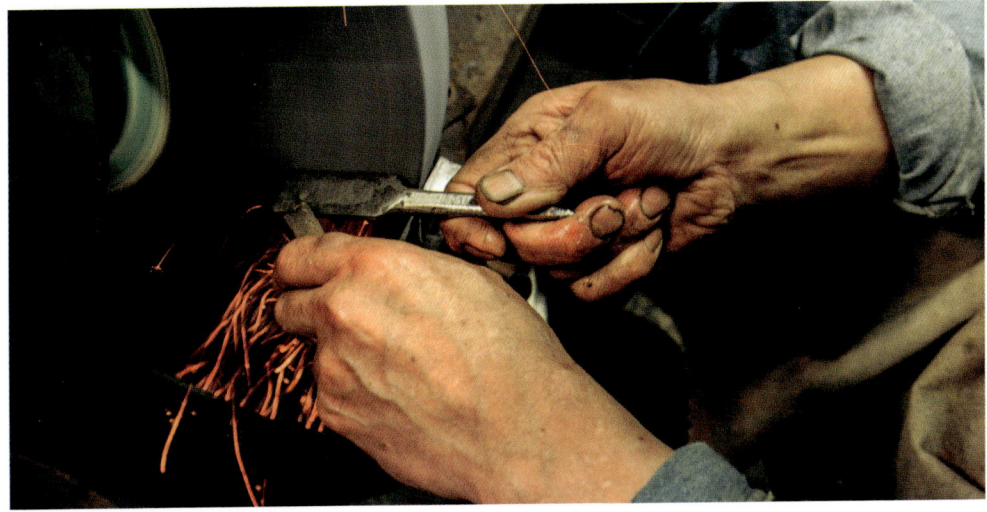

When grinding the side flanks, a taper of 0.5 mm (0.019 in.) over the blade length of 90 mm (3.54 in.) is produced. The edges are beveled.

deepen from the cutting edge to the back but should not be deeper than a maximum of 1.0 mm (0.04 in.) in total. It is important that it does not go all the way to the edge, but that a narrow, closed rim remains. Finally, the white oak

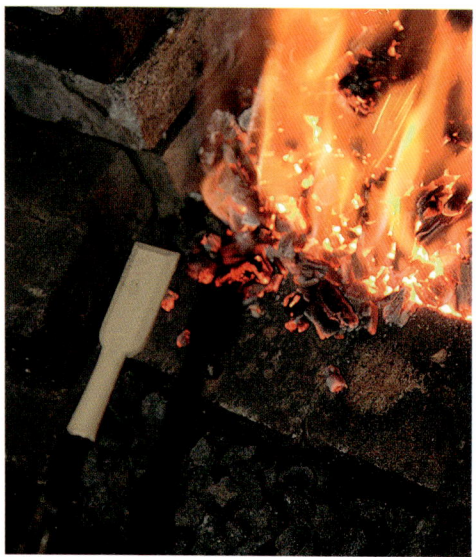

The iron, coated with *tonoko*, is brought to hardening temperature in the charcoal fire.

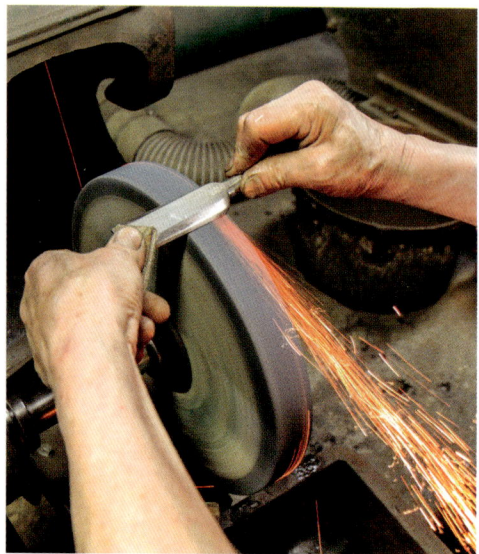

The blade is slightly hollow ground on the mirror side.

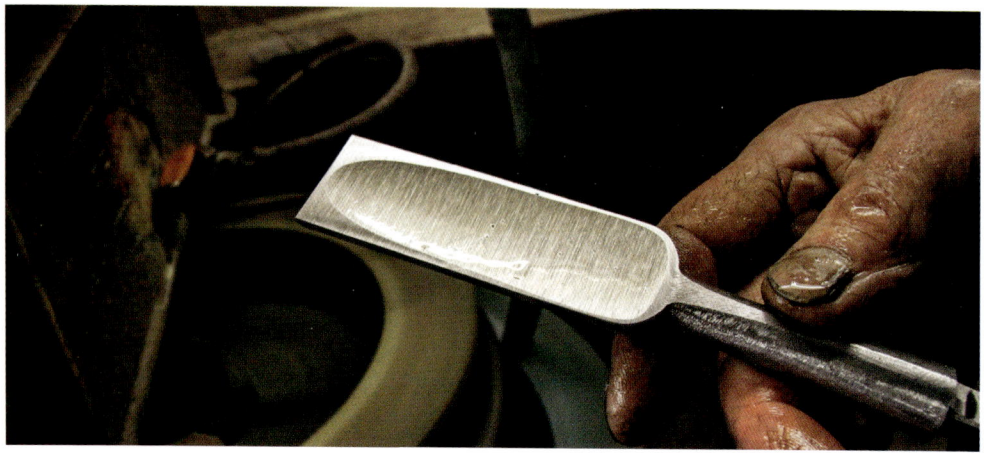

After hardening, the bevel and the mirror side are fine ground on the water-cooled cup wheel.

handle is mounted; it is protected from breakage at the transition to the neck by a conical ferrule.

Mokume Oire Nomi

In designing his finest nomi, Akio Tasai is inspired by the beauty of ancient cedar woods. There, with increasing age, the hard growth rings emerge in relief, retelling the story of the tree in question. To form the body of his nomi, the master mixes hardenable Yasuki steel with old, nonhardening iron. Through folding, twisting, and notching, combined with countless forge welds, he gives this material a vivid pattern that resembles the grain of a cut tree trunk. The term *mokume* (= wood grain) expresses this. The fact that the hard layers stand out in relief on the finished tool makes this nomi not only a visual but also a haptic experience. Technically, this effect is probably due to the fact that the structure of the hardenable steel expands more than that of the nonhardening iron when the workpiece is hardened. The structure is further emphasized by fine burnishing and highlighting of the hard layers by brushing and polishing. To ensure that function does not take a back seat to beauty, the body is forge-welded with a cutting layer of the finest blue-paper no. 2 steel and fitted with a handle of fine sandalwood, topped with a hand-forged head ferrule.

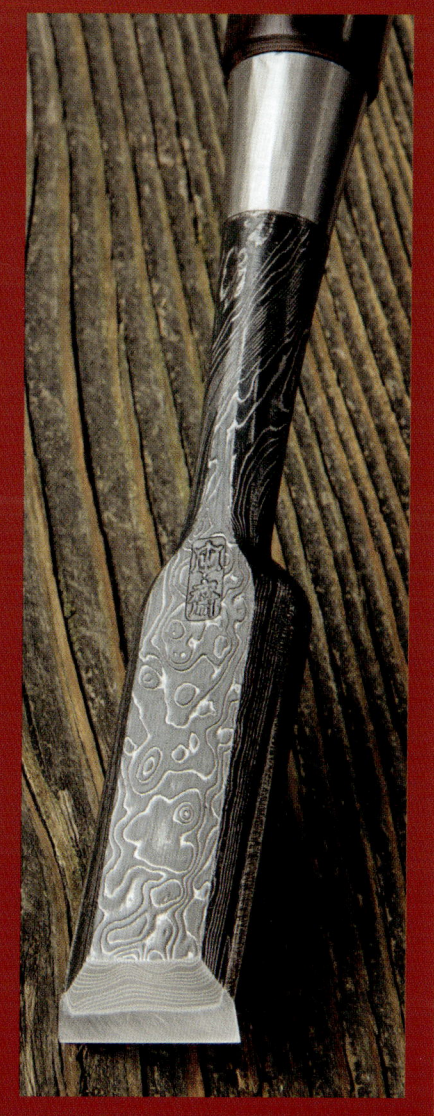

Modeled after nature:
mokume nomi by Akio Tasai.

Bearded Axe and Hatchet (Masakari and Ono)

In a culture that traditionally relied almost exclusively on wood as a building material, the axe was naturally an indispensable tool. Whether for felling trees, hewing logs, or making joints, depending on the use and the region, there were countless variants differing in size, cutting geometry, and shape. In modern times, these tools have been largely replaced by the chainsaw and other machines; consequently, the number of axe smiths in Japan has also declined sharply.

One of the few remaining specialized businesses is the Mizuno brothers' forge located near Sanjo. The company was founded 1937 by the father of its current owners, Isao and Hirofumi Mizuno. The two brothers literally grew up with the blacksmith's hammer. They began playing with fire and iron in their parents' workshop at the tender age of three. Together with around half a dozen employees, they now produce not only a standard range but also various special models typical of the region. The following drawings show some examples of the company's wide range of products.

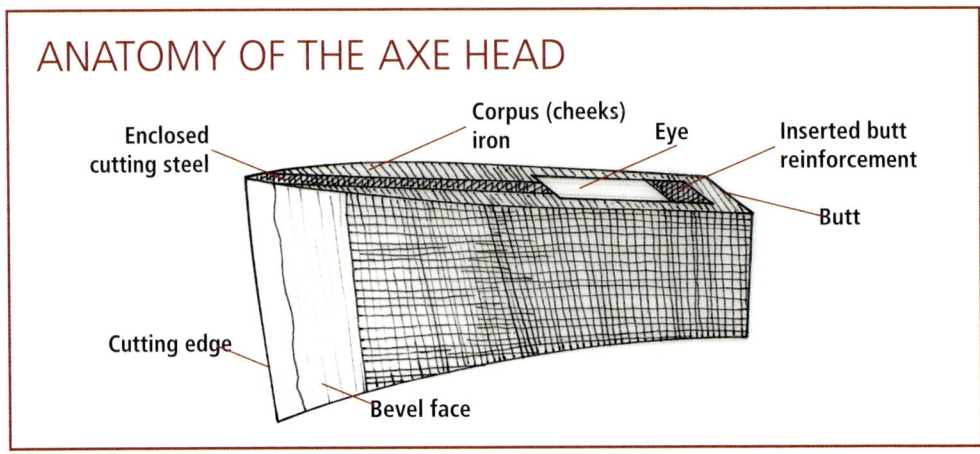

ANATOMY OF THE AXE HEAD

Enclosed cutting steel

Corpus (cheeks) iron

Eye

Inserted butt reinforcement

Butt

Cutting edge

Bevel face

MASAKARI

Axes with prominent beards *(masakari)* **from various regions of Japan.**

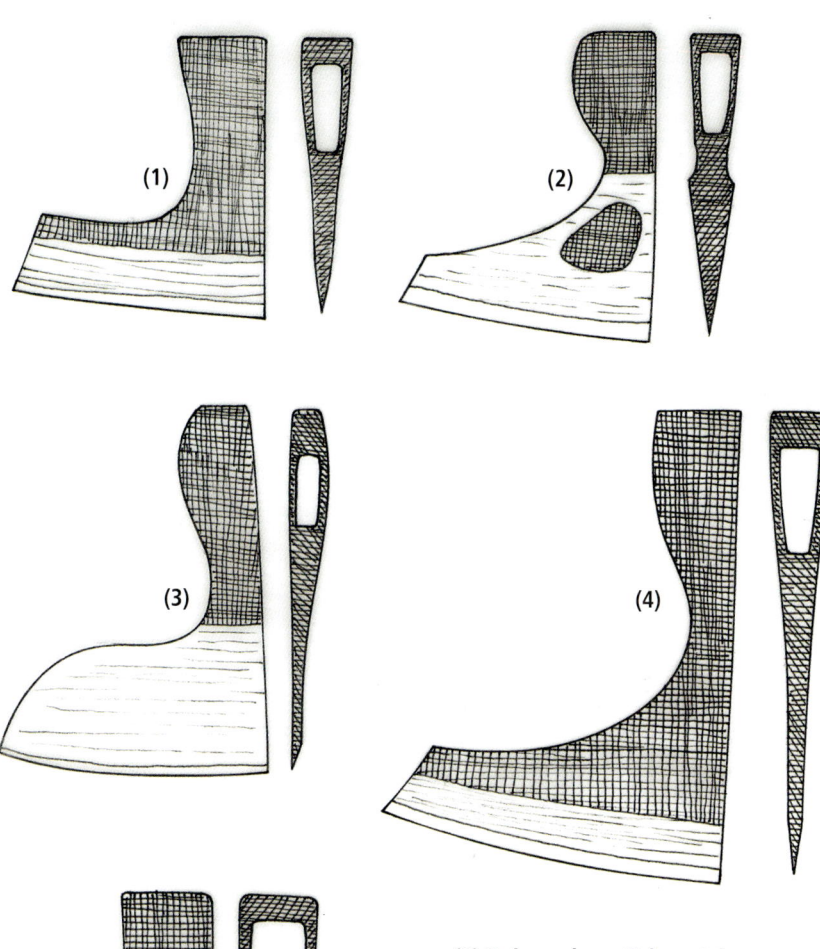

(1) Universal axe, Tokyo style.
(2) Hewing axe in the Chikuzen (old name for the Fukuoka Prefecture on Kyushu) style.
(3) Large carpenter's axe in the Tosa (old name for the Kouchi Prefecture on Shikoku) style. Single bevel.
(4) Large broadaxe in the Umaoi (Yubari region on Hokkaido) style.
(5) Splitting axe in the Chiba style.

FELLING AXES

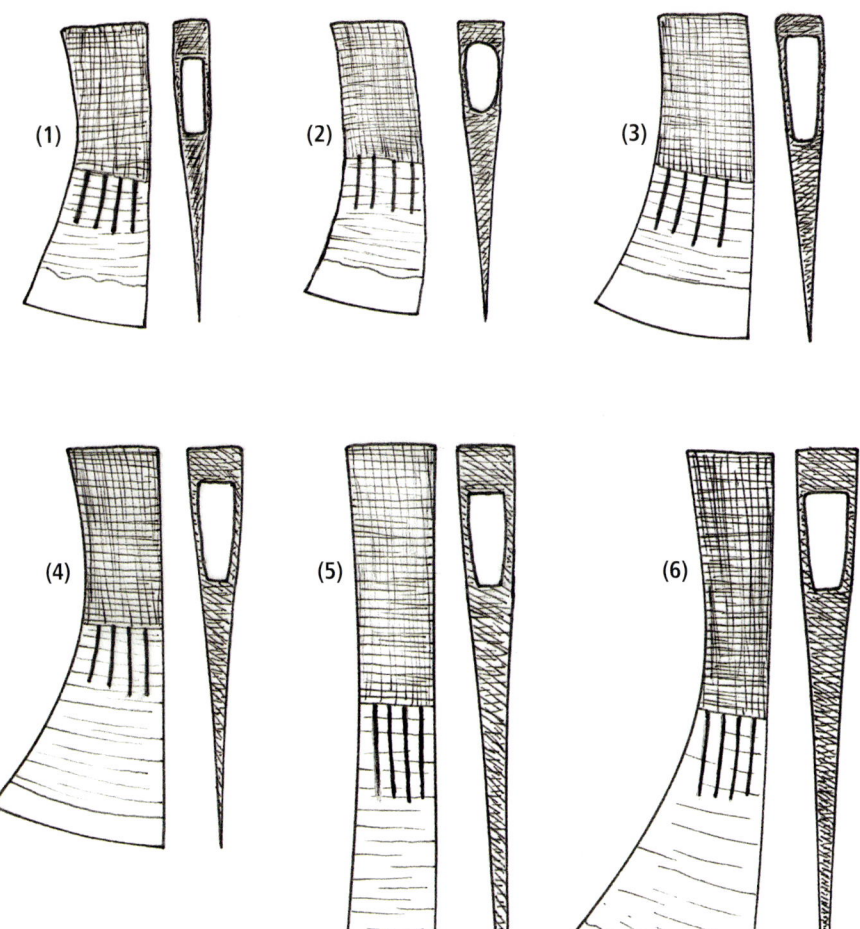

(1) Tosa axe for branches and roots.
(2) Kishu axe for branches and roots. (Kishu is the old name for the Wakayama Prefecture on Honshu.)

(3) Kishu felling axe.
(4) Universal felling and debranching axe.
(5) Mezo axe for wooden joints.
(6) Large woodcutter's axe.

SPLITTING AND EMERGENCY AXES

(1) Hamaguri splitting axe in the Shinshu (old name for the province of Nagano) style.
(2) Firefighter's axe.
(3) Kentsuji firefighter's pickaxe.
(4) Universal axe with hammer poll.

The *ono* (hatchets) and *masakari* (bearded axes) are forged almost exclusively in the traditional laminate technique *(tansetsu)*. While the *masakari* is made by splitting a glowing hot piece of iron and inserting a piece of steel (*warikomi* technique), the head of the smaller ono is usually made by sheathing the cutting-edge steel *(hagane)* in a folded iron bar.

Isao Mizuno, seventy-three years old at the time I compiled this book, demonstrated this technique on a small cleaver with a head weight of 400 grams (14.1 oz.) and a finished size of about 120 x 50 x 20 mm (4.7 x 2 x 0.8 in.). In the folding method, the *hagane* cutting-edge steel as well as a reinforcement at the neck were wrapped ("packed") by folding them in an iron bar and then forge-welded.

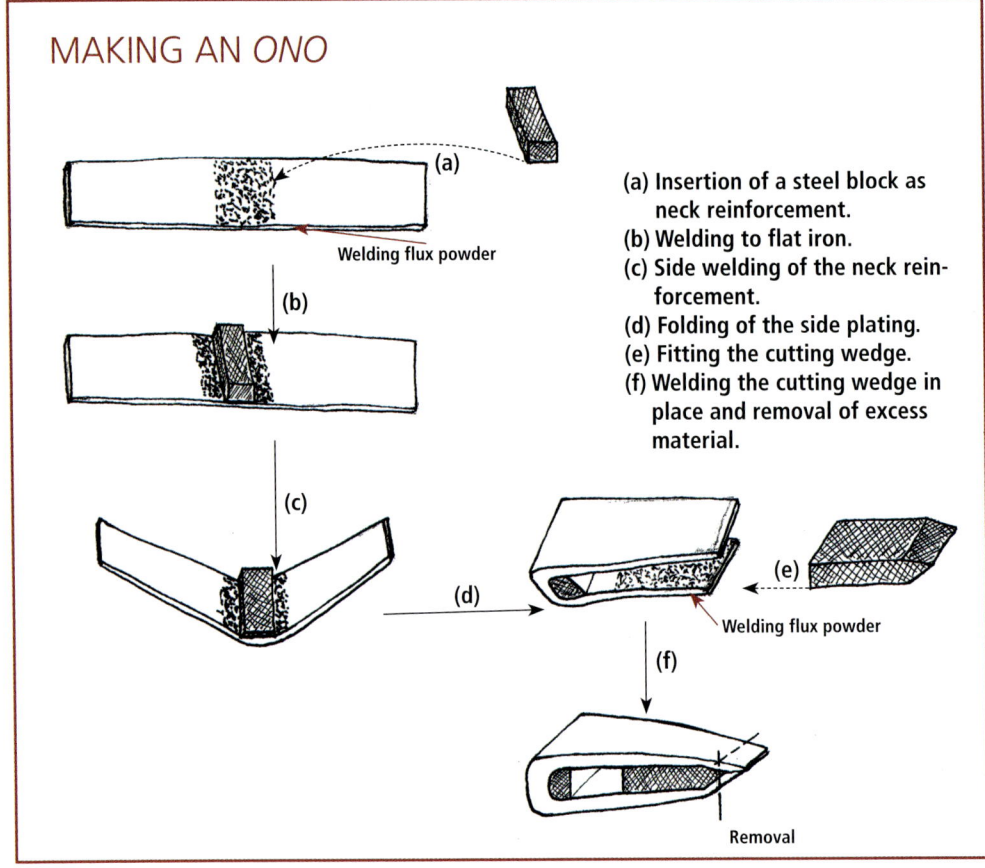

MAKING AN *ONO*

Welding flux powder

(a) Insertion of a steel block as neck reinforcement.
(b) Welding to flat iron.
(c) Side welding of the neck reinforcement.
(d) Folding of the side plating.
(e) Fitting the cutting wedge.
(f) Welding the cutting wedge in place and removal of excess material.

Welding flux powder

Removal

MAKING A *MASAKARI*

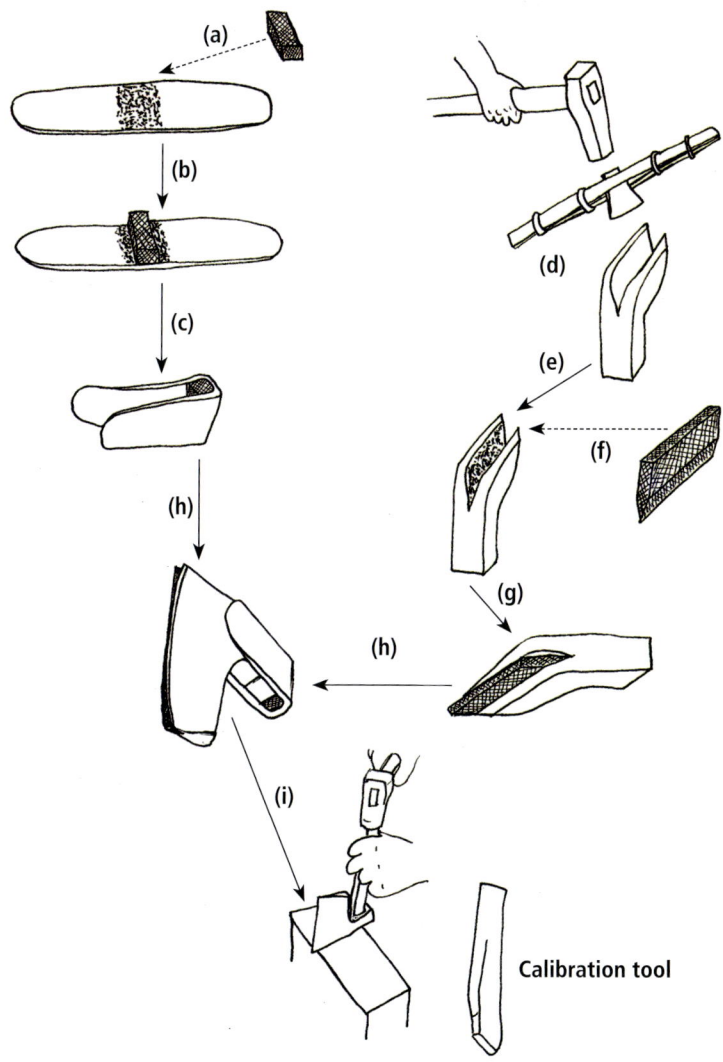

(a) Insertion of a steel block as neck reinforcement.

(b) Welding to the flat iron.

(c) Folding of the side plating and welding of sides.

(d) Spreading the lips with the froe.

(e) and (f) Application of welding flux powder and fitting of the cutting wedge.

(g) Welding the cutting wedge to the corpus.

(h) Fitting the the U-shaped neck plating to the corpus and welding.

(i) Forming the handle hole with the calibration tool.

Compared with a solid block as the starting material, this method has an advantage in that making a handle hole and gouging out the lip is not necessary. However, more precise work must be done in the case of forge welding.

For the body, Isao uses a bar of low-carbon, nonhardening steel (he calls it "SS" steel), 5 mm (0.2 in.) thick, 50 mm (2 in.) wide, and about 260 mm (10.2 in.) long, which is thinned slightly at both ends. Next, he centers a small block (about 6 × 12 × 50 mm, or 1 × 0.4 × 2 in.) as a neck reinforcement. Like the cutting-edge steel, this is made of SK-7 low-alloy carbon steel (C = 0.65%). This steel has a slightly lower melting temperature than iron and is therefore more suitable for forge welding.

The flat iron is heated centrally in the coke furnace until it reaches yellow-white heat, then the composite is placed exactly at right angles with the addition of welding flux powder and pressed on with a hammer. The bond is carefully reheated in the fire to forging temperature (recognizable by the slight sparking) and then forged with at first gentle and later firmer blows. Now the two side cheeks are folded in. With renewed addition of plenty of welding flux powder, the sides of the block are also forge-welded tightly to the cheeks. The cheeks are then driven to fit exactly, using a calibration tool with the same thickness as the cutting-edge steel.

The *hagane* blocks have dimensions of approximately 70 × 40 × 12 mm (2.75 × 1.6 × 0.5 in.), and they are already forged into a wedge shape in the front area before forge welding. A mark is made on the side cheeks for the correct positioning in the body of a hole about 30 mm (1.2 in.) in length. The front edge of the cutting-edge steel should be slightly recessed from the cheeks of the side walls so that during welding it is enveloped by the iron and protected from decarburization. The cutting-edge steel should fit tightly between the side cheeks so that it does not slip during welding.

With a generous addition of welding flux powder, the composite is held in a horizontal position in a sufficiently large bed of coals and uniformly heated to welding temperature, recognizable by the slight spraying of sparks. The initial fixation is achieved by light but rapid hammer blows on the anvil. After welding powder is scattered into the lateral joints, in the next heat the composite is forge-welded over its entire surface on the spring hammer.

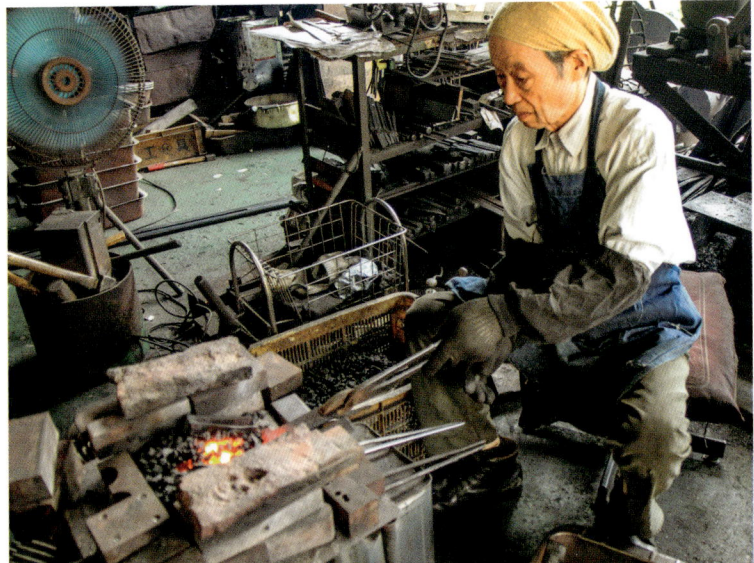

Master Mizuno forges while sitting: the advantage of the loose firebrick forge is its adaptability, since its size can be scaled to suit the forging material and the work requirements.

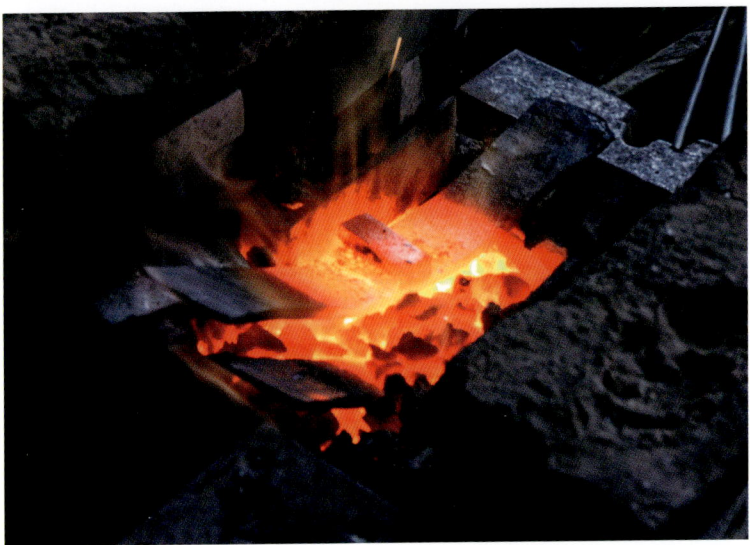

A block of steel is placed in the center of the plating steel, which is thinned at both ends. The block will later serve as a neck reinforcement.

Although any welding defects could usually be corrected by rewelding, this should be avoided if possible, since it leads to decarburization of the steel close to the edge. The axe head is now hammer-forged free-form in rapid succession. Not only for reasons of economy, but above all for quality reasons, the hot working steps should be kept as short as possible. When forging cutting tools, the general rule is that speed is rewarded by edge-holding quality!

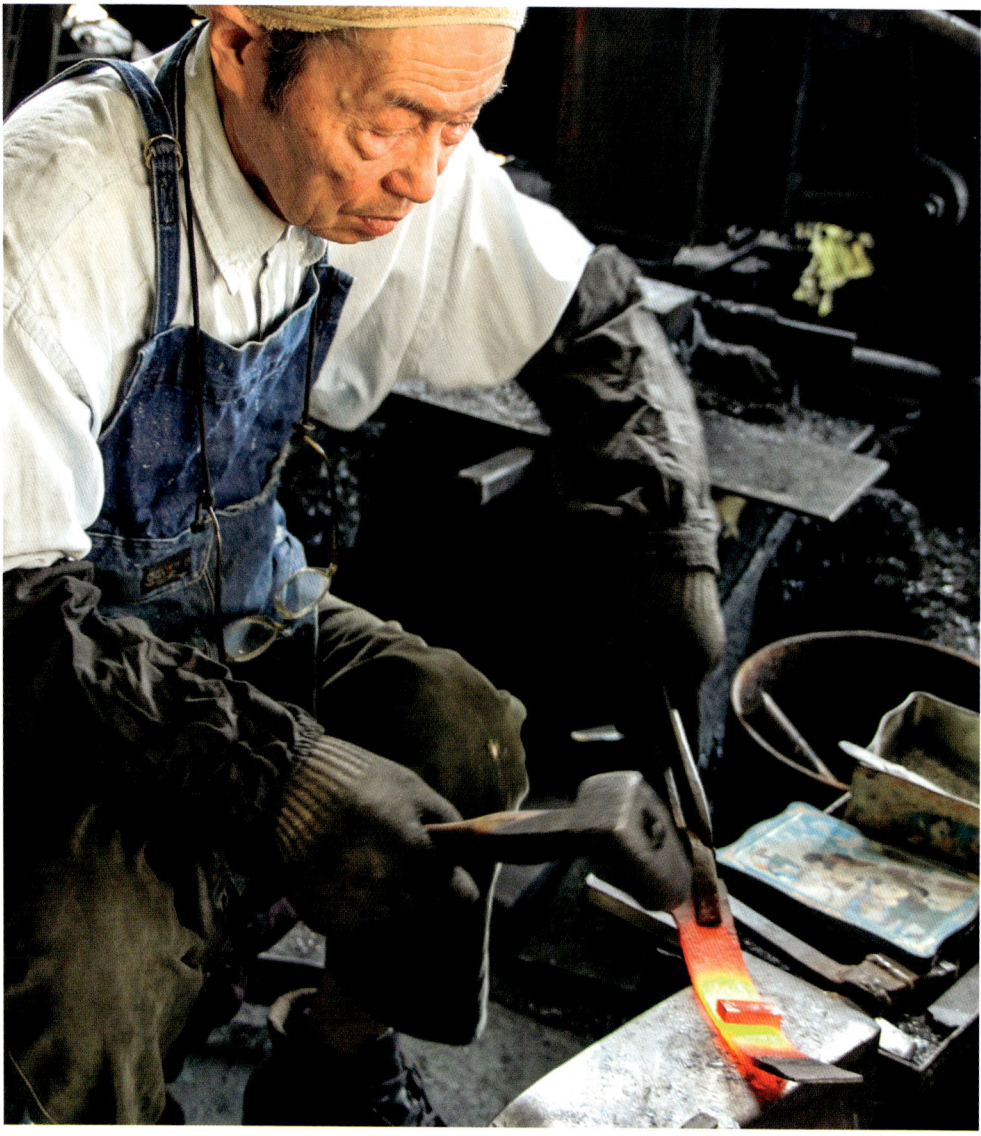

The block of steel is forge-welded with gentle blows.

Tips for Forge Welding (*tansetsu*)

There are a few general rules that should be followed when forge welding steels:

- To the extent possible, the parts to be welded should fit together without gaps. For this purpose, it is advantageous to adapt or pack one part to the other in the heated state.
- Thoroughly descale the surfaces of the parts to be joined by grinding or with acid.
- For forge welding, the forge should be clean and free of slag.
- Give the surface a light texture (coarse grinding or beaten riffling). This improves the bond and prevents small parts from "floating away."
- Ensure that the heating is as uniform as possible by embedding in a sufficiently large pile of embers.
- The fuel (coke or charcoal) should have a fine and uniform grain size.
- First heat the "mother part" to red heat before applying a generous amount of welding flux powder. It should liquify on the joining surface and react with the oxide layer. The mating part can then be placed cold on this surface before the composite is brought to welding temperature.
- Steel (with carbon) is easier to forge weld with iron (without carbon) than steel with steel or iron with iron.
- The melting point of steel decreases with increasing carbon content. While iron must be heated to about 1,300°C or 2,372°F (white heat) for forge welding, temperatures of 1,150°C to 1,250°C, or 2,102°F to 2,282°F (yellow to yellow-white heat) are sufficient for carbon steel, depending on its carbon content.
- A good indicator of the right time is the appearance of light sparks. Keep a small viewing window clear in the ember pile for checking.
- In the case of forge welding, the parts are first tapped lightly with a hand hammer to tack them in place. With the addition of welding flux powder, the parts are then tapped more vigorously by hand or with the aid of a machine in order to achieve a full-surface weld.
- When forge welding cutting-edge steel, avoid decarburization of the sections responsible for the cutting edge (do not heat too often, wrap up, later trimming cut).

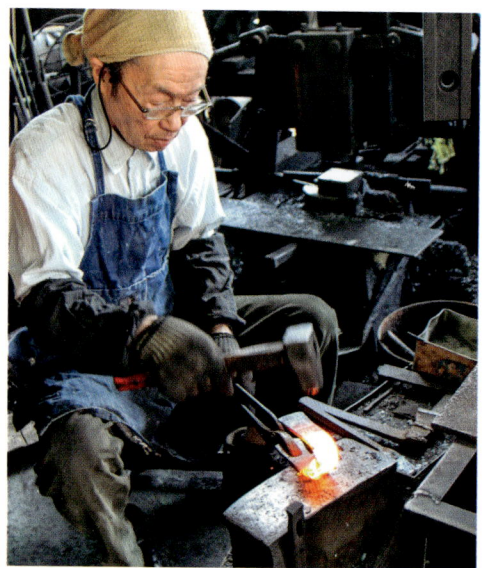

After the neck reinforcement has been welded in place, the plating is formed into a U shape.

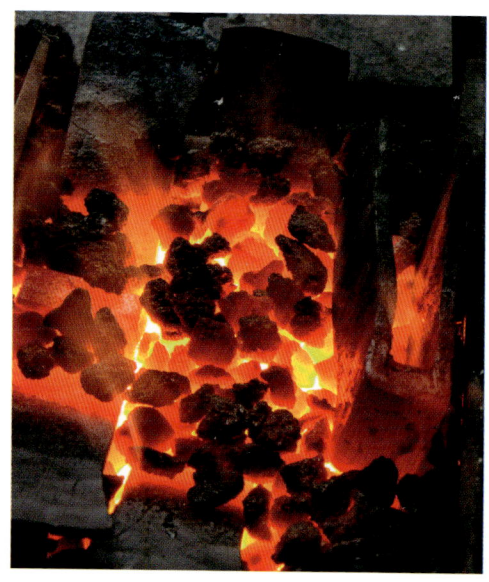

Maximum efficiency: small axe heads are forged in batches of four in one heat.

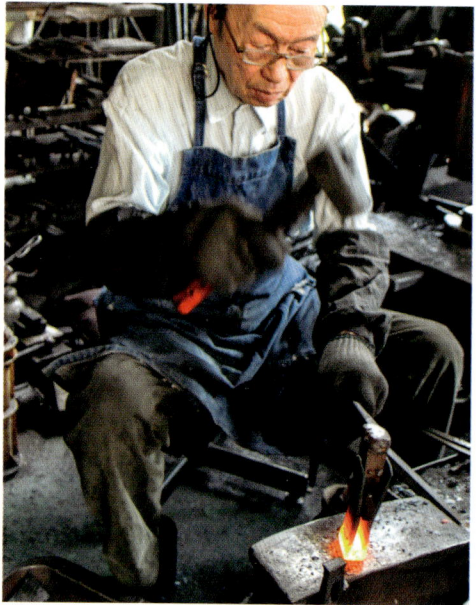

The cheeks are spread apart to accept the cutting-edge steel.

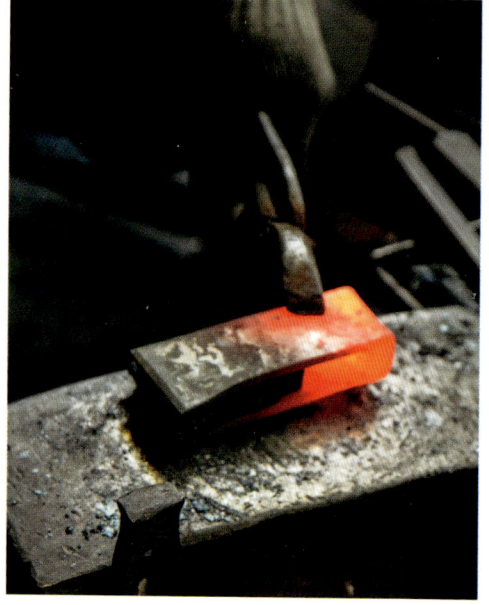

The tapered cutting-edge steel should be enclosed as accurately as possible by the side cheeks.

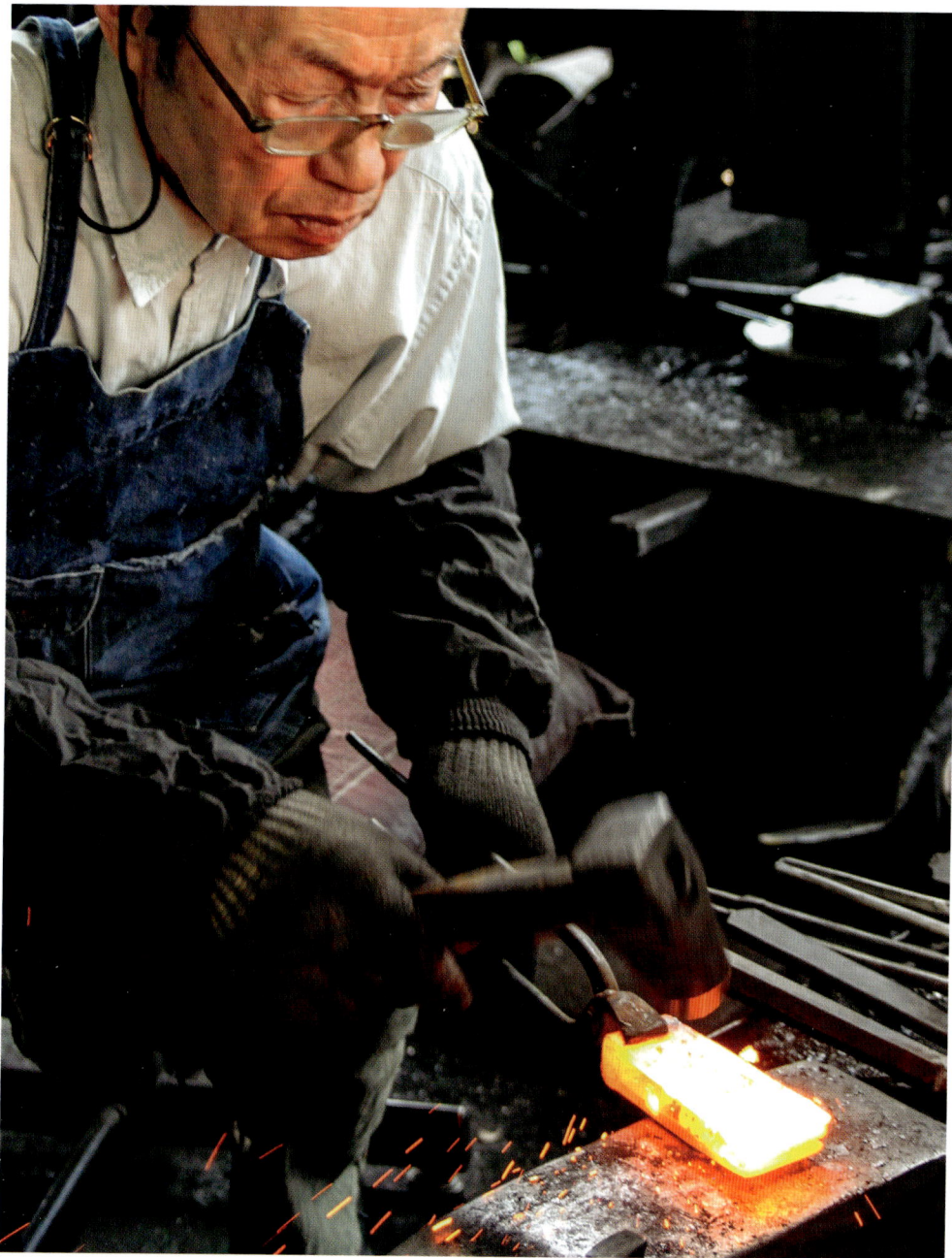

The composite is forge-welded, initially with gentle but rapid blows. The plating layer should completely enclose the cutting steel along the cutting edge, so that it is protected against decarburization. Only later, by means of a trimming cut, is the cutting edge exposed.

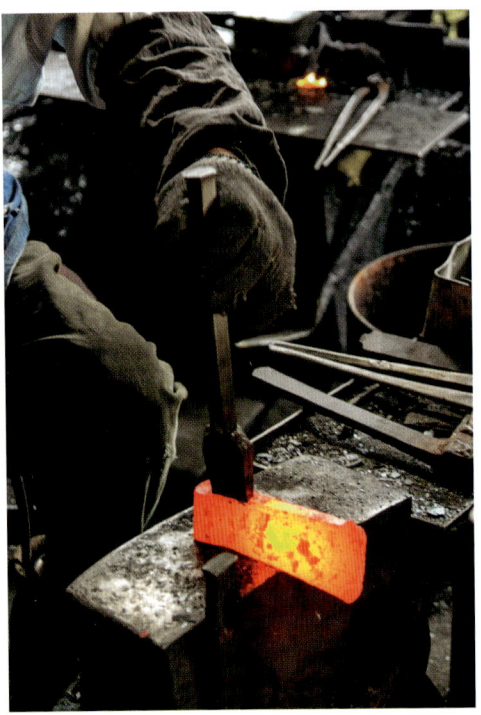

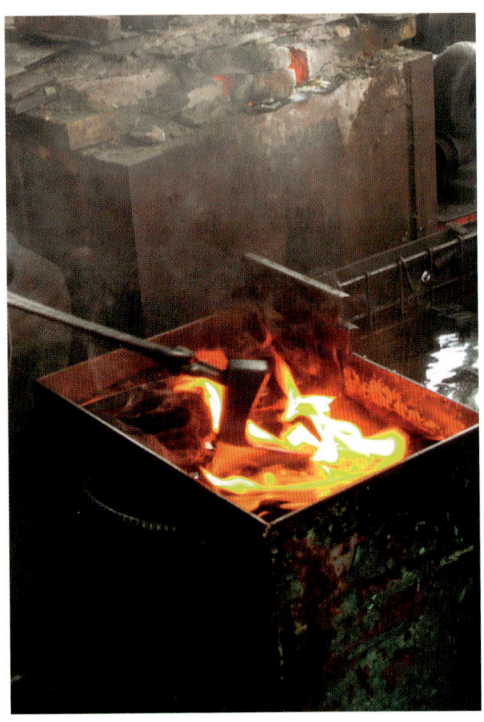

The punch is used to open the handle hole from both sides, resulting in a rectangular shape.

For hardening, the head (in this case a *masakari*) is heated to 780°C (1,436°F) in a lead bath and then is quenched in oil, cutting edge first.

A calibrated punch is used to expand the eye to fit exactly. To do this, the rear area of the head must be heated again to yellow heat to prevent the weld seams from bursting. Also, when finally exposing the cutting edge by removing the protruding lips with the blacksmith's chisel, sufficient heating must also be ensured.

The head is now ground in several passes with finer and finer grits on the wheel and normalized before hardening. This heat treatment serves to reduce the stresses and to produce a uniform microstructure. In the case of a steel with 0.65% carbon, it is heated in a furnace or forge to bright red (about 850°C or 1,562°F) and then slowly cooled in the air or in a bed of sand.

For hardening, the head must be heated to about 780°C (1,436°F). Isao Mizuno uses liquid lead (800°C or 1,472°F), which ensures uniform heating. The lead bath is covered with fine pieces of charcoal to prevent oxidation and evaporation.

Note: Lead vapors are harmful to health; therefore it is recommended that you not use this method (maybe even forbidden commercially in the US)!

Quenching is done with the cutting edge forward, first in oil and then in water. This avoids the heat being drawn from the core. Finally, the head is annealed in oil at 200°C (392°F) for about thirty minutes to a hardness of 55 HRC.

Sharpening takes place on water-cooled discs, whereby the bevel is ground slightly spherical at a cutting-edge angle of about 35°.

The handle, made of Japanese white oak, is fixed with a simple iron wedge that can be redriven. Most axe heads, however, leave Mizuno's workshop without a handle. In Japan, installing the handle is the responsibility of the user, who with this act adds his own personal touch to the tool.

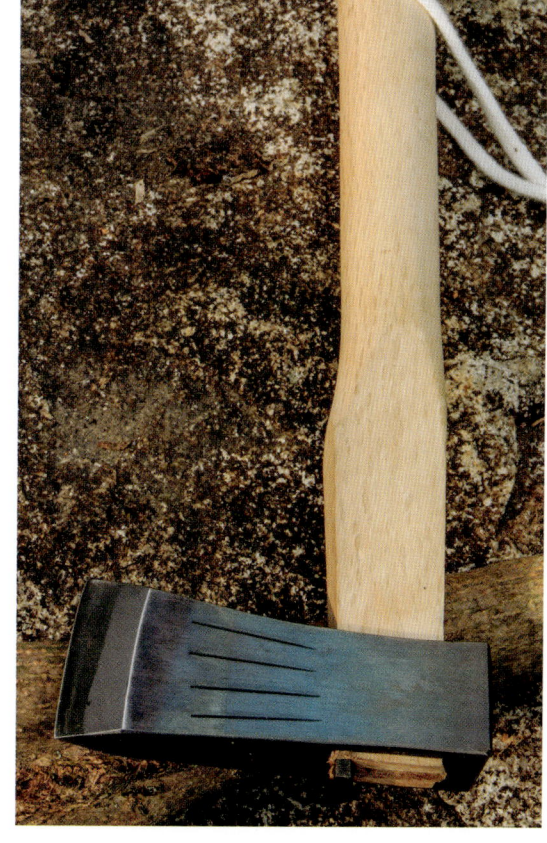

This small splitting axe has been fitted with a handle made of white oak.

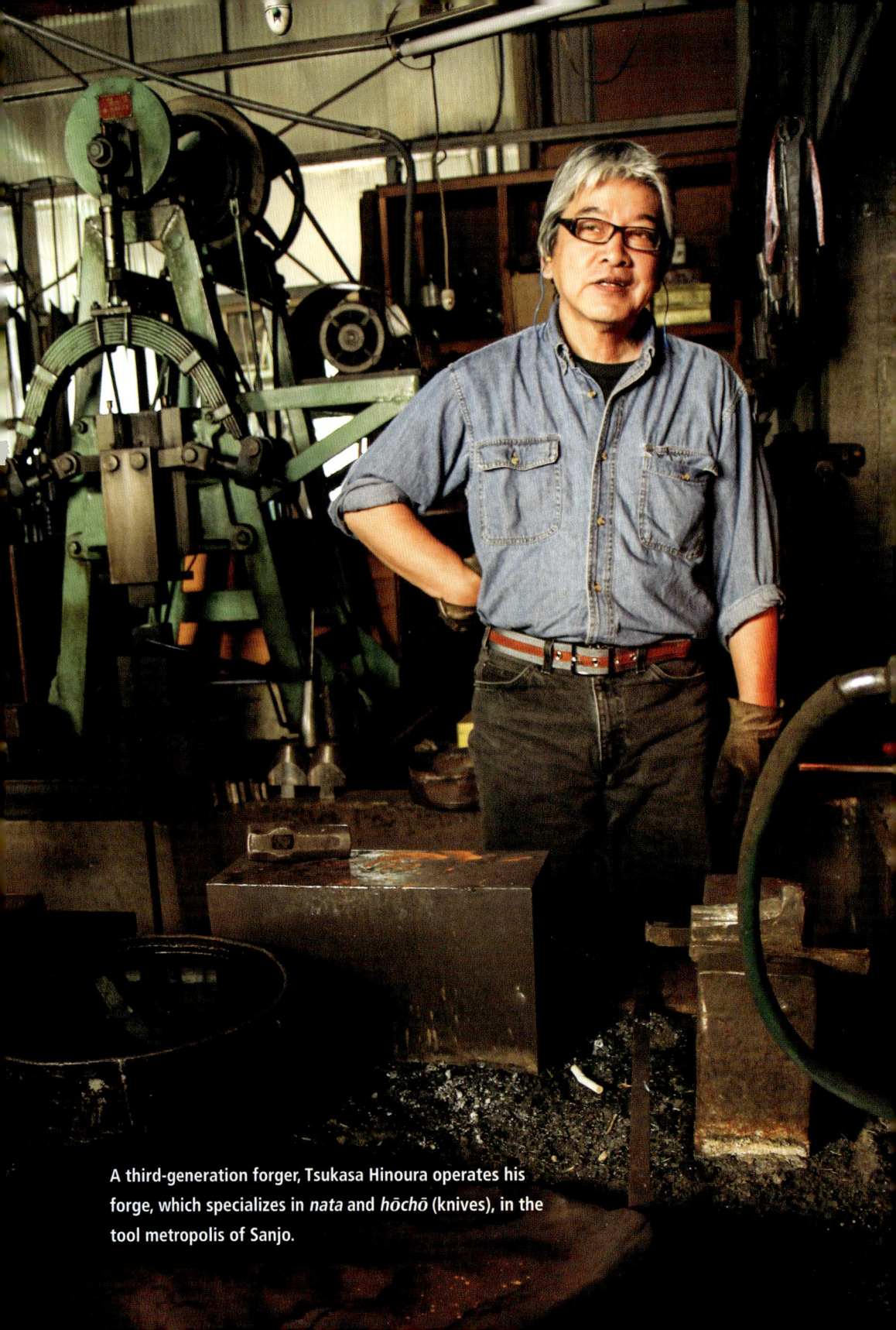

A third-generation forger, Tsukasa Hinoura operates his forge, which specializes in *nata* and *hōchō* (knives), in the tool metropolis of Sanjo.

The Gardener's Machete (Nata)

The *nata* is the standard tool of the Japanese gardener. With its sharp, thick blade, it is highly effective for pruning and trimming trees and shrubs. Its edge, usually single beveled, allows smooth cuts close to the trunk with the minimum possible damage to the plant. In contrast to gardener's machetes with the more common single beveled edge, models beveled on both sides are preferred for splitting firewood or for general outdoor use.

Due to their formal relationship, *nata* are usually made by cutlery makers *(hamono-kaji)*. This is also true of Tsukasa Hinoura, who enjoys a national reputation not only for his *nata*, but also for his hunting and cooking knives. Committed to over a hundred years of family tradition, he pursues his profession with almost scientific meticulousness. The will to perfection was instilled in him by his teacher Shigeyoshi Iwasaki, revered in Japan as the "Pope of Blacksmiths," an expert in traditional forging techniques (see page 93).

To have complete control over the quality of his products—from the first blow of the hammer to sharpening and installation of the handle—they are made in his own workshop in Sanjo, where his son Mutsumi is the only employee. He is particularly interested in optimizing the interactions among the material he uses, the forging process, and the heat treatment. The use of prefabricated, laminated blanks, increasingly used by colleagues, is out of the question for Tsukasa Hinoura. Father and son demonstrated the forging steps involved in the creation of a common *saya-nata* with a blade length of 170 mm (6.7 in.) and a weight of 450 grams (15.9 oz.) on the occasion of my visit in 2015.

The blade of this single-edged tool, which is sharpened on the right side only, is of two-layer construction. The hard *shirogami* cutting-edge steel is embedded in the *shigane* base body made of soft, nonhardening iron. This so-called *kasumi* construction combines two advantages: the tough, damping base material suppresses bounce during impact and makes the blade very resistant to breakage. Second, when the blade is sharpened, only a little of the hard material, which makes up only about a third of the cross section, must be ground.

NATA TYPES

There are three types of *nata* blades:

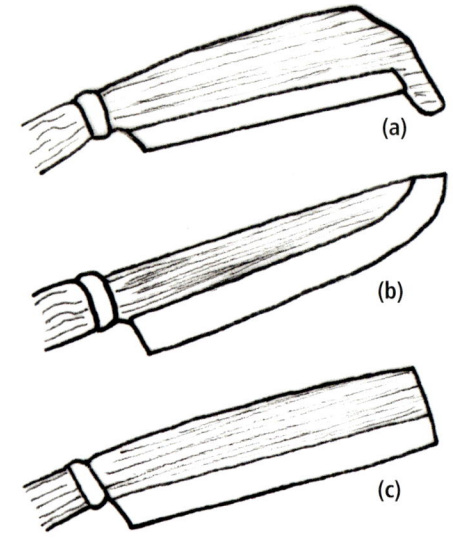

(a)

(b)

(c)

(a) *hashituki-nata*: rectangular blade with a "nose," which is intended to protect the cutting edge if the user misses his target or strikes the ground.

(b) *ken-nata*: pointed blade, used primarily as a bush machete, usually beveled on both sides.

(c) *saya-nata*: the *nata* with a rectangular tip is best suited for garden work.

NATA CROSS SECTION

The *kawagane* cutting-edge steel *(shiro-gami 2)* is embedded in the soft iron body by forge welding.

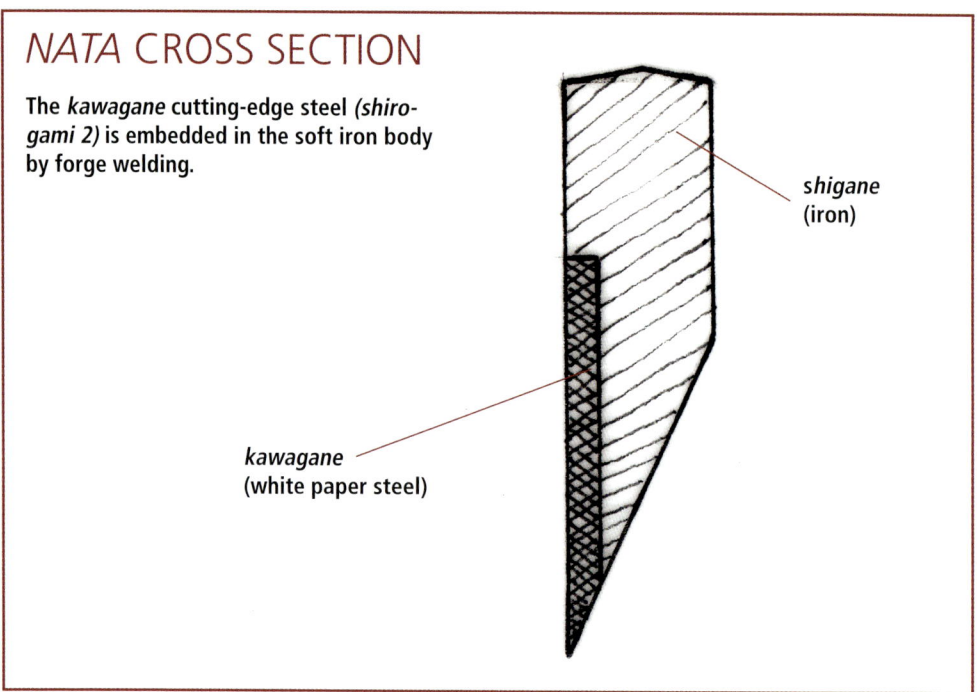

shigane
(iron)

kawagane
(white paper steel)

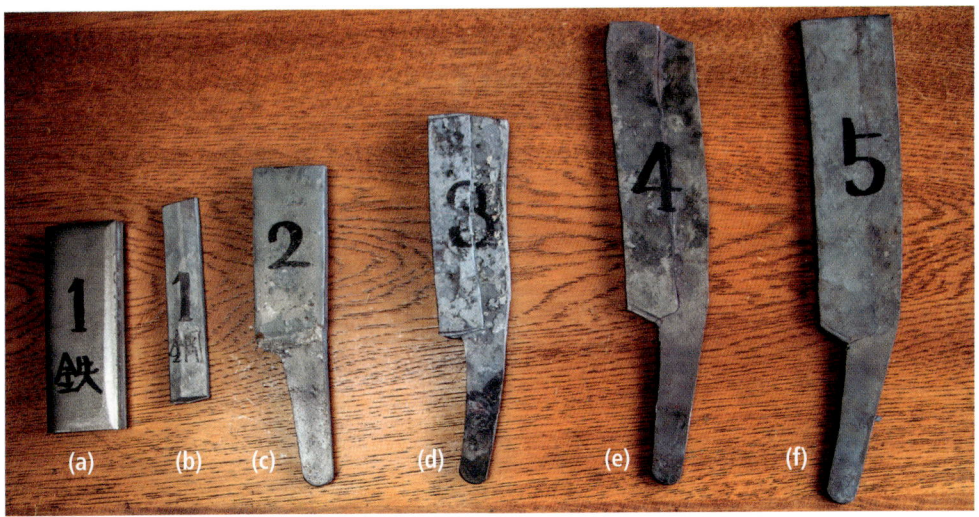

The Stages of Forging:

(a) Iron blank.

(b) Plating steel *(shirogami 2)*.

(c) Iron base body *(kokunanko)*.

(d) Forge-welded composite of base body and plating steel.

(e) Blade forged to thickness and shape.

(f) Blade cut to size, roughly ground and hardened.

The block for the blade body measuring 45 × 110 × 10 mm (1.8 × 4.3 × 0.4 in.) consists of low-carbon iron (C 0.04%), which does not harden and has a slightly higher strength than pure iron. Hitachi's white paper steel, which is specially produced for cutting tools *(shirogami 2)* is used for the cutting-edge steel (C 1.1%, Si 0.16%, Mn 0.25%). The platelet prepared for forge welding, measuring 25 × 105 mm (0.98 × 4.1 in.), was cut from a slightly thicker stock forged down to 5 mm (0.2 in.). This purely martensitic hardening steel has a somewhat lower welding temperature than the base metal and is therefore ideal for laminating techniques. It achieves hardness levels of more than 60 Rockwell C, and its fine microstructure enables extremely sharp cutting edges.

First, material is removed to form a tang approximately 60 mm (2.35 in.) long. This also makes for better handling with roundnose pliers. For the forge welding, the base material is shaped with hammer blows and lightly structured. It is then heated to a uniform red heat (850°C or 1,562°F) in the gas furnace. With the addition of plenty of welding flux powder *(tansetsu-zai),* consisting of borax, boric acid, and pulverized rust, the jacket steel is placed flush with the edge.

The composite is heated in the center of the furnace to the required welding temperature of around 1,050°C (1,922°F). A strong steel plate serves as a base, ensuring uniform heat dissipation. A slight sparking signals the right time for removal and immediate welding with gentle hammer blows. At about 950°C (1,742°F), the cutting-edge steel is then worked flush into the base body on the spring or air hammer. The upper edge of the inserted cutting-edge steel must also be joined seamlessly to the base body. If necessary, one can improve this seam by means of an edgewise weld.

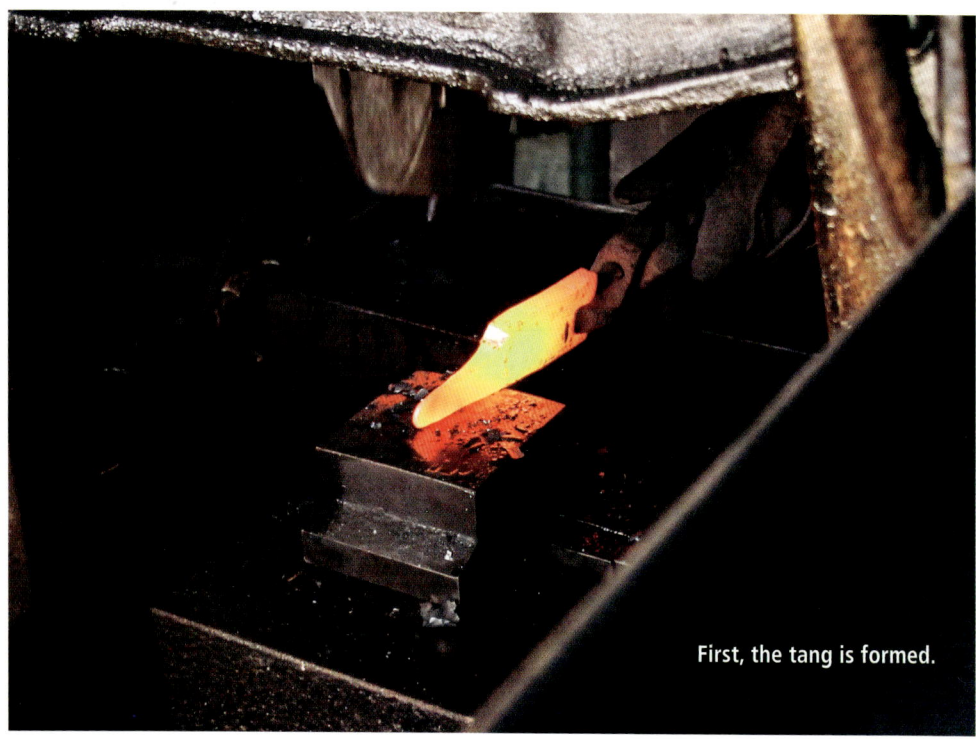

First, the tang is formed.

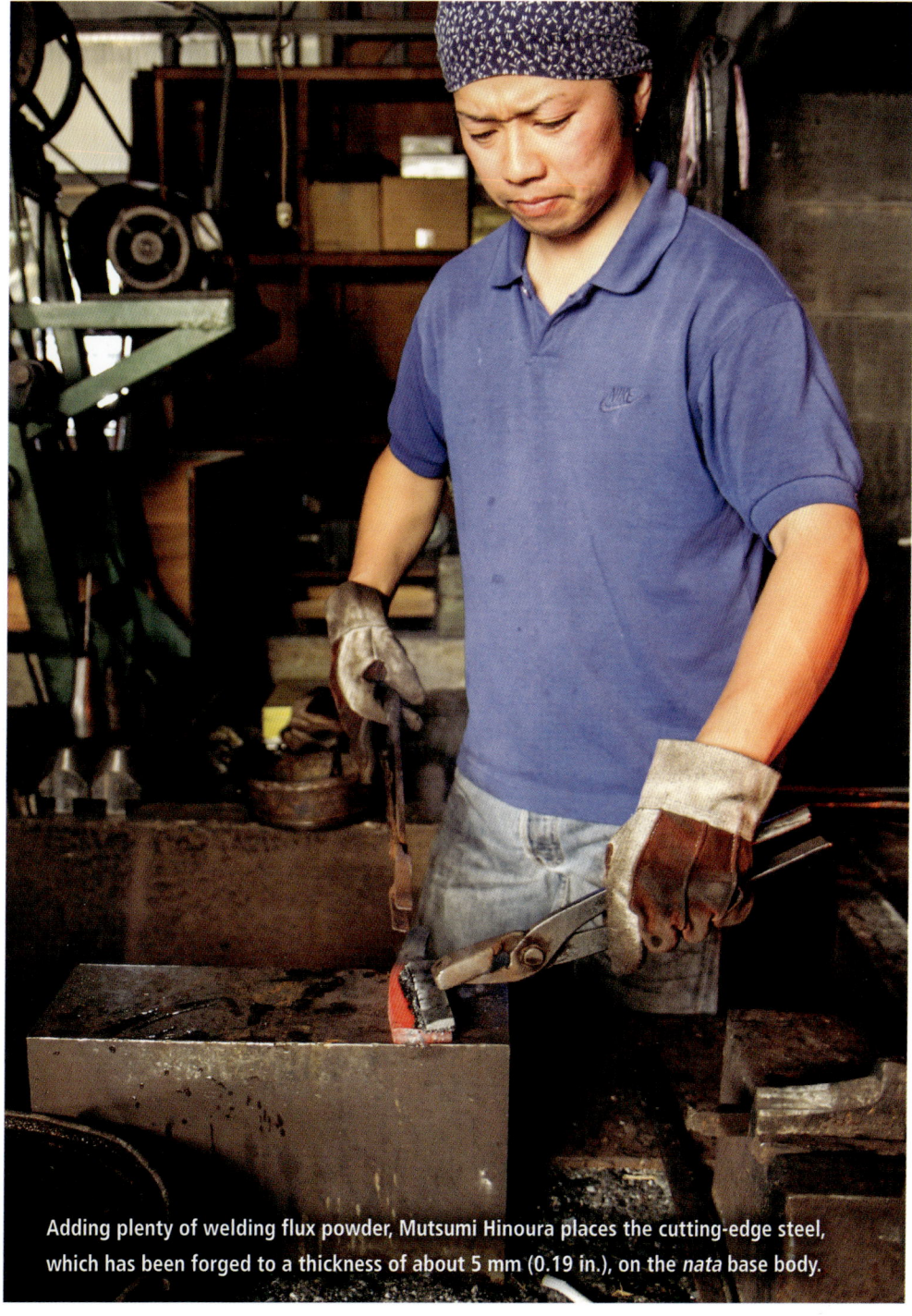

Adding plenty of welding flux powder, Mutsumi Hinoura places the cutting-edge steel, which has been forged to a thickness of about 5 mm (0.19 in.), on the *nata* base body.

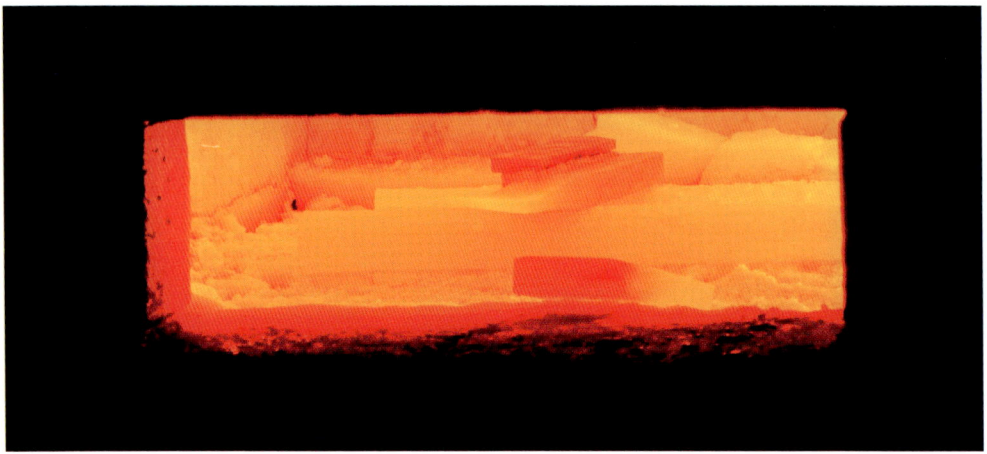

In the gas furnace: the *shirogami* cutting-edge steel, together with a *nata* base body on a thick steel plate, is heated to forging temperature. A second base body (*foreground*) is being preheated.

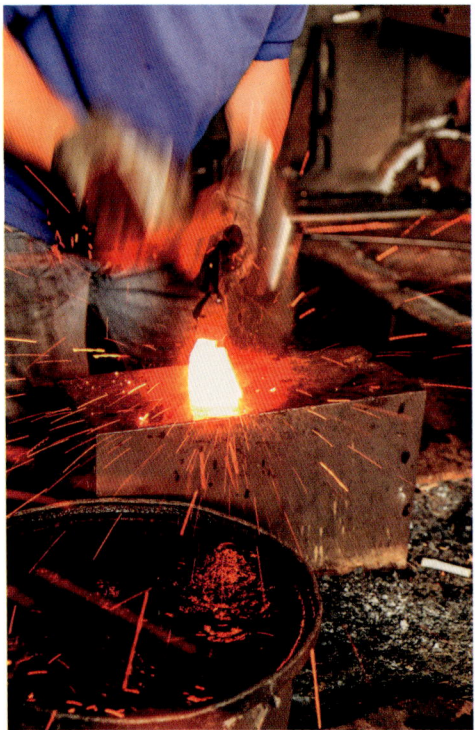

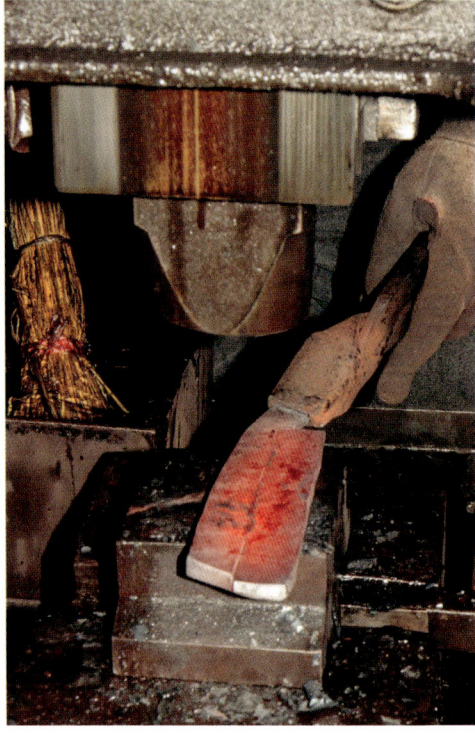

Glowing yellow-white, the composite is welded with not-too-heavy blows.

Drawing out is done on the spring hammer. The bundle of wet straw in the background is used for descaling.

The workpiece is then shaped to a thickness of 6 to 7 mm (0.23 to 0.27 in.) at a somewhat reduced heat, whereby it is mainly machined on the reverse side. Excessively high temperatures are to be avoided, as is too-frequent heating, since both are detrimental to quality. The thickness should decrease somewhat toward the tip, while the blade width increases from 40 to 50 mm (1.6 to 2 in.) from back to front.

In edge forging, the microstructure is compacted along the cutting edge, and the blade is given a slight longitudinal curvature with the aid of a wedge-shaped saddle. The one-sided bevel of about 20° is roughly preforged along the cutting edge. To break off the scale during the forging process, Mutsumi uses a wet bundle of rice straw, which he repeatedly feeds under the spring hammer.

After shaping, the raw blade is cut to size at the tip and along the cutting edge and coarsely ground on all sides on the dry-running grinding wheel. The blade is then normalized at about 750°C (1,382°F) and slowly air-cooled, which re-lieves the stresses and produces a uniform microstructure.

In preparation for hardening, Mutsumi coats the blade with a clay slurry *(to-noko)* mixed with charcoal powder. It is intended to prevent superficial carbon removal in the embers and improve wetting with water during quenching.

After the coating has dried, the blade is heated in the workshop to cherry red heat (about 780°C, or 1,436°F). The smith uses a special forge, which he fires with finely chopped charcoal. It contains no sulfur, unlike forge coke or molten lead, which can affect the steel structure through red brittleness. Quenching takes place in a basin of stagnant water at 15°C to 20°C (59°F to 68°F), which results in hardly any bubbling due to the lack of oxygen in the water. The resulting very hard martensitic structure is subsequently annealed by tempering at 180°C (356° F) and adjusted to a final hardness of approximately 61 Rockwell C.

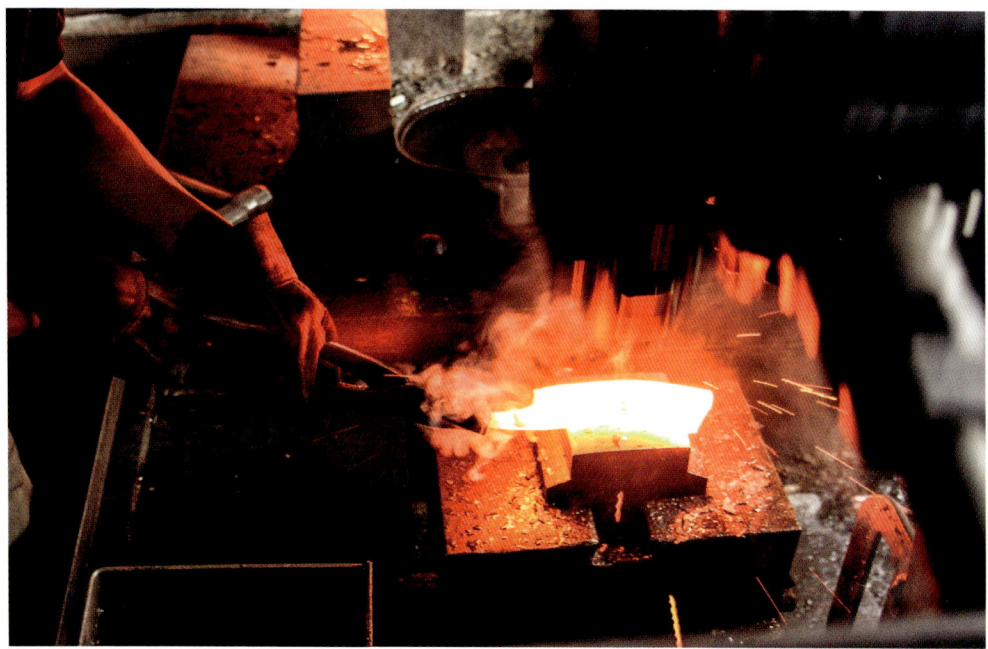

Upright forging gives the *nata* a slight curvature and refines the microstructure in the area of the cutting edge.

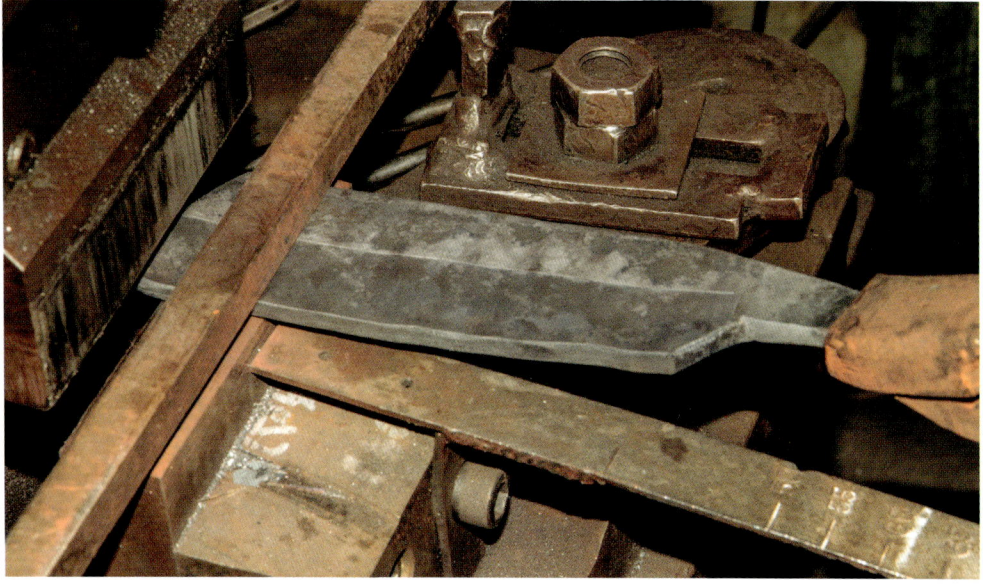

The blade blanks are cut at the tip and along the cutting edge.

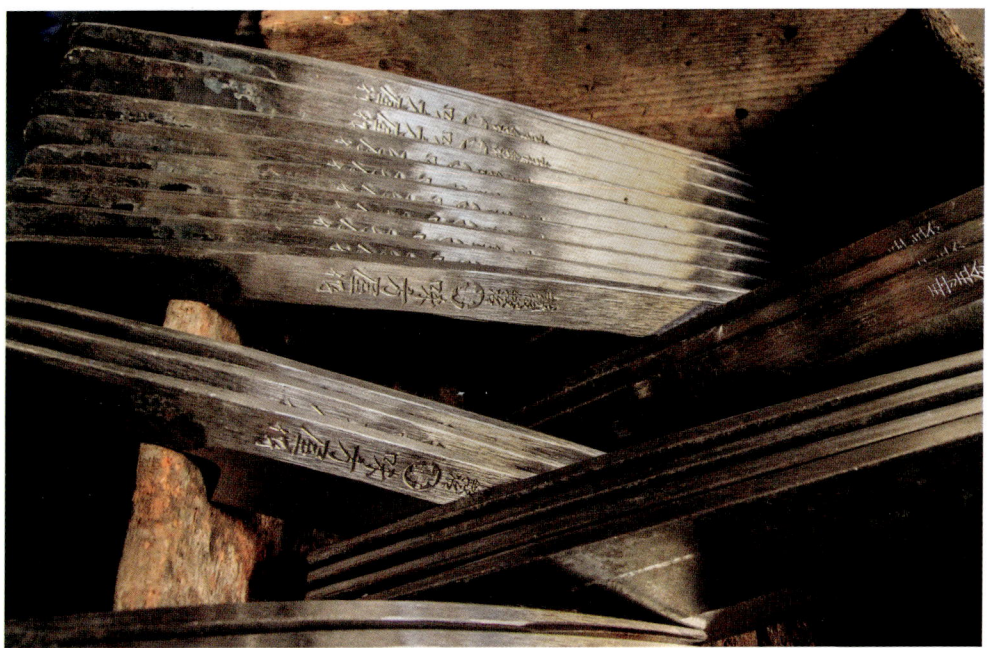

Produced in small batches, completed *nata* blades wait for the hardening process.

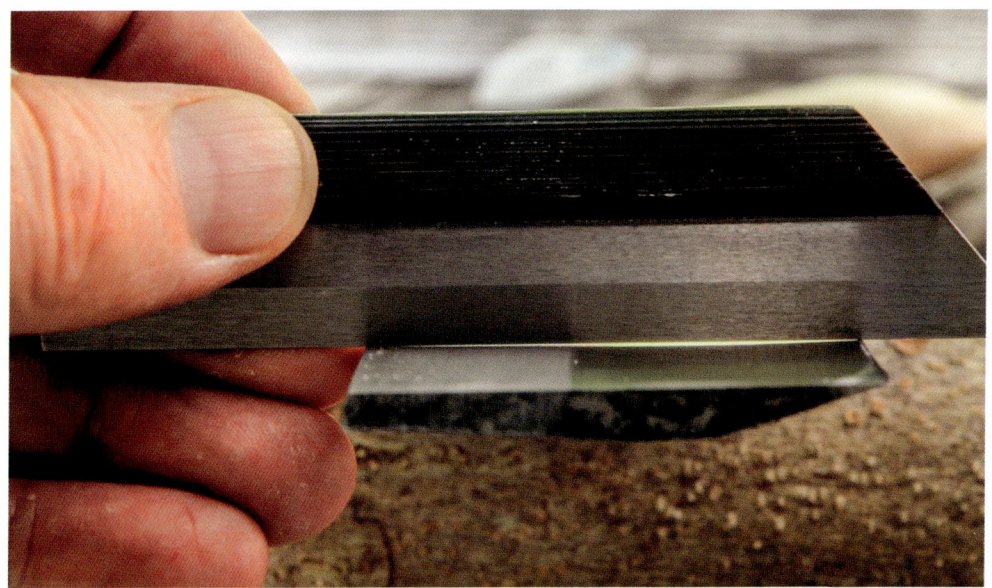

The slight hollow grind *(ura)*, about 0.55 mm (0.021 in.) deep, on the reverse of the blade, facilitates sharpening.

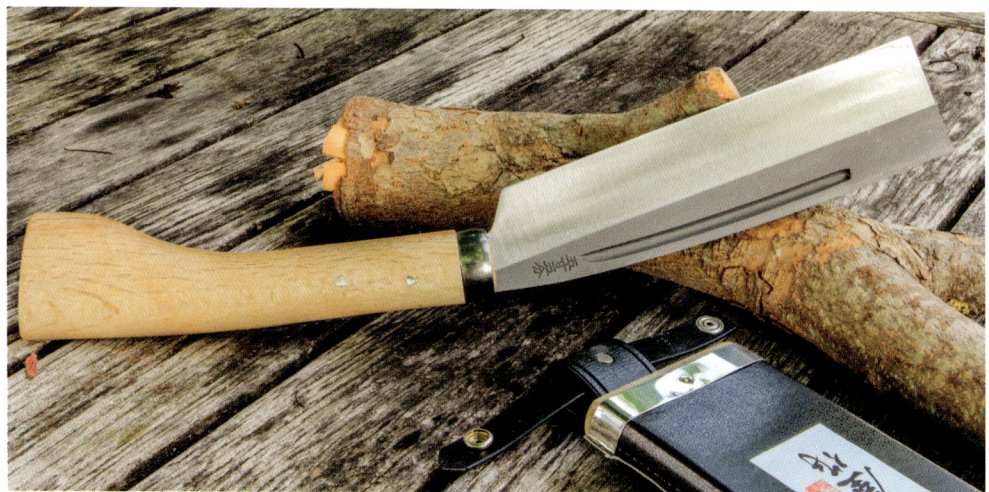

The groove on the back of the blade is a design feature with which Tsukasa Hinoura pays homage to his stylistic model, the Japanese sword *(katana)*.

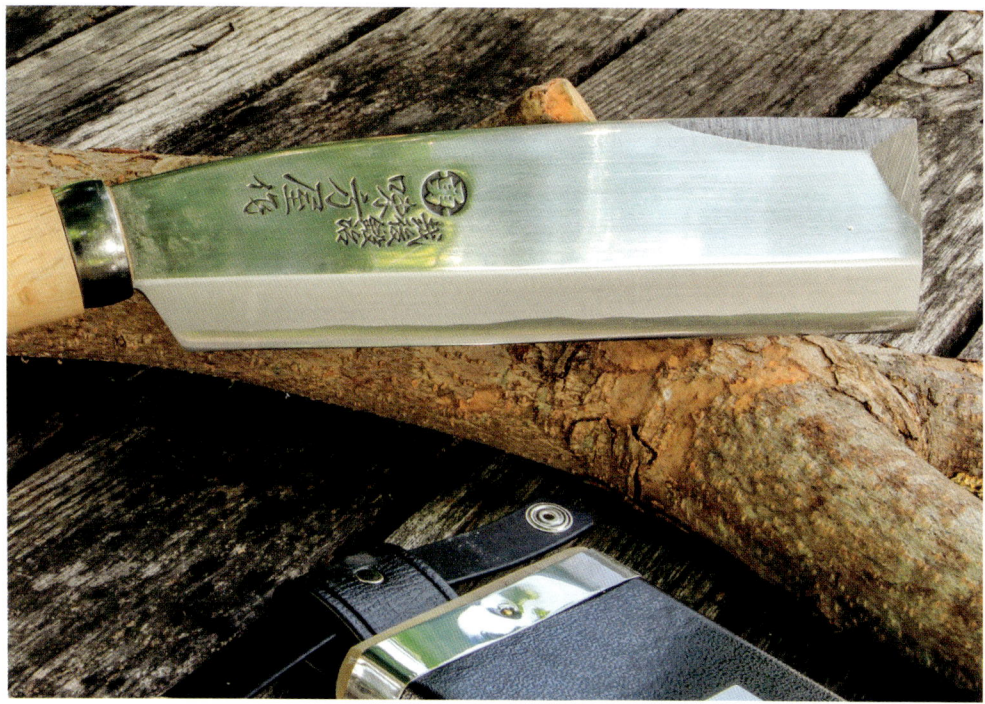

The blade back's lines are continued in the handle. The blade tip is slightly beveled, which makes it easier to insert into the scabbard. The *nata* is stamped with the trademark *(ajigataya)* and the place of manufacture, Echigo (old name for the prefecture of Niigata).

Due to the 4 percent increase in volume of the martensite compared to the base material, significant warping occurs during the hardening process. The next step is therefore the careful straightening of the blade on the anvil. This is done by tapping only on the soft front side to avoid cracks in the cutting-edge layer.

The flat reverse side is then slightly hollow ground on the water-cooled wheel. This feature, typical of many Japanese tools, serves primarily to facilitate sharpening. After several grinding passes with progressively finer grits, the cutting edge is finally sharpened on waterstones, and the blade is signed with the stamp. The knob-shaped handle, riveted to the tang and made of natural white oak, is designed with a solid head ferrule for heavy use in gardening.

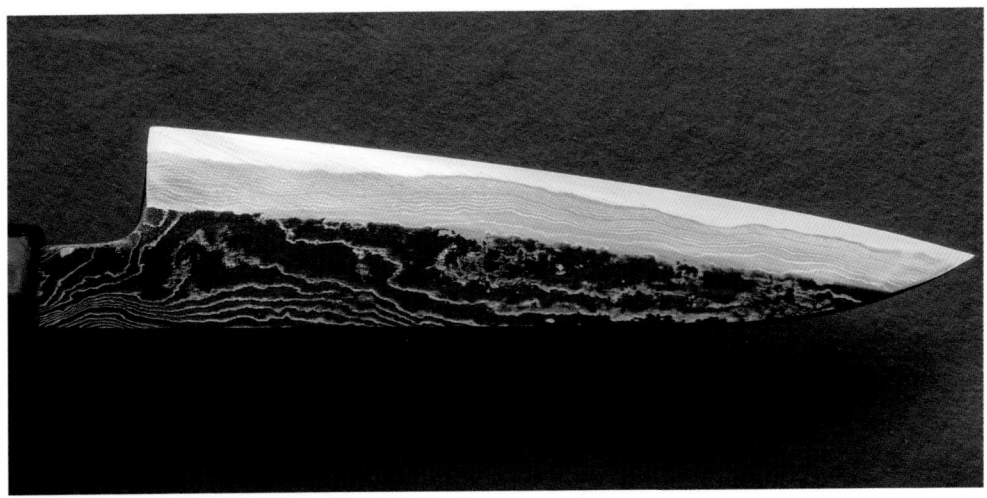

Not only *nata* but also magnificent *hōchō* are created in the Hinoura workshop. Here is an example made of multilayer *mokume* steel.

(1)

(2)

(3)

(4)

(5)

(6)

(7)

(8)

(9)

(10)

(11)

(16)

(15)

(14)

(13)

(12)

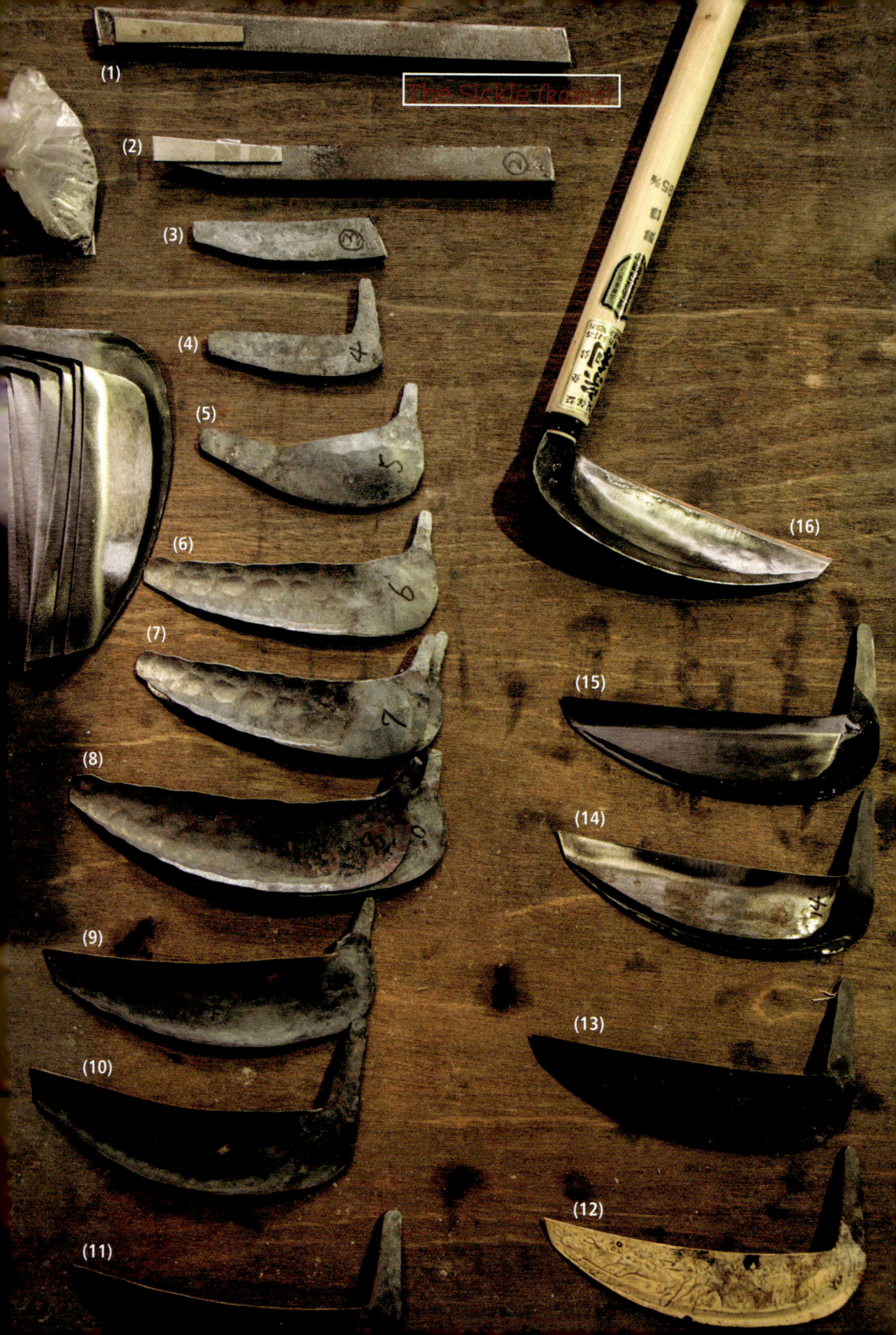

The Sickle (*Kama*)

Today, cutting tools for the garden are largely produced in automated production, with hardly any human presence. With purely mechanical processing, however, it is impossible to achieve the fine dimensioning, balance, and, above all, a steel structure that is designed to withstand stress, which can be achieved by a skilled blacksmith.

When someone spends an entire working life making nothing but sickles, it is safe to assume that he has refined this craft to the highest degree. This is undoubtedly true of Koichi Tsurumaki, who is considered one of the last of his profession in his home country. His sickles, forged by hand from double-layer steel, are held in the highest esteem by professional gardeners in Japan. The accompanying sequence of photographs documents the numerous steps that go into making a traditional *kama* with a blade length of 180 mm (7 in.).

Opposite: The making of a traditional *kama* with a blade length of 180 mm comprises about 16 working steps:
(1) Preparing the starting material: soft flat iron for the body and 3 mm thick white paper steel (*shirogami* 2, C 1.1%) for plating.
(2) The flat iron is forged conically toward the tip on the spring hammer.
(3) The two components are forge welded and cut to length.
(4) Forming of the offset tang.
(5–8) Shaping and thinning the sheet on the spring hammer, shaping the back.
(9) Trimming.
(10) Fine forging with a hand hammer (*narashi* process).
(11) Rough grinding.
(12) Coating with hardening paste.
(13) Hardening in a lead bath at about 700°C (1,292°F) and annealing at approx. 270°C (518°F), final hardness 60 HRC.
(14) Fine grinding, water-cooled.
(15) Sharpening and polishing.
(16) Mounting the handle.

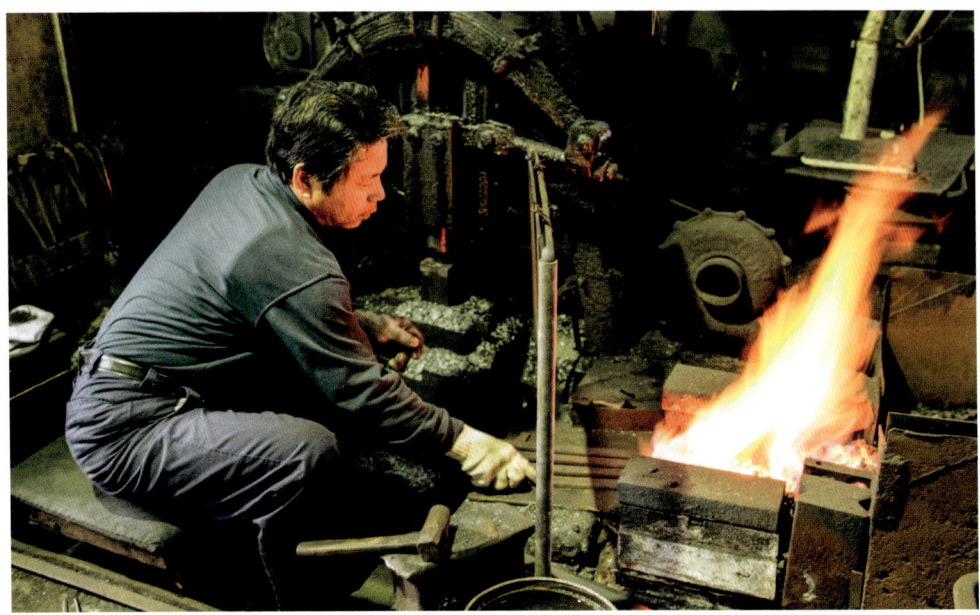

Koichi Tsurumaki forges sitting on a stool in a pit, which is adapted to the ground-level construction of his tools. The forge, bordered with loose stones, is variable in size.

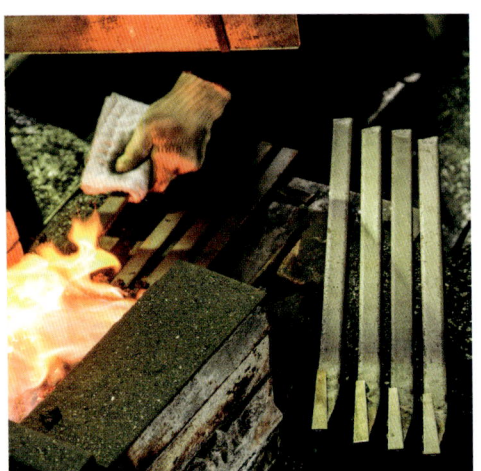

The workpieces are ready for fire welding. The cut steel plates, measuring approx. 180 x 15 x 3 mm (7 x 0.59 x 0.11 in.), were placed on the workpiece with the addition of welding flux powder—protruding slightly at the tip.

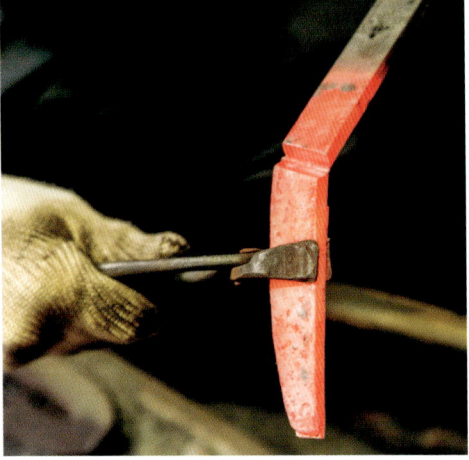

The laminated blade blanks are separated from the holding bar for further processing.

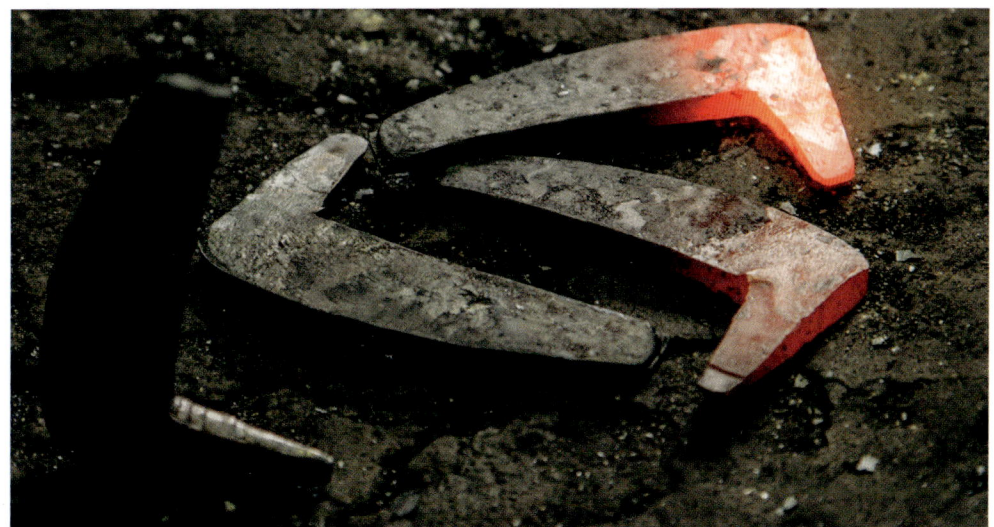

First, the tang is stepped and roughly shaped.

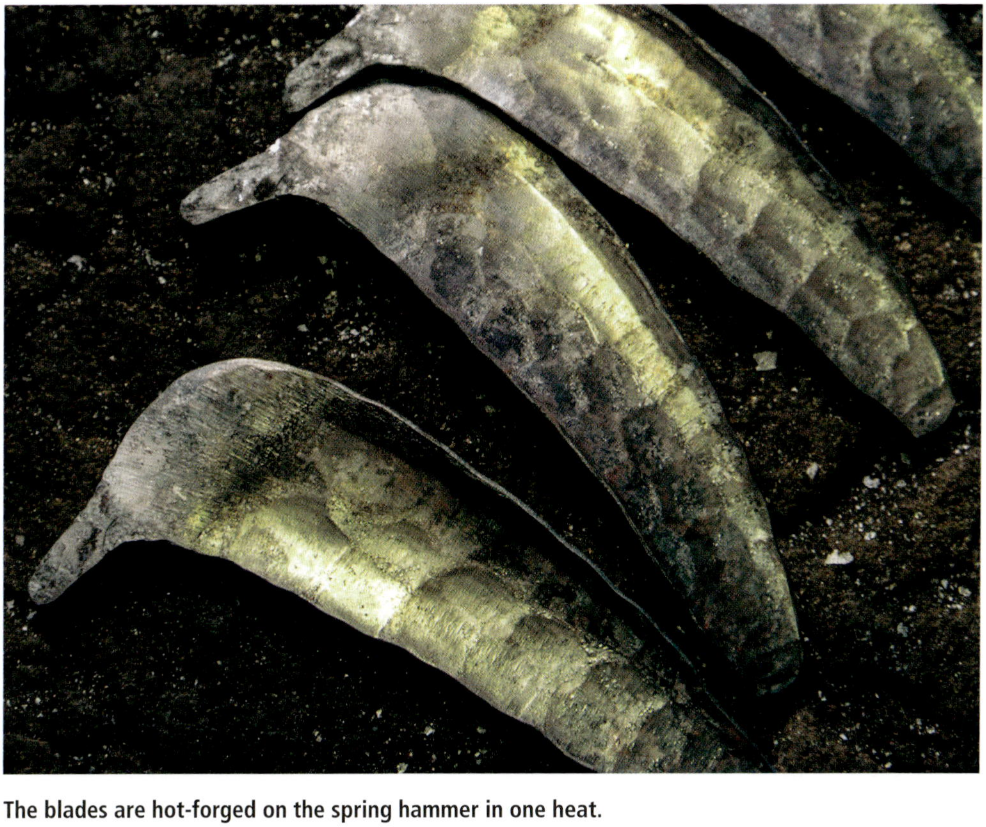

The blades are hot-forged on the spring hammer in one heat.

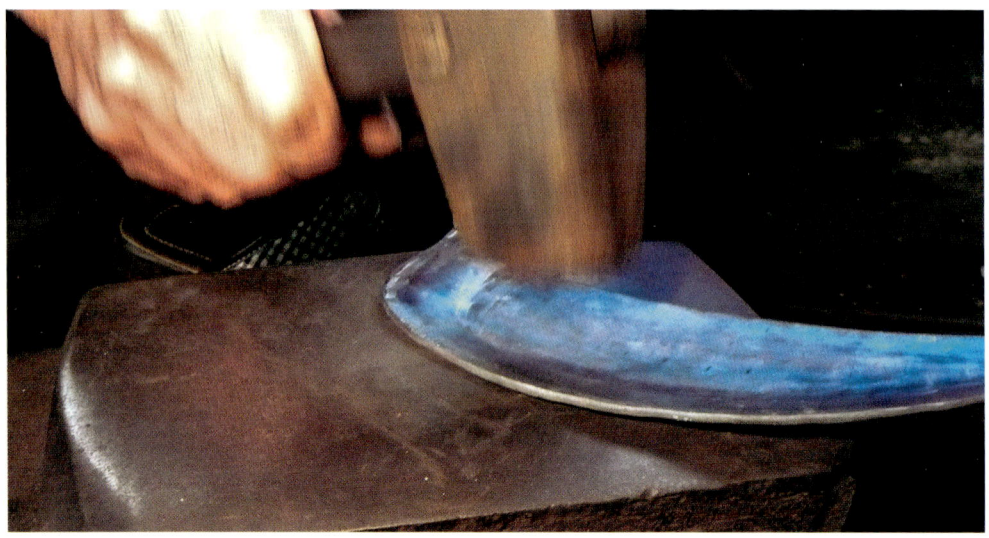

After stress-relieving annealing, the sheet is further thinned at a reduced temperature (approx. 330°C, or 626°F) and shaped into its final form with delicate strokes.

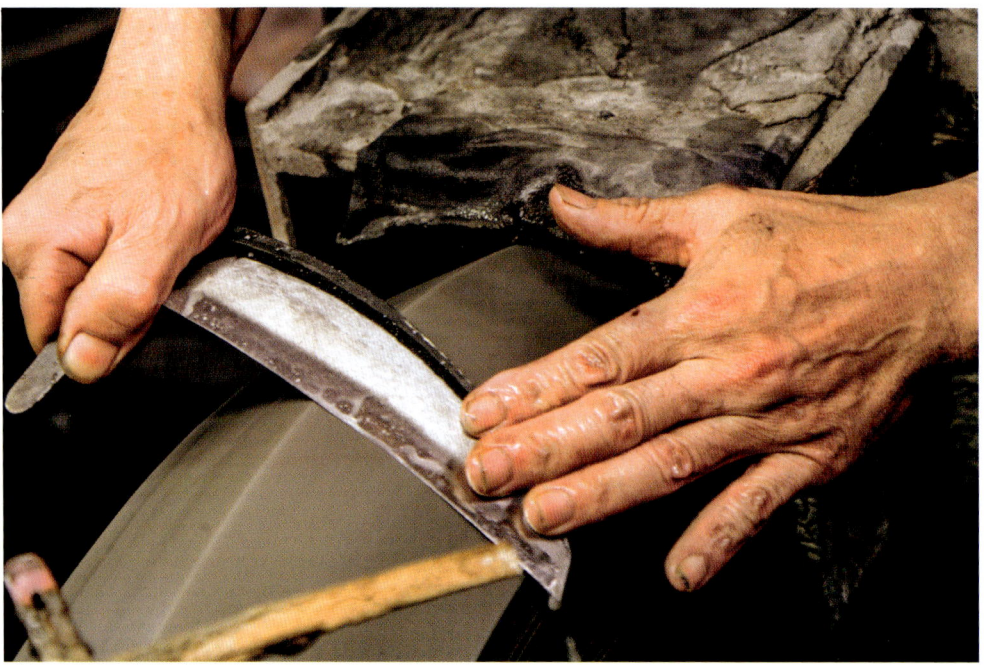

The straight edge is ground on both sides on the face of a large waterstone. The bevel has an angle of 12°; unlike the western sickle, it is not peened.

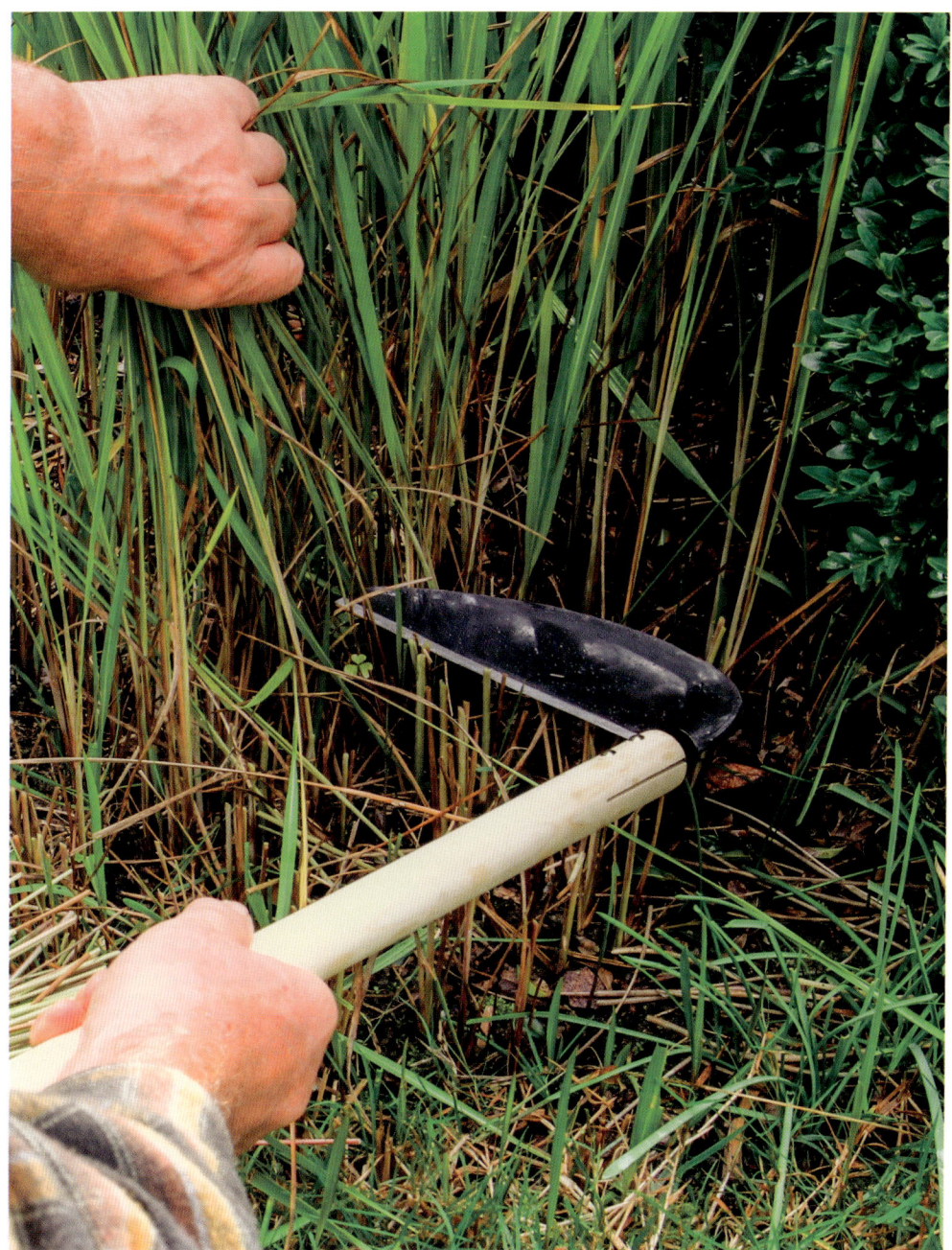

Equipped with a handle made of untreated magnolia wood *(ho)*, the *kama* is a feather-light (250 grams, or 8.81 ounces) and highly efficient cutting tool for grasses and herbs.

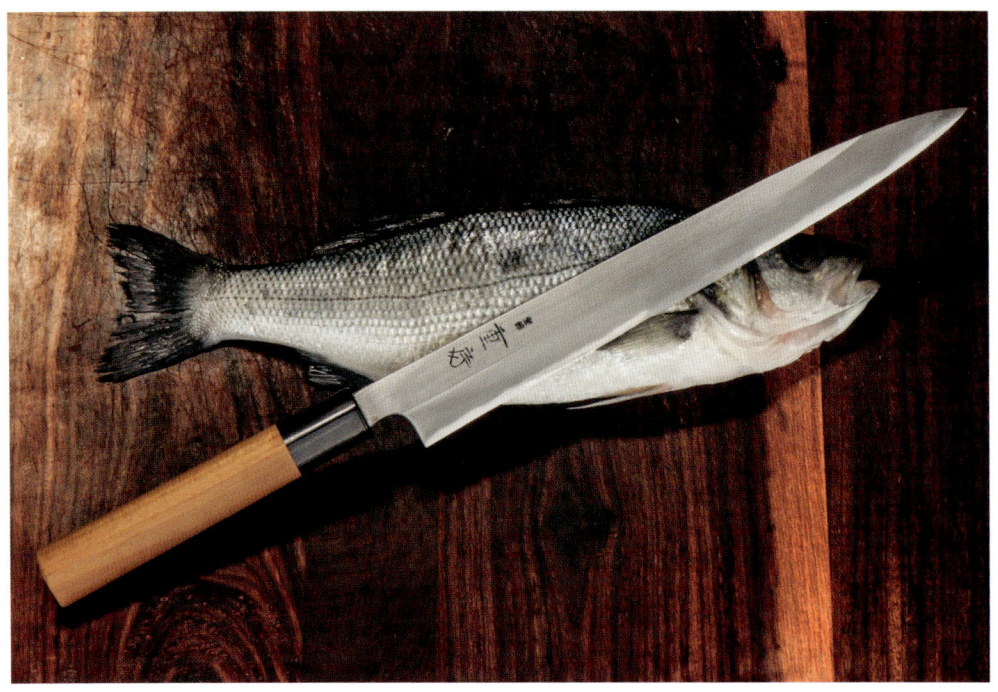

The beauty of the useful: a *sashimi hōchō* from Shigefusa.

The Fish Knife (*Sashimi Hōchō*)

No other object expresses the skill of the Japanese bladesmith as clearly as the *sashimi hōchō*. With it, the chef celebrates the art of cutting, turning raw fish into a treat for the eye and the palate. To achieve this, the blade must not only be razor sharp but also allow for highly precise cuts. For this purpose, the sashimi *hōchō* has a long, slender blade that is guided with a pull stroke. It cuts through even the most delicate food in a way that is extremely gentle on the tissue, while at the same time bringing out its flavor to the fullest. The knife's single edge is also well suited for precise handling; for example, when skinning fish.

For the bladesmith, the challenge is to create a knife with great hardness and thus the finest steel structure which, despite its length, has little risk of breaking. In addition, it must not be too heavy and must be well balanced in the hand. Cutting tools of this kind are born solely out of function. Their blade shape, named *yanagi ba* after the willow leaf, is correspondingly puristic. The *hamono-kaji*, a bladesmith with a strong sense of tradition, makes every effort to meet the expectations of his customers. With his products, he symbolically bows to the things that nature has given us.

Tokifusa Iizuka's forge in Niigata Prefecture is one of the few workshops that still pay uncompromising homage to pure manual labor and the associated work ethic. Under the company name Shigefusa, he has been supplying Japan's most demanding chefs with cutting tools in keeping with their standards for over fifty years. With the support of his sons, Yoshihide and Masayuki, as well as his wife Kyoko, Tokifusa, born in 1942, relies on the traditional methods of steel processing, which have their origins in sword forging. His teachers were Munenori Nagashima and Shigeyoshi Iwasaki (see page 93), both icons of Japanese blade forging. Stylistically, he follows the example of the legendary Chiyotsuru Korehide, whose purist blades are revered by connoisseurs as the epitome of Japanese aesthetics.

The elder of his two sons, forty-three-year-old Yoshihide, demonstrates the forging process used to produce a *sashimi hōchō* blade with a cutting length of 240 mm (9.4 in.) in the classic kasumi construction method. This refers to the one-sided bonding of a hard cutting-edge steel *(hagane)* with a basic blade body made of nonhardening iron-steel *(shigane)*. The thickness of the cutting-edge steel should not exceed 10% to 15% of the blade thickness.

Yoshihide uses a high-carbon Swedish tool steel with relatively low alloying contents (C 1.25%, Cr 0.17%, Si 0.20%, Mn 0.4%) as the cutting-edge steel. This is from an old stock of a material that is no longer commercially available in this composition and was probably still smelted with charcoal. From this flat material, Yoshihide forms a platelet about 1.5 mm (0.06 in.) thick and 85 mm (3.3 in.) long, which is beveled at the edges and slightly curved. A gradation toward the heel is intended to improve the breaking strength of the blade at the transition to the tang. The base material for the body is Japanese wrought iron with a very low carbon content (C 0.04%), called *kokunanko* by Yoshihide, which under the spring hammer is forged out to a thickness of about 8 mm (0.3 in.) and a width of 30 mm (1.2 in.).

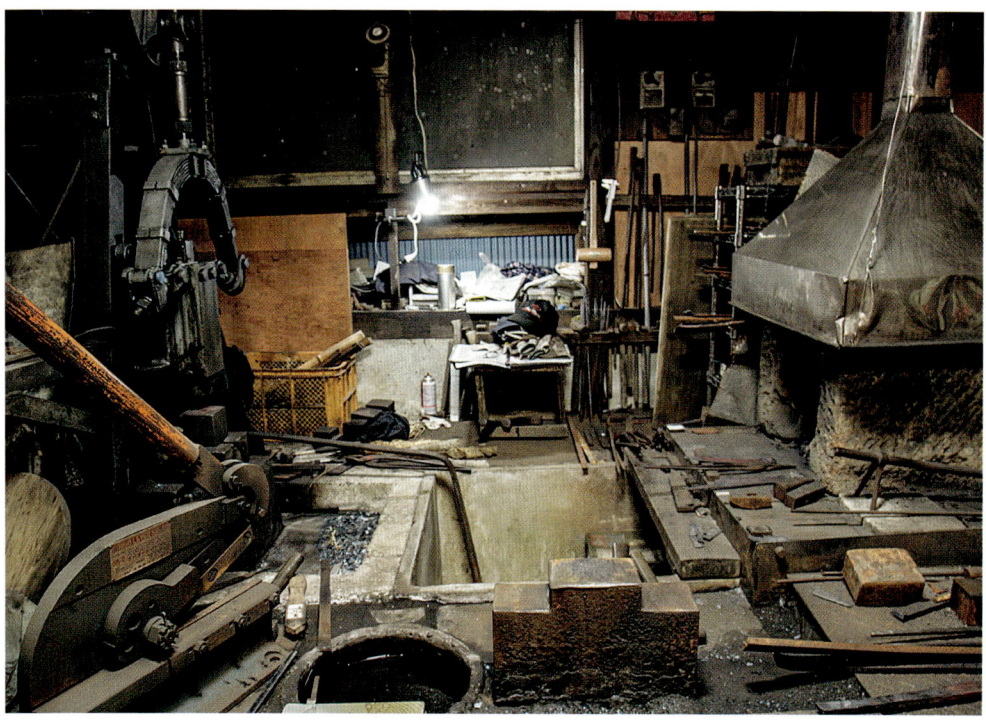

The workplace: the pit allows the blacksmith to work in a standing position at equipment traditionally designed for a seated posture (spring hammer, anvil, forge, etc.).

After fitting the plate to the flat iron, both parts are heated and liberally sprinkled with welding flux powder, a mixture of borax, boric acid, and iron oxide powder. The powder melts on the hot surface, forming an oxidation barrier. Now the composite is brought to the welding temperature of about 1,250°C (2,282°F) in the coke oven. A slight sparking signals the moment when the composite is removed from the furnace and forged with, at first, gentle hammer blows.

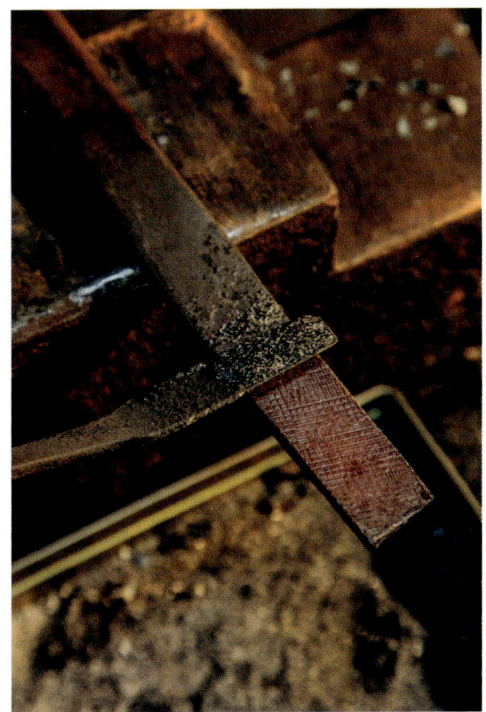

Welding flux powder is applied to the grooved flat iron, which has been heated to dark red.

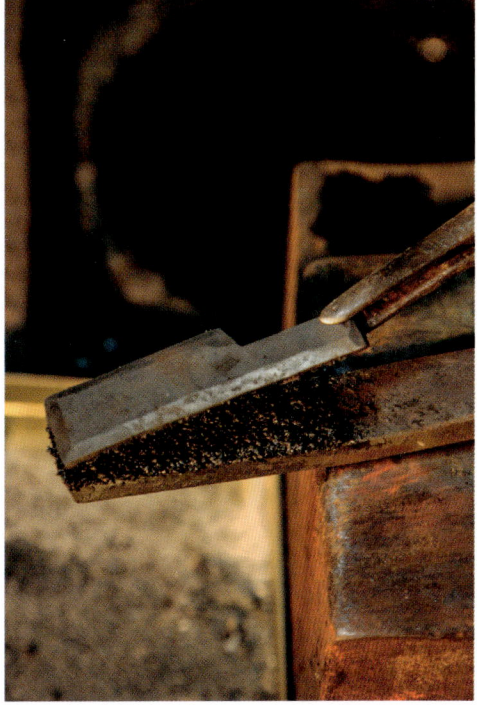

The plating steel, chambered at the edges and stepped toward the tang, is fitted to the basic body.

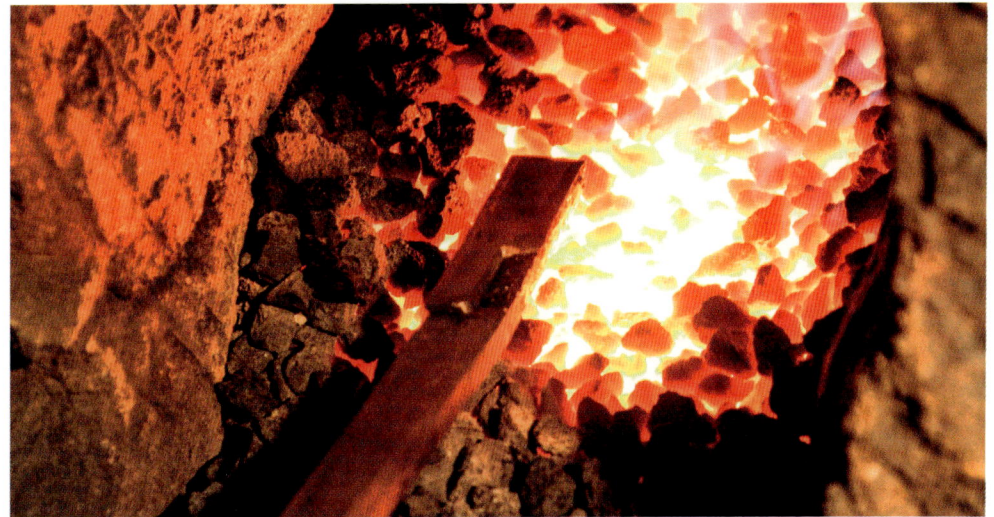

An evenly heated bed of embers is necessary for forge welding.

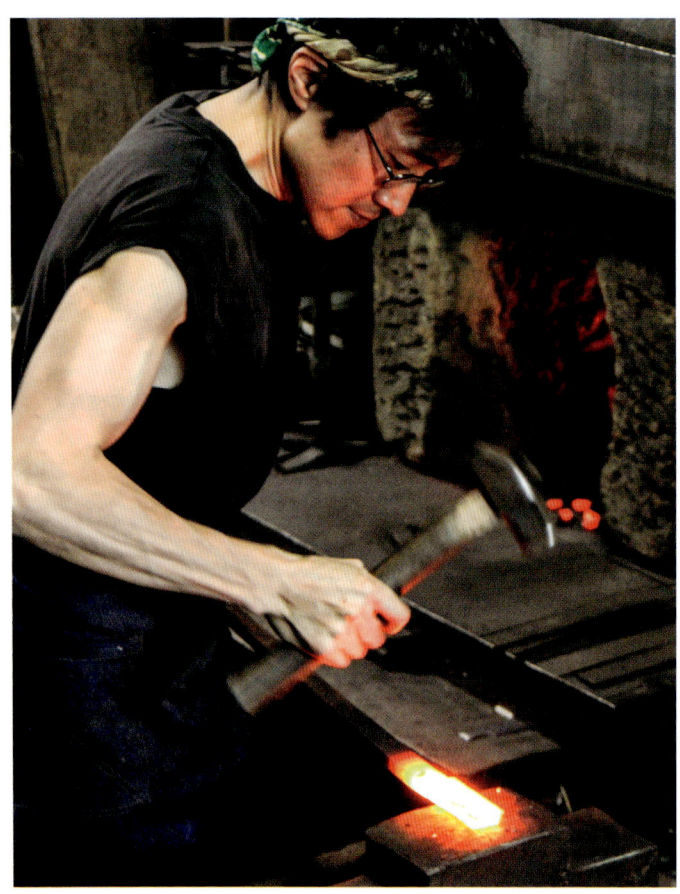

The steel is forge-welded with gentle blows.

The tang is shaped behind the plating and forged to a length about 90 mm (3.54 in.).

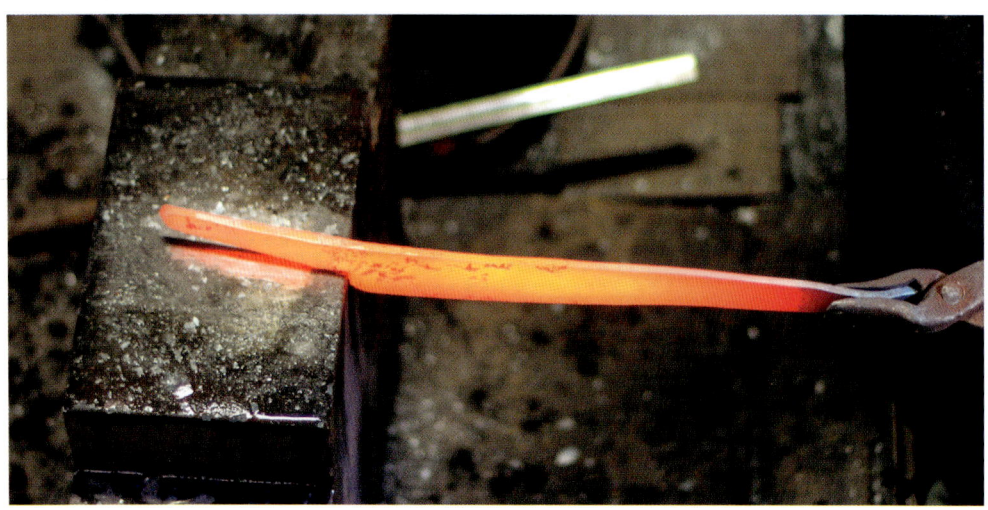

The Japanese Chisel *(tagane)*

Japanese blacksmiths use the tagane for cutting, splitting, piercing, or boring. When making this traditional tool, the chisel is clamped between two bamboo handles. This allows it to be guided by the smith without bouncing and with good thermal insulation. In the event of mechanical or thermal wear, the handles can be replaced quickly and inexpensively. In the event of high stress, steel slats can also be used as handles instead of bamboo.

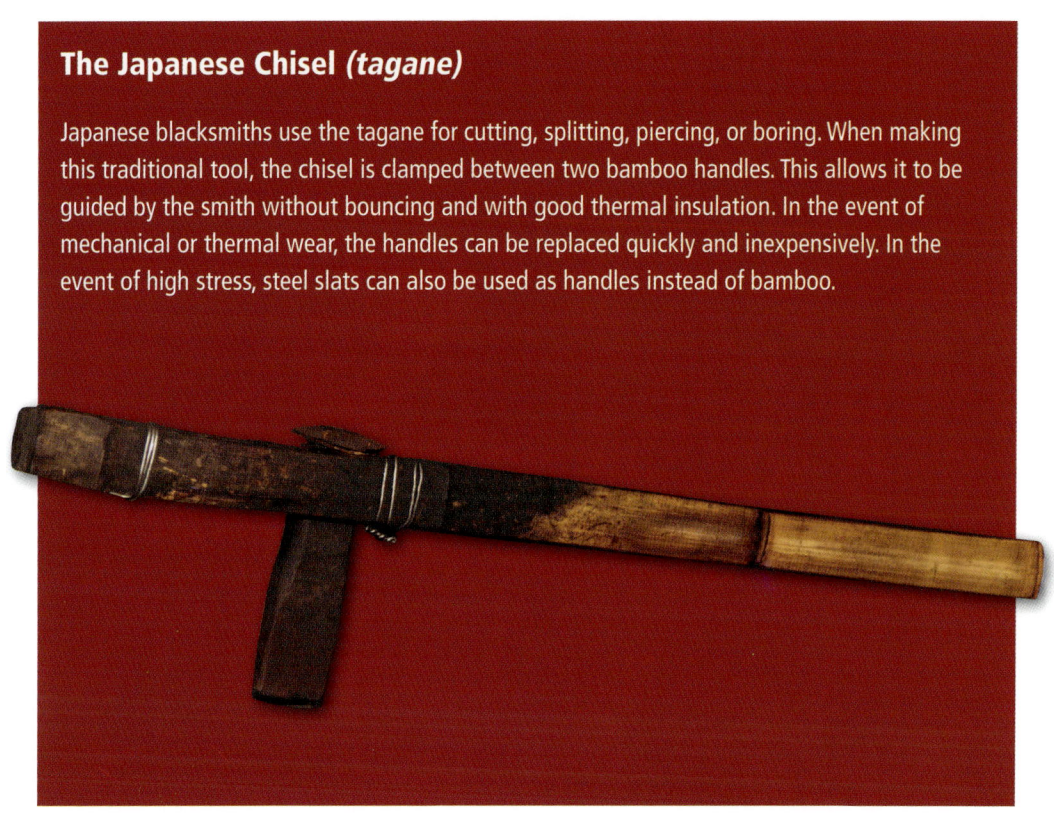

In the next step, the laminate is stretched to a length of 30 cm (1.18 in.) on the spring hammer at about 950°C (1,742°F) and then cut to length. To shape the tang, the excess material is first cut off with the shot chisel. In the process, Yoshihide's mother, Kyoko, delivers an impressive display of female clout. She wields the large *kozuchi* sledgehammer, whose overall length is almost equal to her height, while her son wields the shot tool. To avoid structural defects at the functionally very important tip, called the *kissaki*, the edge is also cut off here.

For the following fine forging, Yoshihide switches to the gas forge. First, the tang is conically forged to a length of about 90 mm (3.5 in.). Since the tang is heated and burned into the handle bore with a positive fit during subsequent handle assembly, its dimensions are not critical.

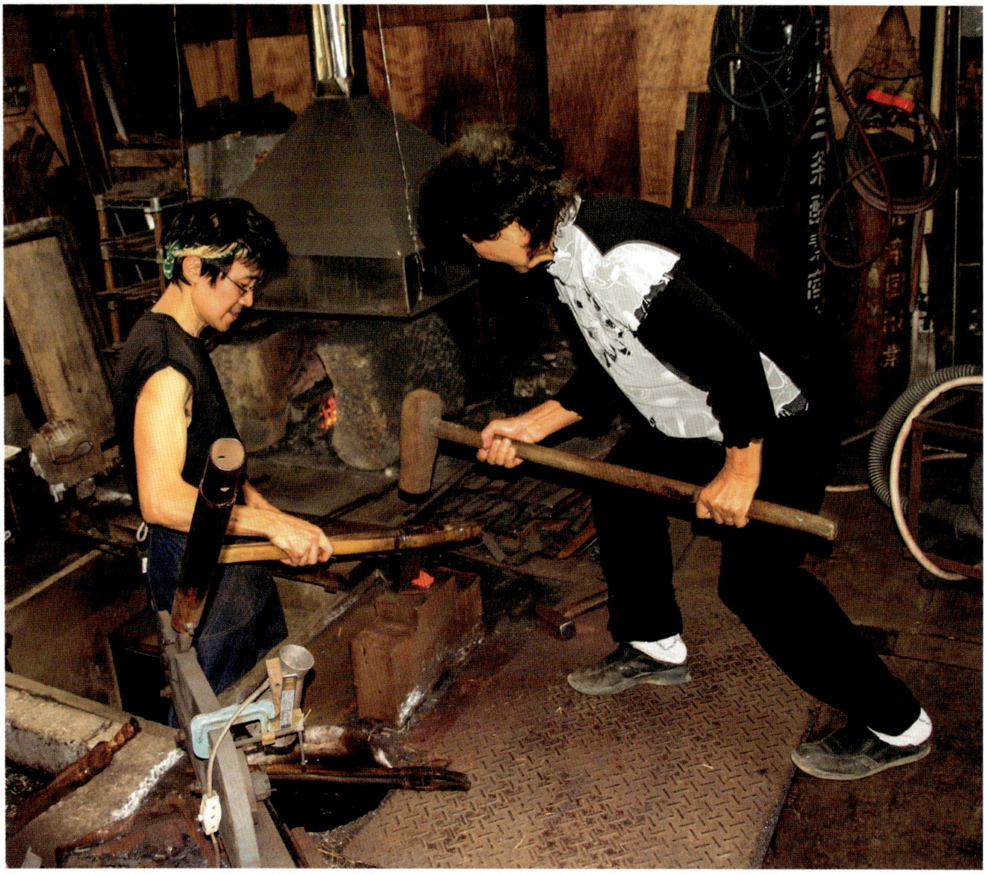

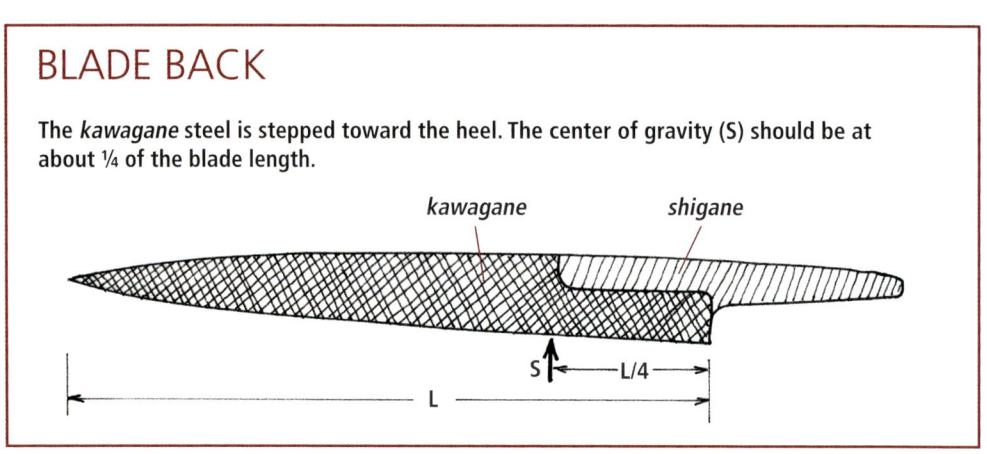

With the help of his mother, who wields the sledgehammer, Yoshihide shapes the blank to create the tang.

BLADE BACK

The *kawagane* steel is stepped toward the heel. The center of gravity (S) should be at about ¼ of the blade length.

kawagane   *shigane*

S↑ ←L/4→

L

The end of the tang is slightly cranked so that the blade can be better gripped with pliers during the subsequent shaping process. For fine forging, the blade is heated to yellow heat (950°C, or 1,742°F) only once, if possible. Working quickly at not too high a temperature is particularly important in this process to avoid decarburization of the cutting-edge steel. At the same time, this reduces scaling. As the temperature drops and the brittleness of the steel increases, the blows must be delivered more carefully.

With the hand hammer, the blade is continuously thinned from about 5 mm (0.2 in.) in thickness at the tang to 2 mm (0.08 in.) at the tip, primarily with blows to the iron side of the blank. The blade must not become too top-heavy. Ideally, the center of gravity should be about ¼ of the blade length from the rear cutting edge. The tip is formed first, and then the slender blade edge is worked out with quick, high edge strokes. The extremely flat bevel of about 10° is also predefined as precisely as possible, so that only a little material has to be removed later

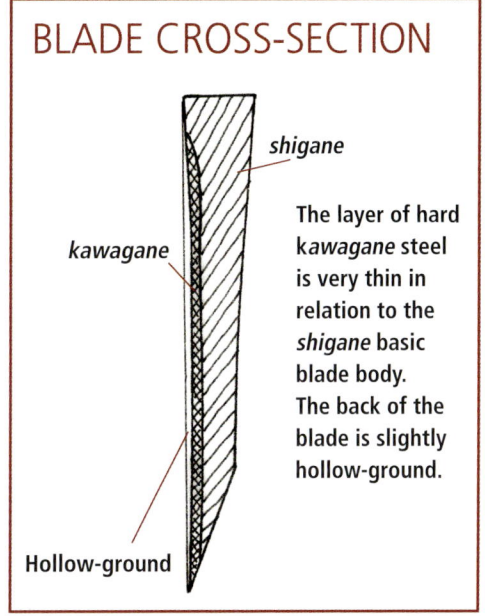

BLADE CROSS-SECTION

shigane

kawagane

The layer of hard kawagane steel is very thin in relation to the shigane basic blade body. The back of the blade is slightly hollow-ground.

Hollow-ground

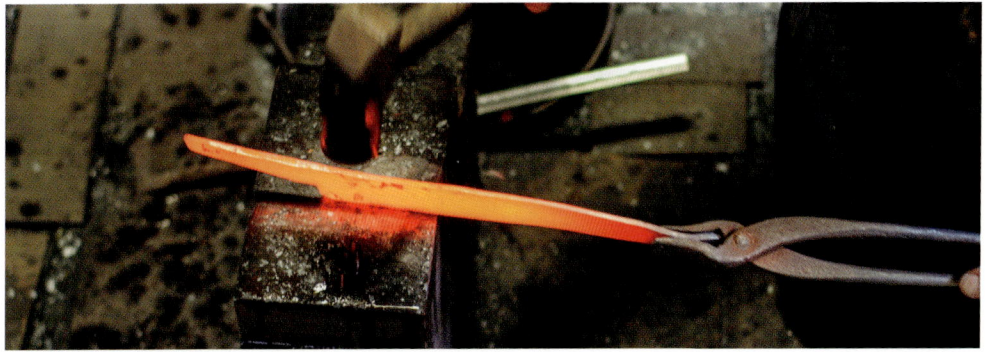

Upright forging emphasizes the willow leaf shape of the blade and improves the microstructure along the cutting edge.

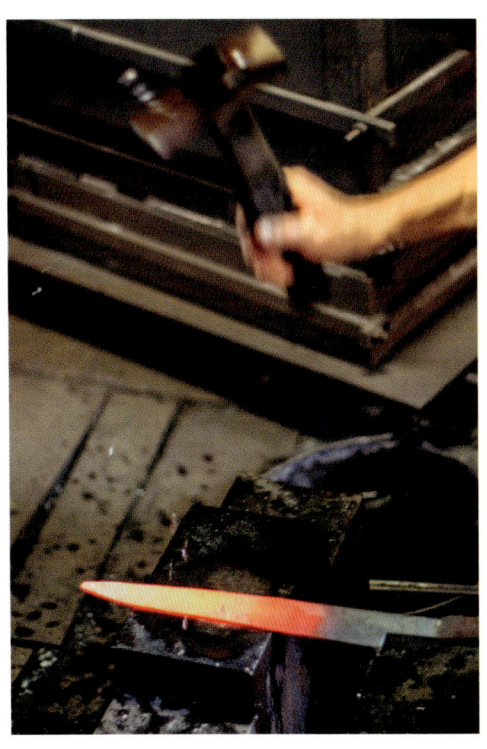

The blade is forged out slenderly toward the tip at temperatures that are not too high (750°C–950°C, or 1,382°F–1,742°F). The blade must not become top-heavy.

The finished forged blanks of various lengths are ready for grinding and hardening. The tangs are cranked for better handling.

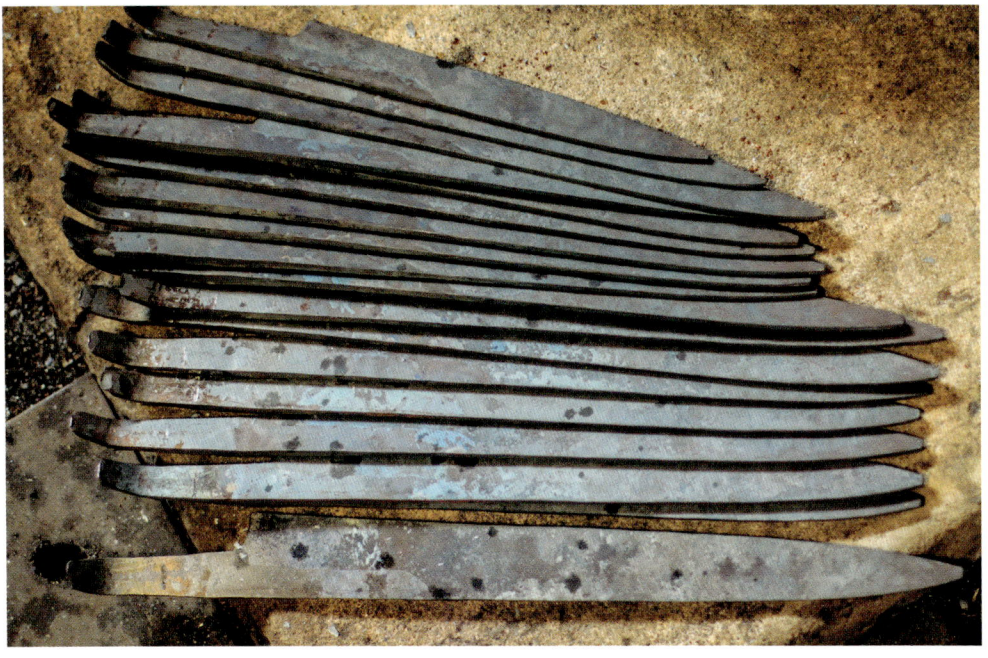

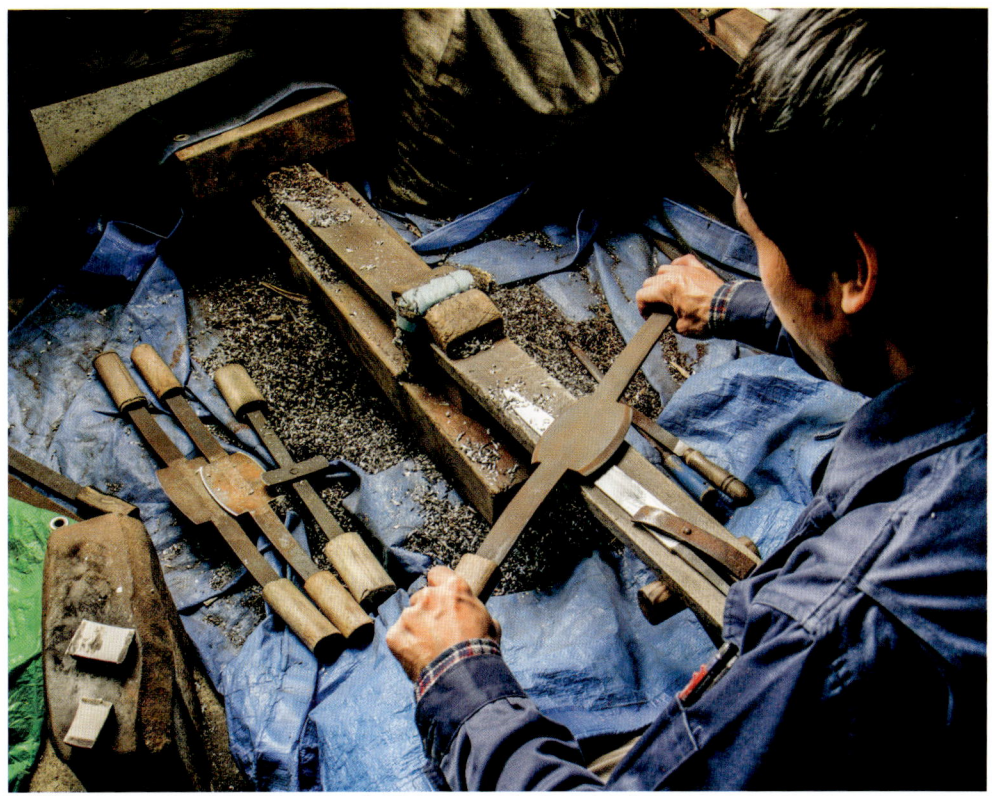

Sen scraping irons are used to smooth the front and back sides of the blades.

during grinding. In order to achieve the cleanest possible surface, Yoshihide always dips the hammer briefly in water, which promotes flaking of the scale.

After shaping, the blade is hammered again at about 600°C to 800°C (1,112°F to 1,472°F) in a process called *narashi*. This process, which serves solely to refine the grain, is not associated with any material deformation.

After forging, the blank is normalized at 780°C (1,436°F), which produces a homogeneous structure. After a short holding time, it is allowed to cool slowly in a bed of sand and rice straw ash.

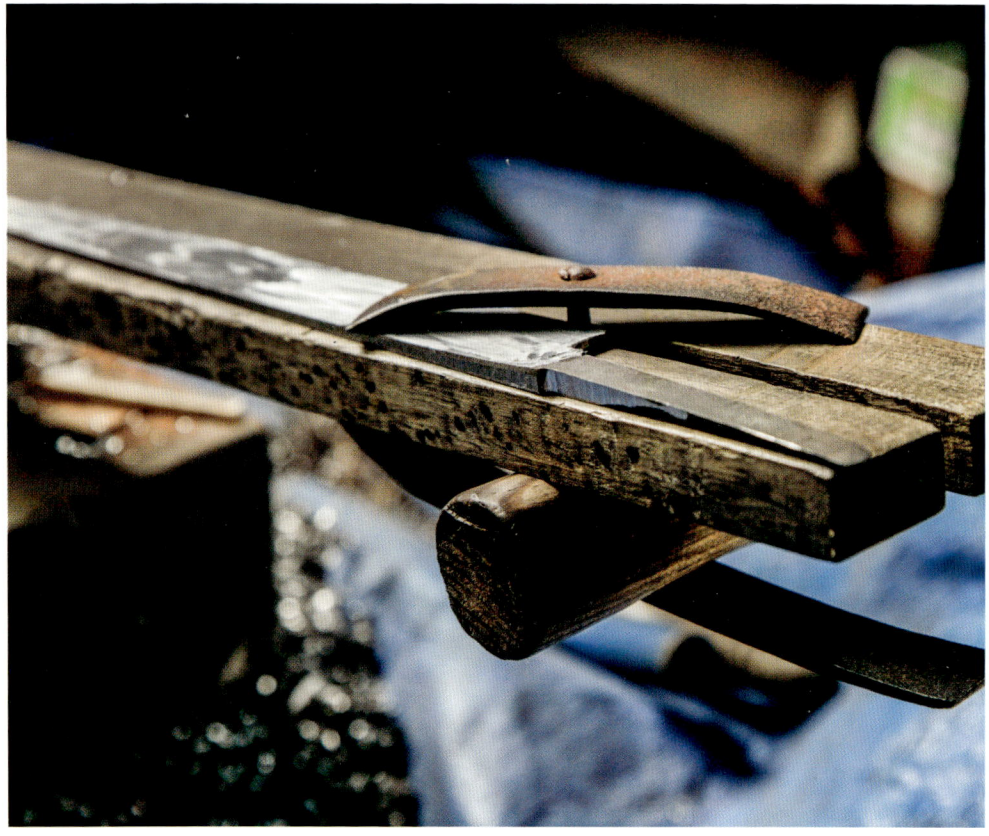

For scraping, the blade is fixed with a special clamp.

Now the surface is scraped with a scraping iron, called a *sen* in Japanese. This is a machining operation in which the unevenness left by forging is removed. Unlike grinding, this traditional process produces an exceptionally smooth, closed surface.

This convex-shaped steel tool is also used to create the hollow *(ura)* on the back side of the blade. It should not be deeper than 0.5 mm (0.02 in.) and should be limited by a narrow, closed edge, which lies on one level. This hollow, which is also found on other single-edged tools such as Japanese chisels, facilitates sharpening and reduces cutting resistance.

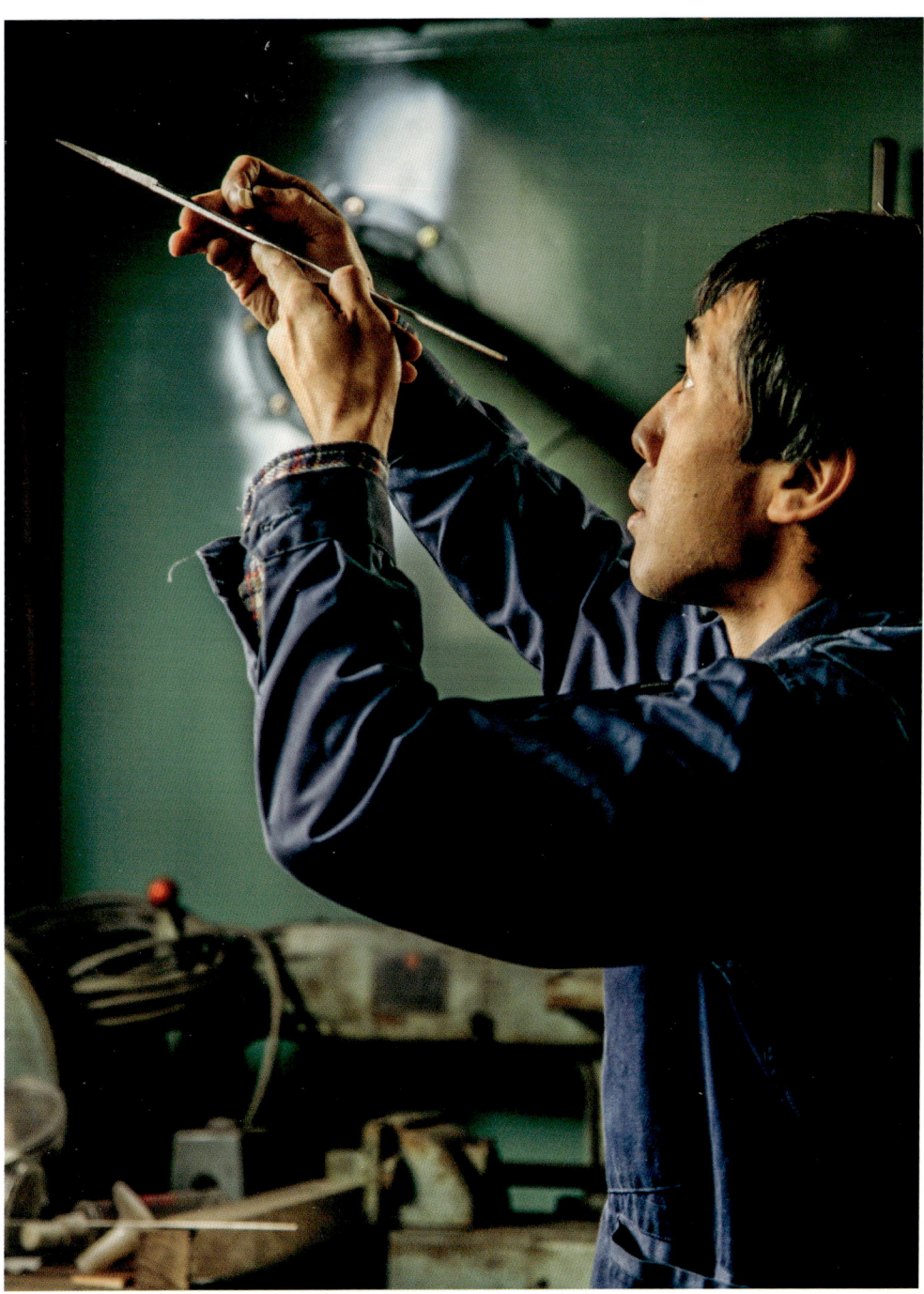

Both the shape and the balance of the blade are perfected during the finishing process.

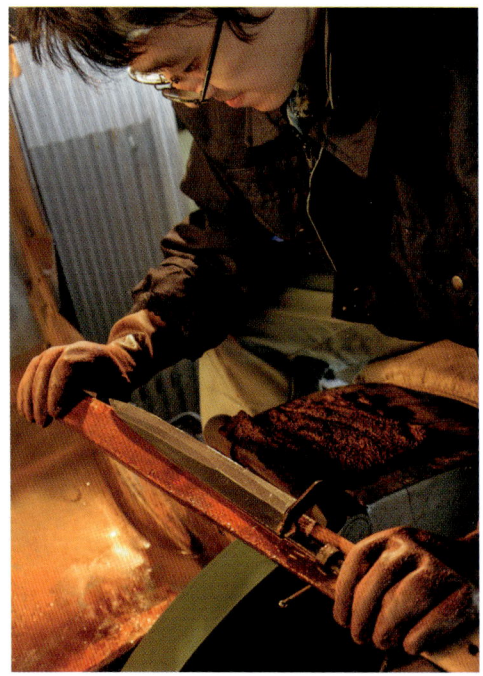

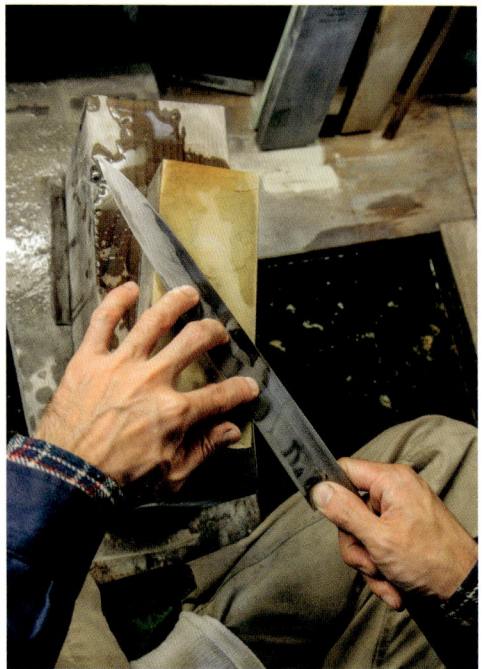

The bevel is reworked on a large-diameter water-cooled corundum wheel.

When honing on the fine natural stone, the fingers of the left hand exert pressure near the cutting edge, while the right hand guides the longitudinal movements of the blade.

The beveled edge is reworked freehand on the grinder, with the blade clamped on a wooden support for better handling and to avoid deflection.

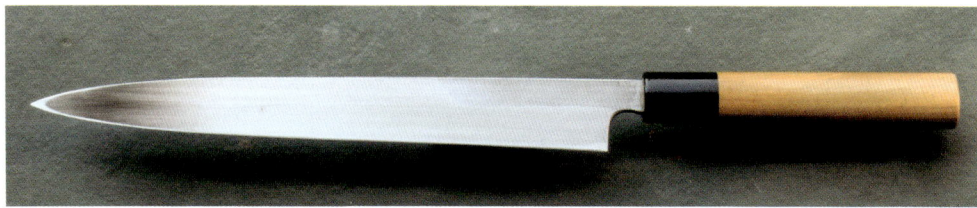

The back of the blade has a slight indentation bordered by a flush edge.

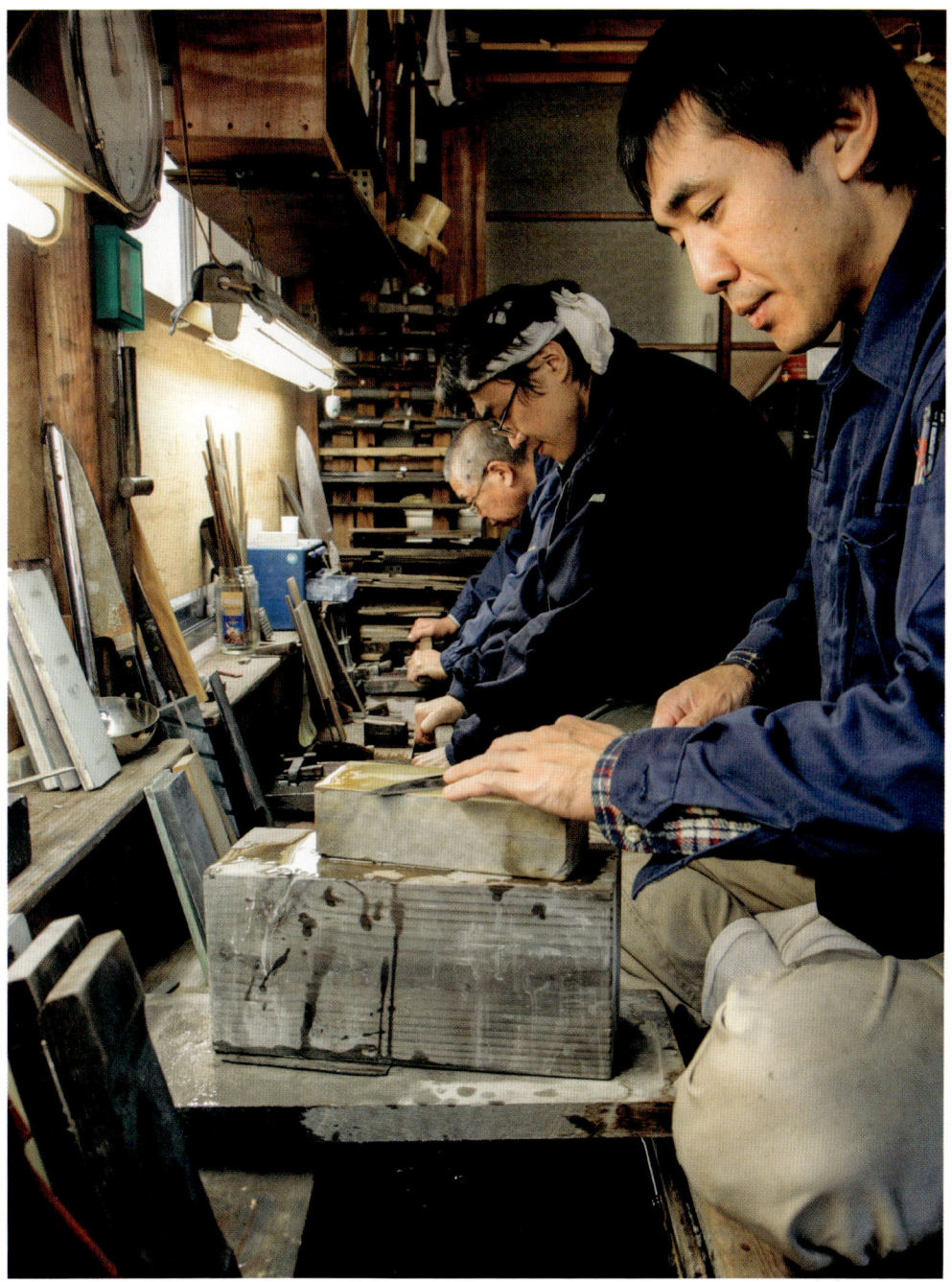

The finishing touches require the full concentration of the master and his two sons. The block stones rest securely on pedestals above a water basin.

Utmost Specialization

The Japanese chef usually has an entire arsenal of knives, each designed for a very specific purpose. For example, there is a version of the fish knife with a particularly thin blade that is used exclusively for gutting and cutting up the puffer fish *(fugu)*, the so-called *fuguhiki hōchō*. With this ultimate precision tool, the specially qualified chef ensures that the fish's highly toxic innards are removed completely, so that dinner does not become the "last supper."

A more common model for Western cooking is the so-called *santoku hōchō*, a multipurpose knife with the "three virtues" (fish, meat, and vegetables). Its blade is relatively high in order to be able to guide it close to the finger for julienne cuts, as well as being sharpened on both sides for universal use. To give the blade a lively effect, Master Iizuka prefers the *suminagashi* construction method for this knife shape. In this process, the Swedish carbon steel that serves as the cutting-edge steel is embedded in a multi-folded carrier material consisting of unalloyed and low-alloy iron. The resulting discreet cloud pattern looks as if painted with ink *(sumi)*.

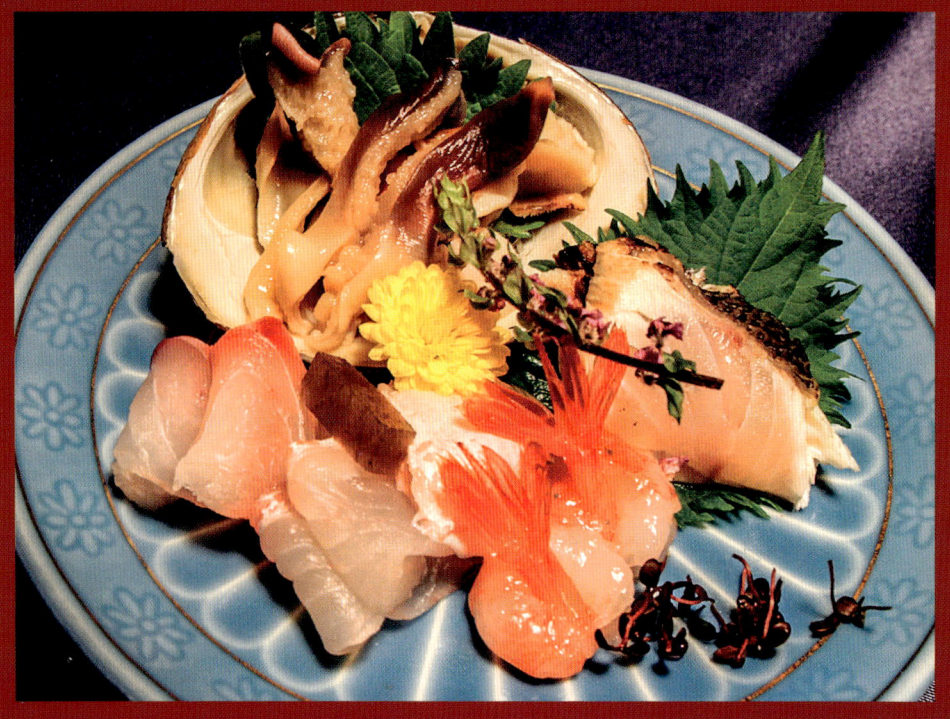

In preparation for hardening, the blade is coated with a thin clay slurry. After it has dried, it forms a separating layer to prevent surface oxidation and decarburization during heat treatment. The hardening temperature is 820°C (1,508°F) for the low-alloy carbon steel. A magnetic test on the red-hot blank shows whether the magnetic, ferritic structure has completely transformed into nonmagnetic austenite. After quenching in hardening oil at about 50°C (122°F), the blade is tempered for two hours at 180°C (356°F) to a cutting-edge hardness of 62 Rockwell C. Since the resulting martensite has a higher specific volume than ferrite, distortion during hardening is unavoidable. The resulting deflection is corrected by stretching the soft material with a straightening hammer before fine grinding and sharpening.

On Japanese waterstones of increasingly fine grain, the 10° beveled edge, which tapers "to zero," is ground by hand and finally honed to a mirror polish with natural *awaseto* whetstones. Only when the work satisfies the master's unerring eye does an engraver sign it with the brand name Shigefusa, a compound of the first names of his master Shigeyoshi and his own, Tokifusa. Finally, the knife is fitted by the master's wife with a light magnolia wood handle with a buffalo horn ferrule handle, to finally be used for its sole purpose: to transform the finest fish into edible works of art!

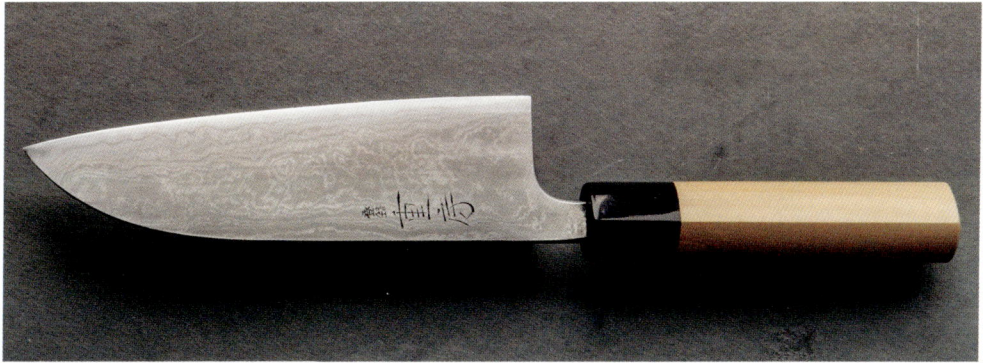

Another example from the Shigefusa knife forge: the *santoku hōchō* (multipurpose knife) in the *suminagashi* design. The blade, sharpened on both sides, has a discreet cloud structure.

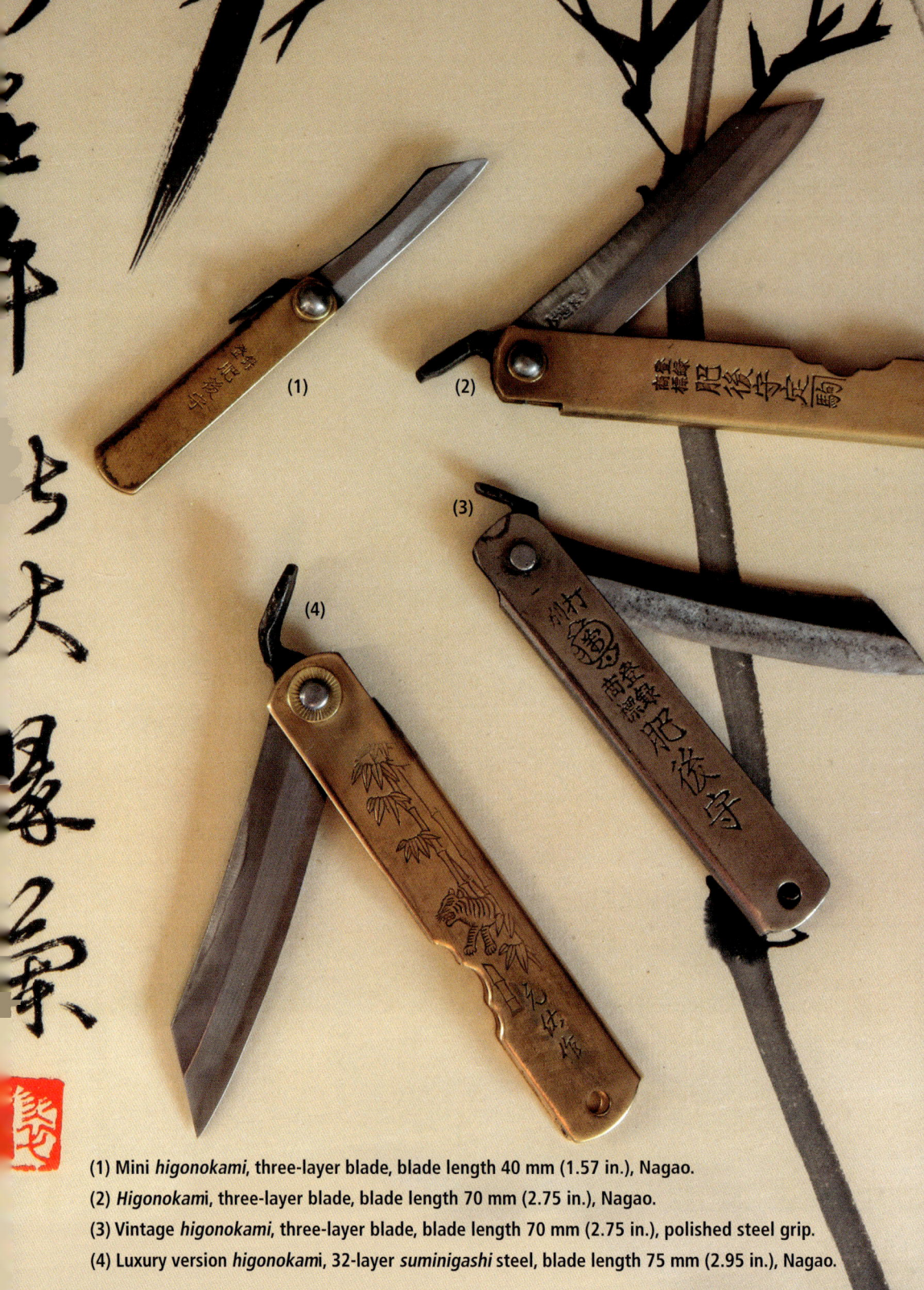

(1) Mini *higonokami*, three-layer blade, blade length 40 mm (1.57 in.), Nagao.

(2) *Higonokami*, three-layer blade, blade length 70 mm (2.75 in.), Nagao.

(3) Vintage *higonokami*, three-layer blade, blade length 70 mm (2.75 in.), polished steel grip.

(4) Luxury version *higonokami*, 32-layer *suminigashi* steel, blade length 75 mm (2.95 in.), Nagao.

The Folding Knife
(Higonokami)

Higonokami literally means "the lord of Higo"; Higo is the old name of the Japanese island of Kyushu. However, the noble character of the Japanese folding knives so named is not apparent at first glance. Rather, they have a rather rustic appearance with visible machining marks and a mechanism reduced to the elementary. Consisting of just three parts—the blade, the folded metal handle, and the rivet—the *higonokami* exemplifies a culture of omission that is typical of the traditional Japanese canon of forms.

After the disempowerment of the samurai by the so-called Meiji Restoration and the associated public ban on carrying swords, many swordsmiths were forced to reorient themselves in the second half of the nineteenth century. In many cases, they switched to the camp of the knife makers, which thus experienced a special blooming of craftsmanship.

In Miki, one of the centers of cutlery production, worked the former swordsmith Teji Murakami. In 1896, a traveling tool merchant named Tasaburo Shigematsu gave him a primitive peasant folding knife with a U-shaped folding sheath that also served as a handle when unfolded. He had acquired the knife, originally called a *tosu*, on the island of Kyushu (formerly Higo). Despite good sharpness, however, its utility was severely limited by the lack of any kind of blade lock.

By adding a bent lever at the rear end of the blade, which also served as a stop when unfolded, Master Murakami quickly corrected this flaw. He thus paved the way for the enormous success of this inexpensive and versatile knife, which was henceforth called the *higonokami* after its place of origin. The Higonokami Knifemakers Guild was founded in 1899, with up to two hundred employees in its heyday, and in 1907, the name was officially registered as a trademark.

Because of its blade shape, which is based on the Japanese sword, the *higono-kami* is often called the "the katana's little brother." However, it never functioned as a weapon but instead served in the first half of the twentieth century as an everyday tool that was a vital part of almost every household. It was just as indispensable for craftsmen, hunters, and fishermen as it was for schoolchildren, who used it to sharpen bamboo nibs. The sharper the nibs, the more beautiful the *kanji* characters. For this reason, for a long time there were even nationwide sharpening competitions!

The spread of the *higonokami* came to an abrupt end in the 1960s, when a prominent politician was assassinated by an attacker armed with a sword—not a folding knife. This nevertheless led to a drastic tightening of the weapons laws in Japan. Even the small *higonokami* fell victim to the rigid measures— and it was henceforth banned from students' schoolbags. As a result of the ensuing collapse in demand, only two of the more than fifty workshops in Hyogo Prefecture that existed at the time of the folding knife's heyday are still in existence today. The author visited them in June 2015.

Nagao Seishakusho

Knifemaker Komataro Nagao was one of the first manufacturers of the *higono-kami* at the end of the nineteenth century and cofounder of the knifemakers' guild of the same name. His descendant Mitsuo Nagao, who now runs the Miki-based company, is currently the sole owner of the trademark rights. Equipped with a small park of mostly self-designed machines and with the expert assistance of a small staff, he produces fifty to two hundred *higonokami* a day, depending on the design and quality.

There are about thirteen different production steps:
1. Punching out the brass sheet blank for the handle.
2. Stamping the brand name, usually accompanied by a mythological character; for example, the *kanji* character for "dragonfly" *(tombo)*, which enjoys special esteem in Japan.
3. Folding of the handle plate.
4. Punching and perforation of the blade blank from three-layer steel sheet *(sanmai)* 3 mm (0.11 in.) thick. The middle cutting-edge layer is made of Hitachi No. 2 blue paper steel *(aogami 2)* embedded in unalloyed iron. For deluxe versions, a 5 mm thick (0.19 in.), thirty-two-layer *suminagashi* steel is used. Here, too, the center layer is made of *aogami* 2. Both laminate steels can be obtained in Japan as hot-rolled semifinished products. The cranked lever at the end of the blade is then hot set on the same press.
5. Forging the beveled edge on both sides.
6. Rough grinding of the beveled edges, using an automatic grinding machine
7. Fine sanding by hand on a stone grit of 46.
8. Hardening: in simple versions of the knife, the blade is heated by hand in the gas flame and then quenched in oil. High-quality models are heated in a lead bath, which allows more accurate temperature control (790°C, or 1,454°F).
9. Tempering in the furnace (180°C [356°F] for one hour), final hardness 59 HRC.
10. Assembly of the blade and handle, and riveting.
11. Fine grinding of the flanks and beveled edges (60/160/240 grit).
12. Grinding "to zero" by means of a faceplate and sandpaper (320 grit).
13. Honing and polishing on the felt wheel (red and green paste of Koyo brand).

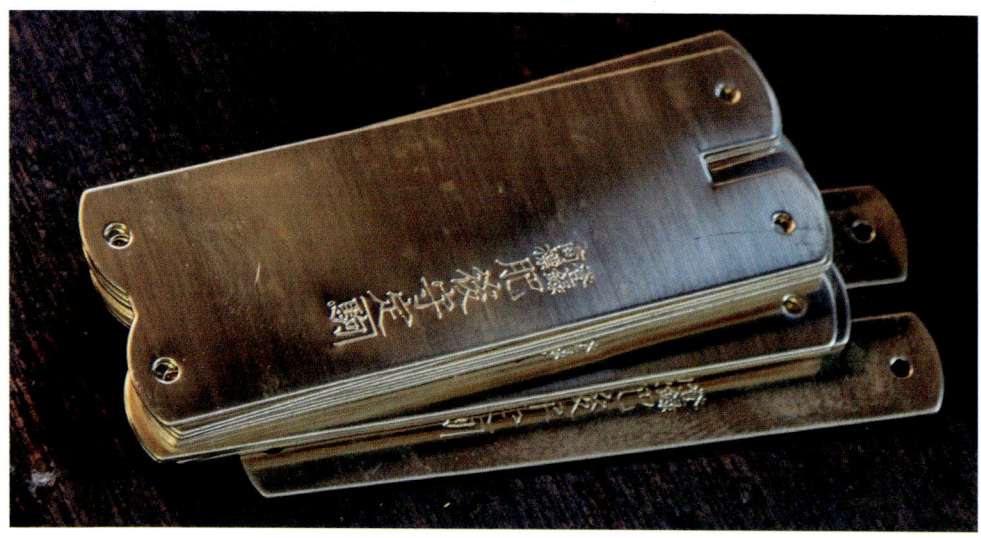

The sheet brass blanks for the handles, ready to be folded.

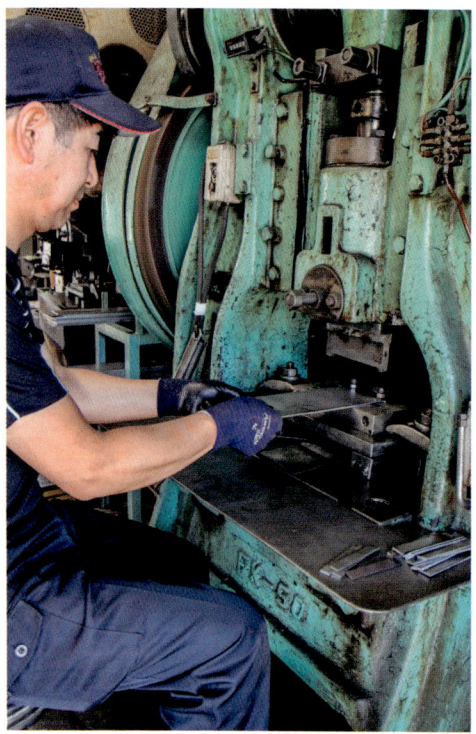

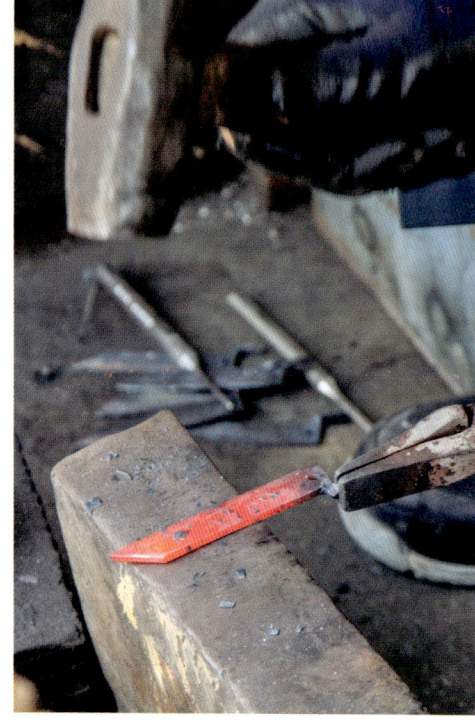

The blade is punched out of three-layer sheet metal.

The flanks and bevels are forged by hand on the anvil close to the ground.

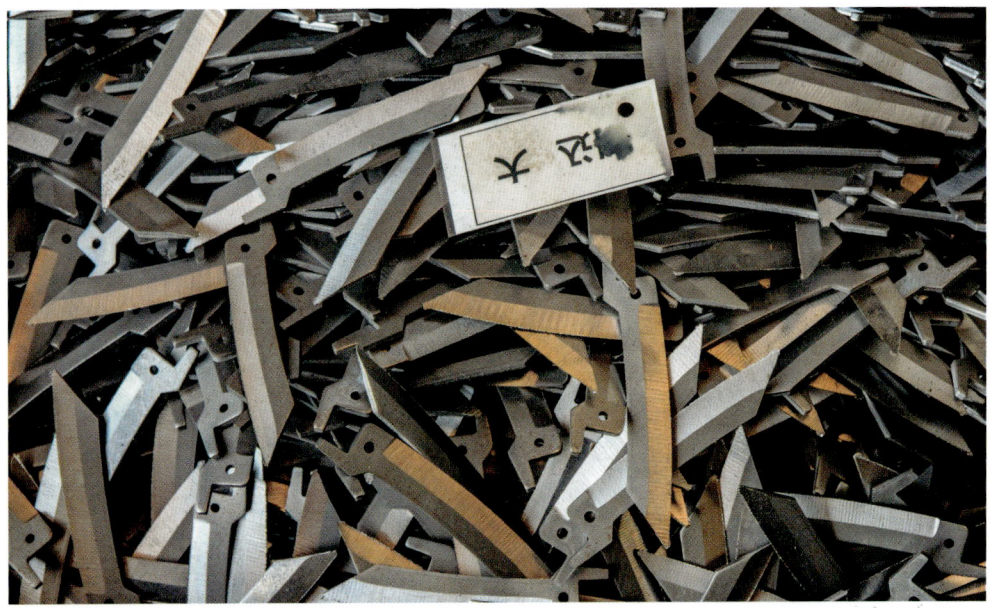

After rough processing on the grinding machine, the blades are ready for fine grinding.

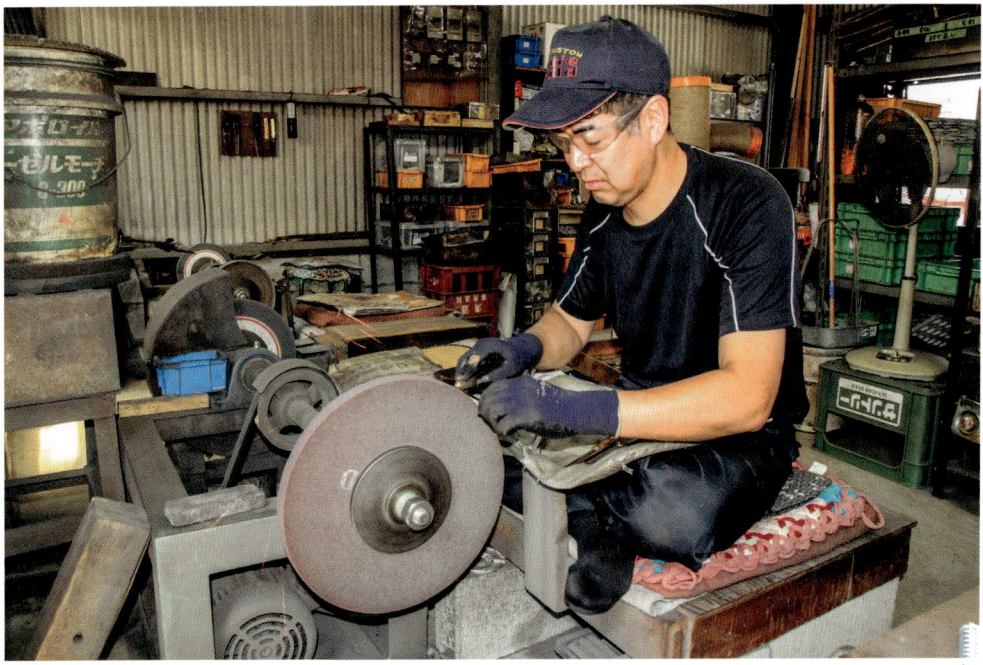

Forty-seven-year-old Mitsuo Nagao, shown here fine-grinding, is the fifth generation to run the business. Note that even in the workshop he has removed his shoes!

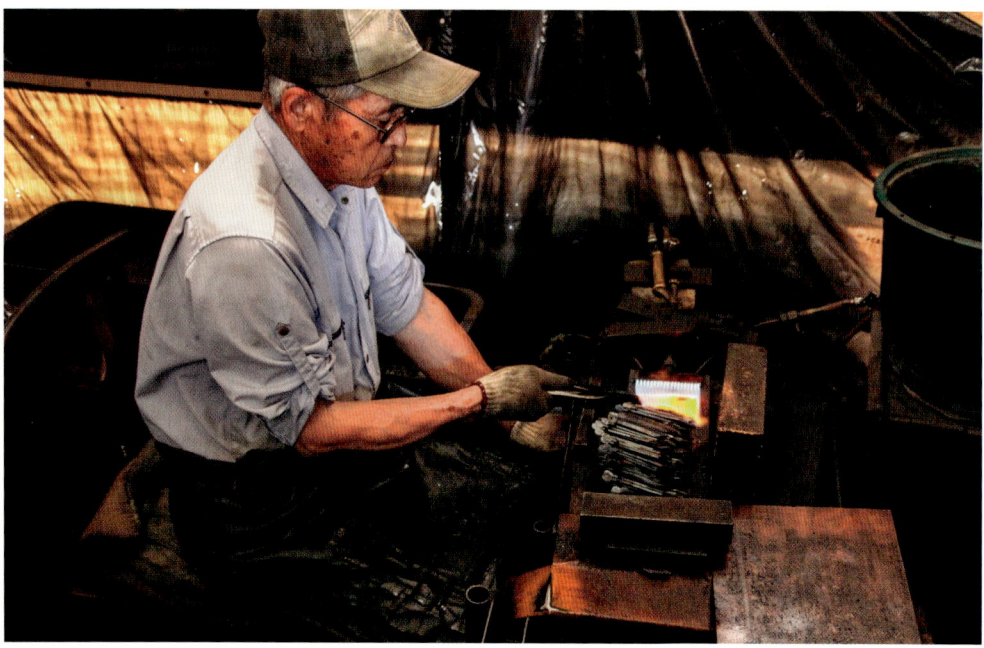

The experienced employee can tell when the metal has reached the correct hardening temperature by its color. The blade must be heated at a uniform temperature and not for too long: these are decisive factors for the quality of the blade.

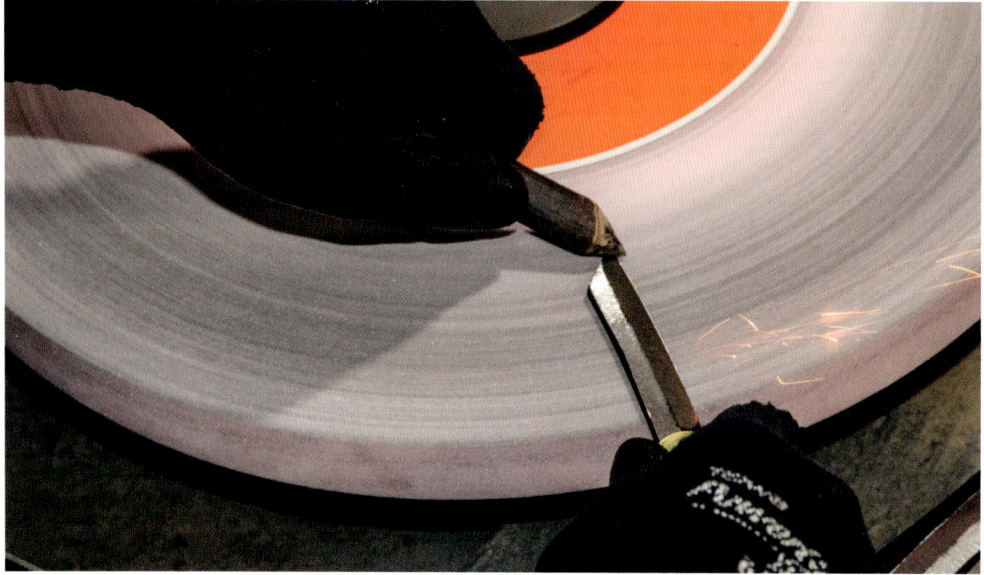

Sharpening is performed on a sandpaper-covered faceplate.

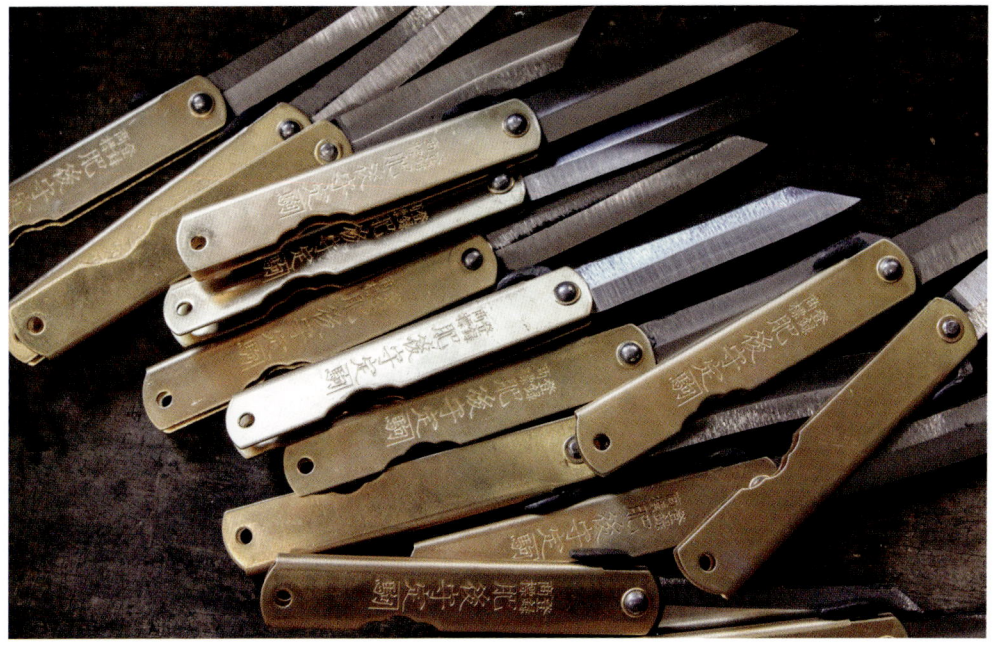

After being honed on the felt wheel, the knives are ready for packing.

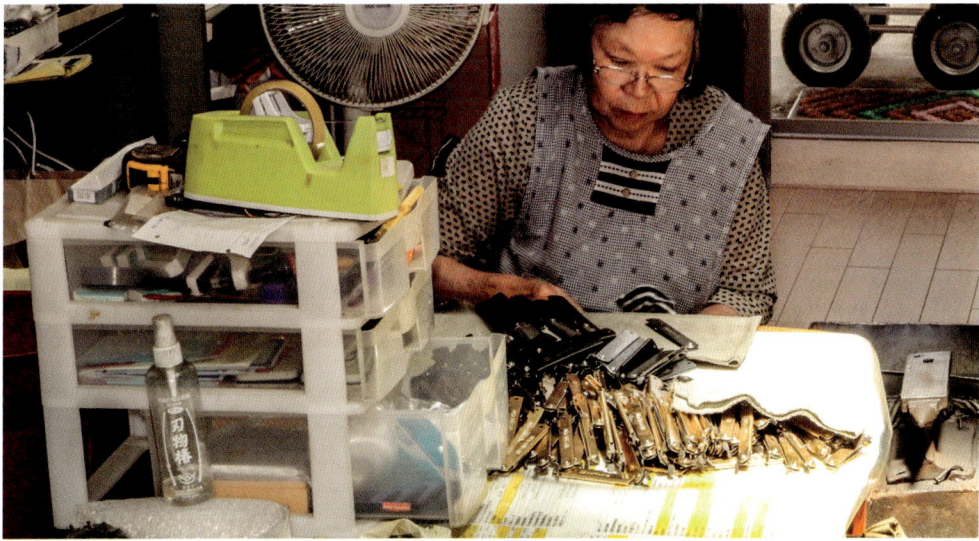

Packaging and final inspection is the job of Nagao's seventy-six-year-old (at the time visited) mother. There is a system to the fact that she ignores minor machining marks: according to Japanese tradition, the final finish of the cutting tool is always the responsibility of the owner, who makes it a "part of himself."

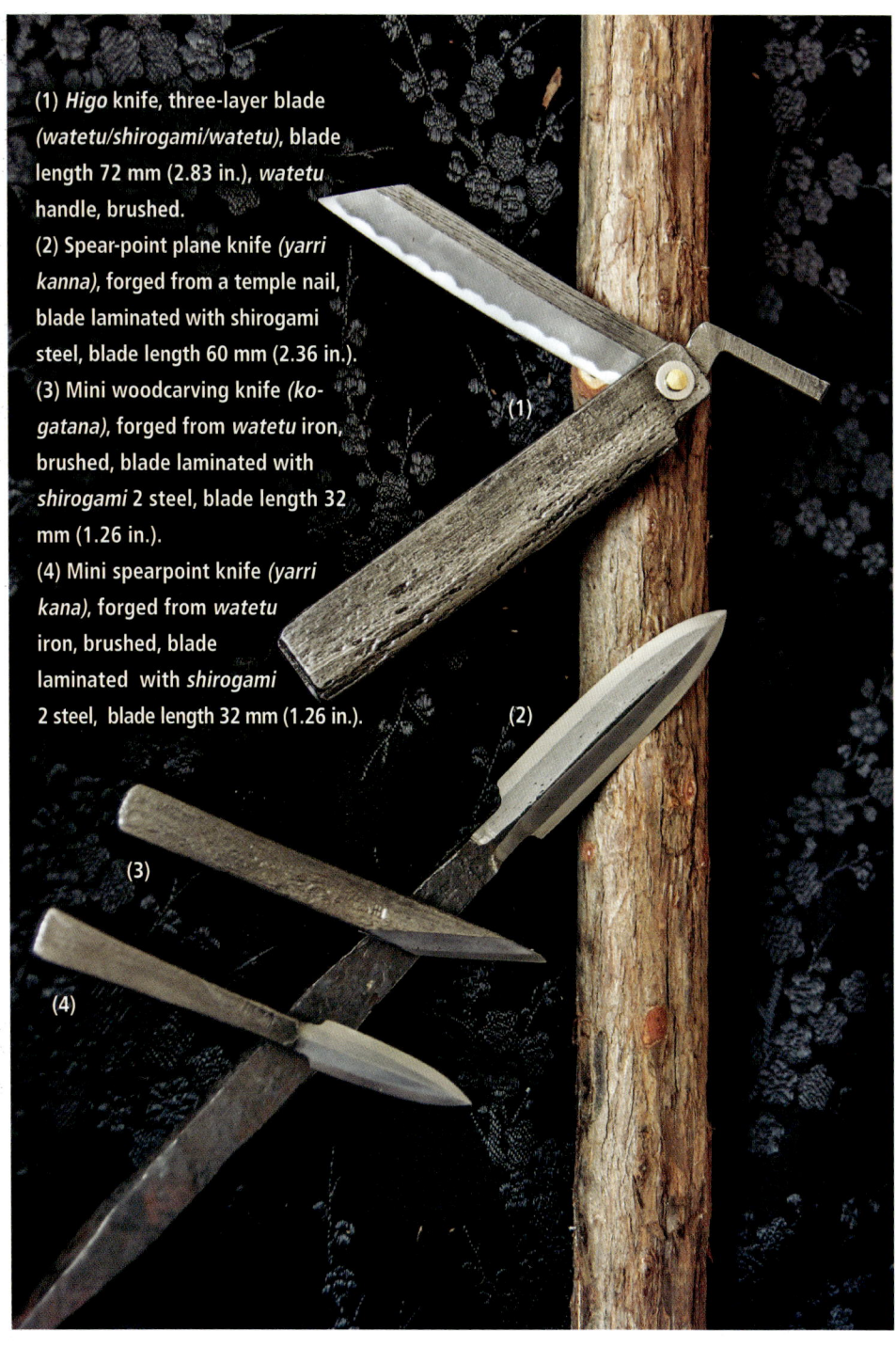

(1) *Higo* knife, three-layer blade *(watetu/shirogami/watetu)*, blade length 72 mm (2.83 in.), *watetu* handle, brushed.

(2) Spear-point plane knife *(yarri kanna)*, forged from a temple nail, blade laminated with shirogami steel, blade length 60 mm (2.36 in.).

(3) Mini woodcarving knife *(ko-gatana)*, forged from *watetu* iron, brushed, blade laminated with *shirogami* 2 steel, blade length 32 mm (1.26 in.).

(4) Mini spearpoint knife *(yarri kana)*, forged from *watetu* iron, brushed, blade laminated with *shirogami* 2 steel, blade length 32 mm (1.26 in.).

Osamu Tomita

In Osamu Tomita, we meet a master of "the old school," who also runs his quaint workshop near Miki. Here, he produces not only *higonokami* (which he calls "*higo* knives" for trademark reasons), but also traditional woodworking tools, mainly by hand. A new product line consists of mini tools, which are manufactured with the same precision and quality as their big brothers. They go mainly to collectors in the USA.

As a tradition-conscious maker of tools and knives, he refuses to use prefabricated laminate steels, thus relinquishing control over the most important steps in the process: the selection, preparation, and forge welding of the blade steel. Osamu prefers to use old *watetu*, once produced in a bloomery, as the starting material for the knife bodies. The material, which is comparable to our historical puddled iron, is excellent for forging and sharpening.

Above all, however, *watetu* can be used to create wonderful surface structures that lend the tool created with it a highly individual character. One should therefore not be surprised to find various boxes of rusty temple nails, door hinges, or anchor chain links in Tomita's workshop, obtained through contacts with scrapping or restoration companies. But these sources are gradually drying up, so that he increasingly has to resort to industrially produced iron.

Tomita uses mainly *hirogami* 2, a high-carbon steel produced by Hitachi from iron sand, as the cutting-edge steel; occasionally he uses real sword steel *(tamahagane)*, which he obtains from a swordsmith friend. Sword steel is not officially sold to toolsmiths. The rough forming work and the forge welding are carried out on the oil forge, while further processing is carried out in the coke forge on the ground.

Before hardening, the blades are coated with a thin clay slurry *(tonoko)* to prevent surface decarburization of the steel. Charcoal obtained from pine trees, chopped into uniformly small pieces, is the most suitable fuel for the hardening fire. After quenching in the hardening oil, the blades rest for three hours in a box filled with rice straw ash while still hot, which reduces the residual stresses and results in a final hardness of about 61 Rockwell C. The blades are then sharpened and tempered. The subsequent sharpening and assembly work follows the usual pattern.

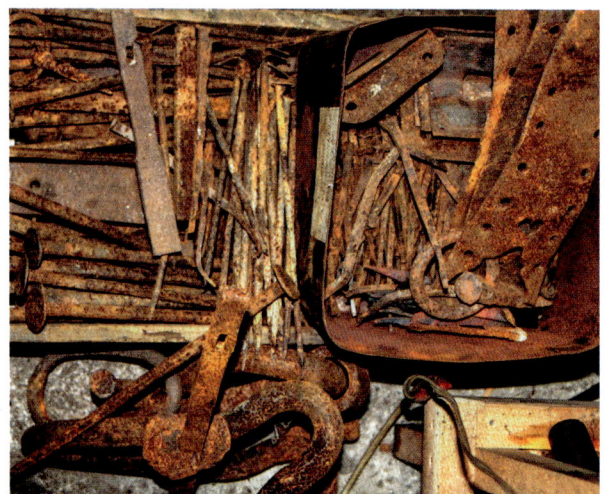

Valuable scrap iron: fittings and nails from demolished buildings, at least a hundred years old. They form the basic material for *higo* blades, handle scales, and tool bodies. Not only is this material excellent for forge welding, it also has advantages when it comes to sharpening.

Striking appearance: folded and forged flat, *watetu* reveals a distinctive grain that in the final product is further enhanced by brushing.

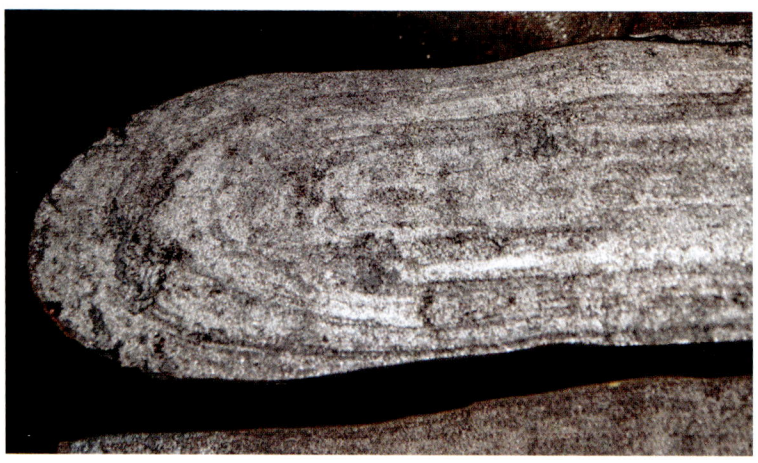

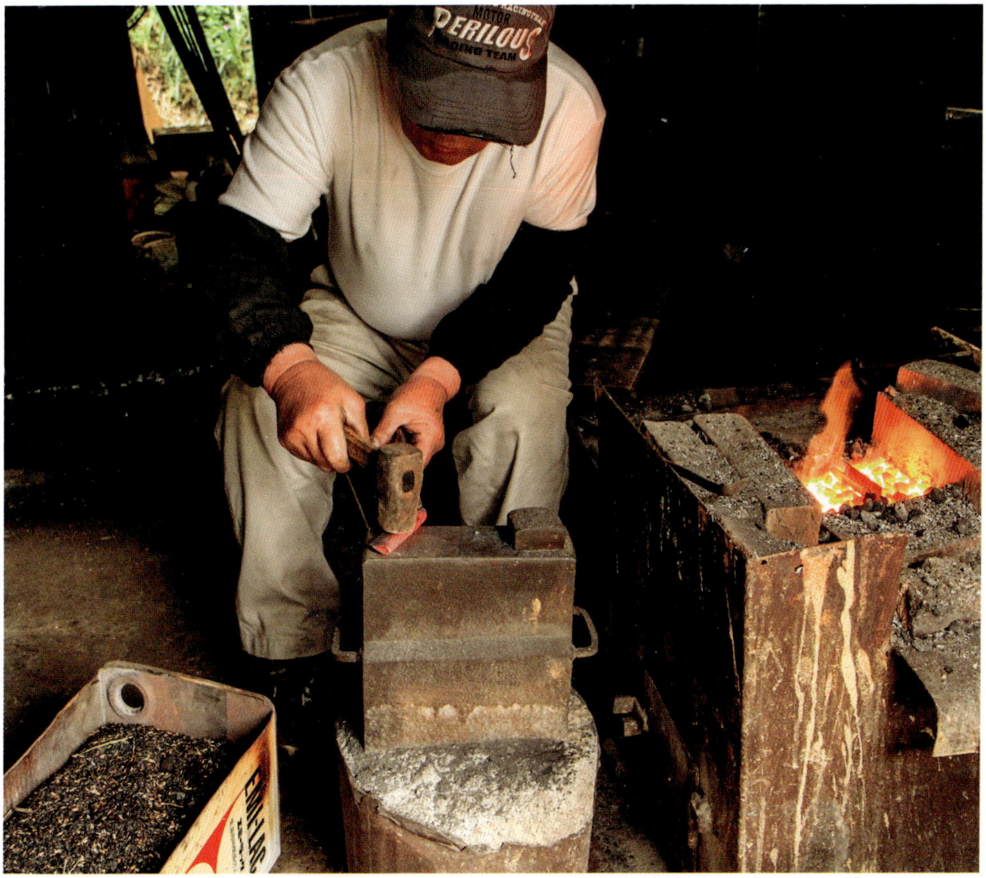

Osamu Tomita shapes the handle scales for his *higo* knives freehand on the anvil from thinly forged recycled iron.

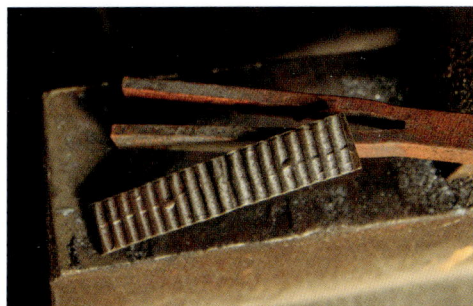

Striation of the core steel prevents movement during the subsequent forge welding process and improves the bond.

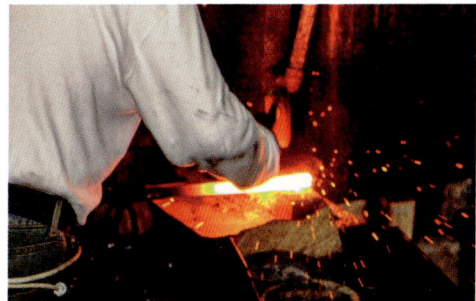

The composite, heated to white heat, is forge welded on the anvil with blows that are not too heavy.

Osamu Tomita's products bear witness to how versatile and creative the black-smith's profession can be. Nevertheless, the knifesmith, who was born in 1945, has no successor—despite a good order situation. But the virtuoso master is not thinking of quitting: "What else could I do? After all, forging keeps you young!" Anyone who has had the opportunity to observe him at work has no doubt about this.

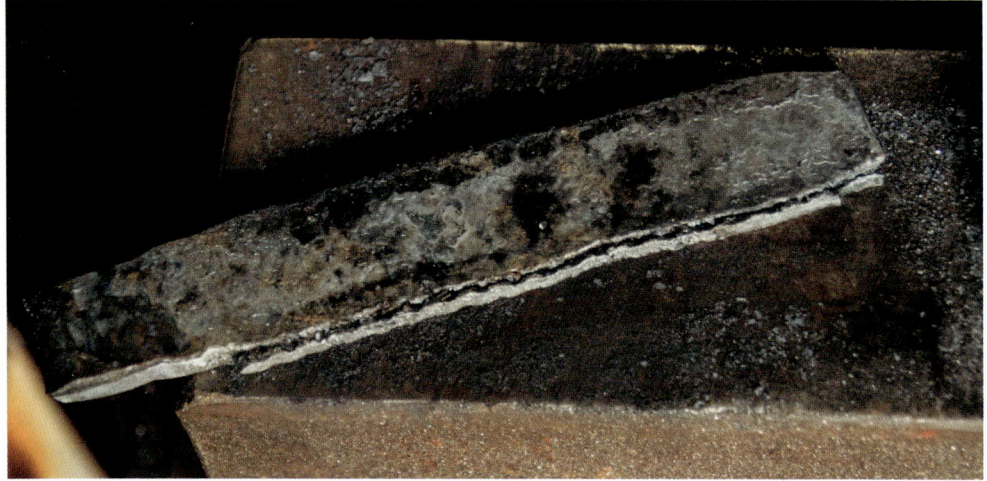

Each forge welded blank produces two *higo* blades.

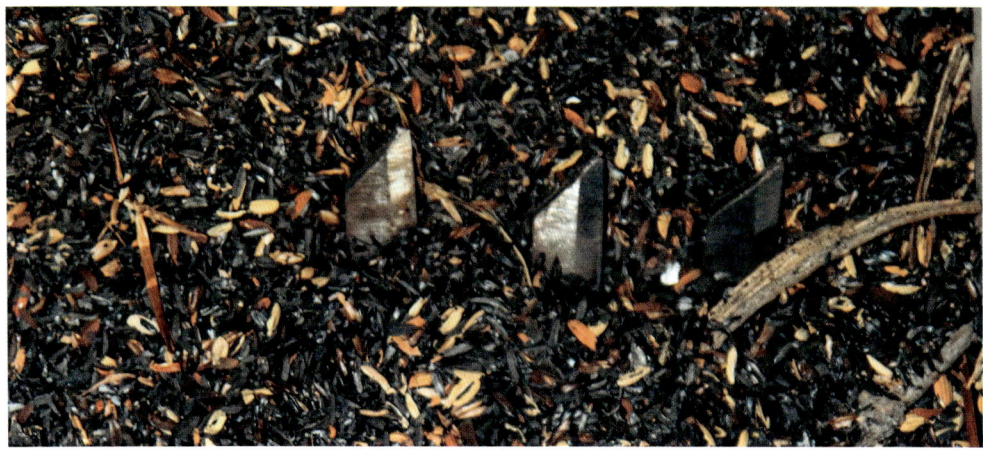

The hardened blades rest in a bed of rice straw ash.

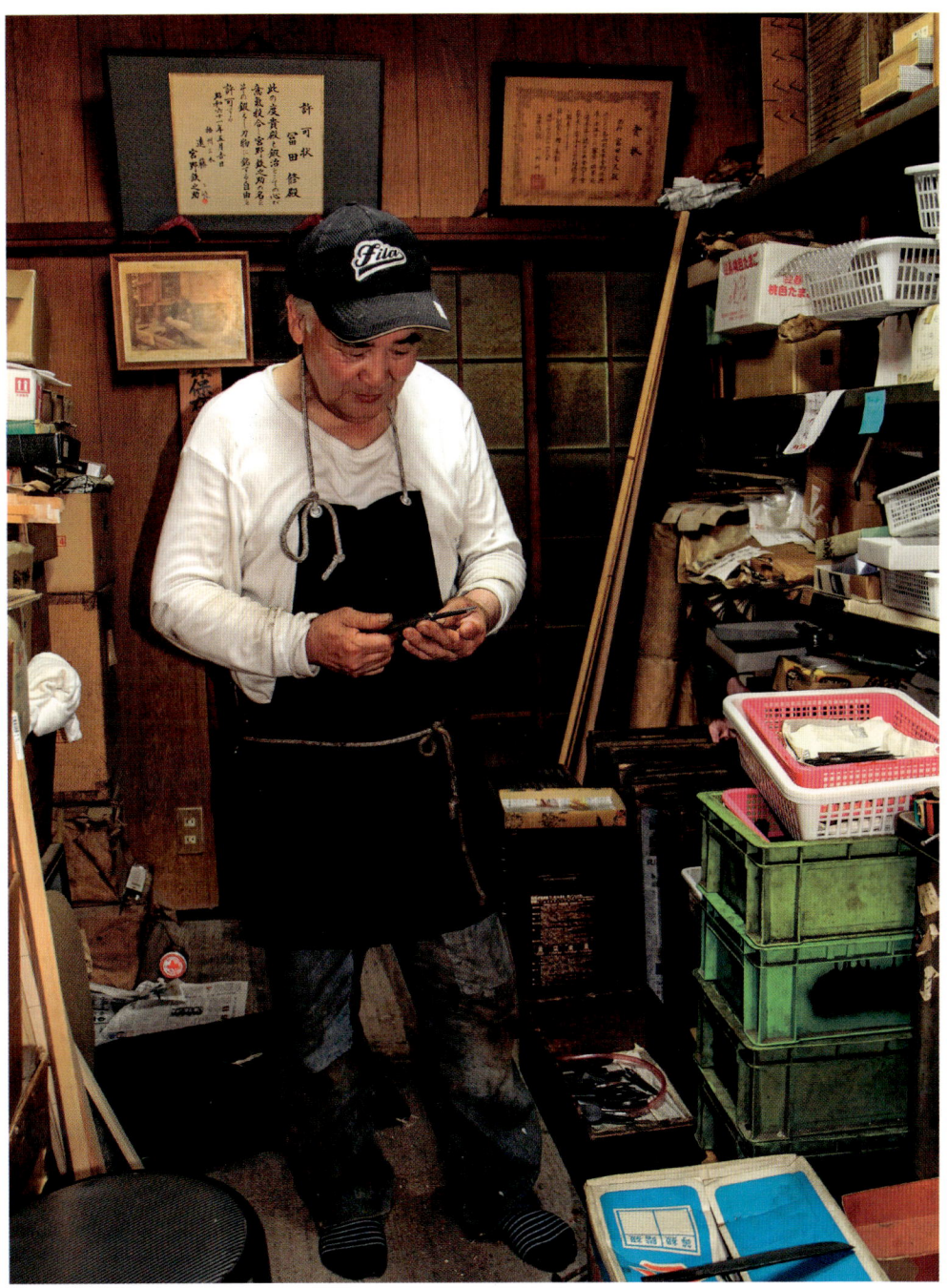

The office, decorated with certificates, is both a warehouse and a reception room.

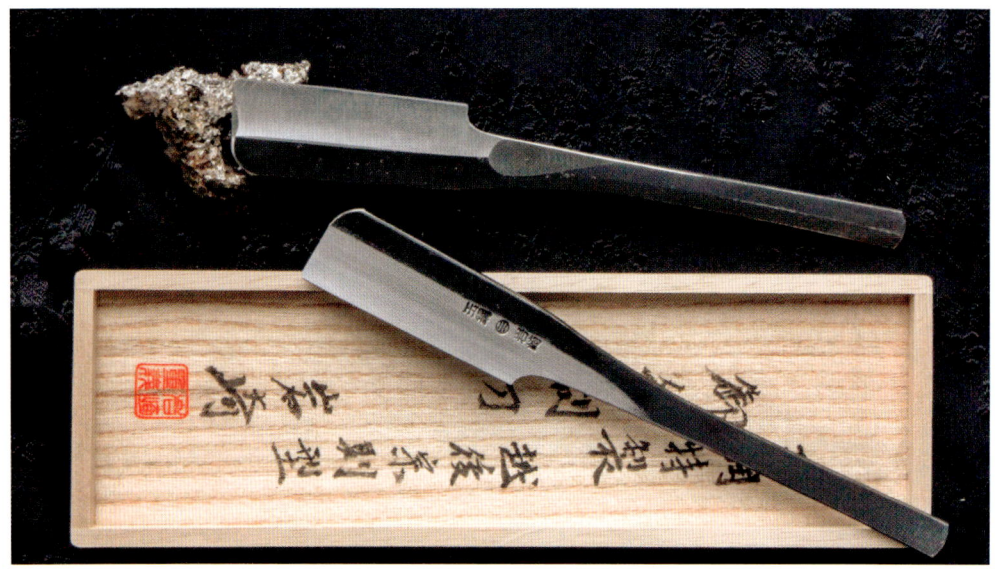

Iwasaki *kamisori* and *tamahagane*: the puristic appearance of the Japanese straight razor reveals little of the effort involved in its manufacture.

The Razor
(Kamisori)

The making of a good *kamisori* is nothing less than a technical tightrope walk. On the one hand, it goes hand in hand with a maximum thinning of the beveled cutting edge, and on the other hand, it requires an extremely high level of hardness so that the wafer-thin cutting edge does not fold over when shaving. Bladesmith Ryuichi Mizuochi masters these conflicting goals by using a two-layer construction method in which a thin steel plate is embedded in a relatively strong base body made of iron.

There are two variants of the *kamisori*, which are largely identical in form but differ in steel composition. In the case of the *tamahagane* version, both the base body and the plating are made of historical sword steel smelted under the aegis of Kosuke Iwasaki. For this purpose, low- or high-carbon *tamahagane* is forged in plate form and compacted by repeated folding and forging, similar to that used in the Japanese sword *(katana)*.

Master Blacksmith: Shigeyoshi Iwasaki

Shigeyoshi Iwasaki received his training from Munenori Nagashima, one of the most respected swordsmiths and cutlers of the Showa period (1926–1989), before joining the business of his father, metallurgist Dr. Kōsuke Iwasaki. The latter's scientific interest was in the Japanese sword and the methods used in its manufacture. It was in this context that Iwasaki, acknowledged as the leading expert of his time, was allowed to examine the *katanas* of the Shōsoin Repository in Nara (eighth century), which are classified as national treasures. His book *Hamono no Mikata (How to Judge a Blade)* is considered a standard work.

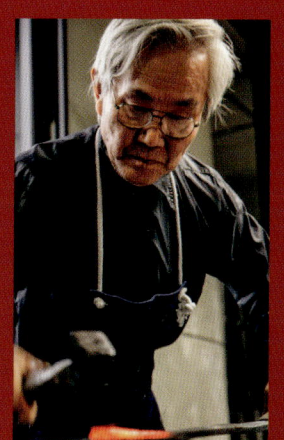

On the basis of the acquired knowledge, Kōsuke developed special *tamahagane* steels for his business, optimized for razors. No less ambitious, his son Shigeyoshi continued his father's legacy as a *kamisori* and *kogatana* (carving knife) smith. Not only as a craftsman, but also as a charismatic teacher and cultural ambassador of Japan abroad, he enjoyed the highest recognition in professional circles. He also founded a state training center for young smiths in his hometown of Kaijdojo. His former students include Tokifusa Iizuka and Tsukase Hinoura, who are among the Japanese smithing elite. During the last decade of his life, he handed the hammer over to his longtime student and colleague Ryuichi Mizuochi and confined himself to quality control. Today, the Iwasaki forge is regarded as Japan's only manufacturer of classic *kamisori* in the *Echigo* style.

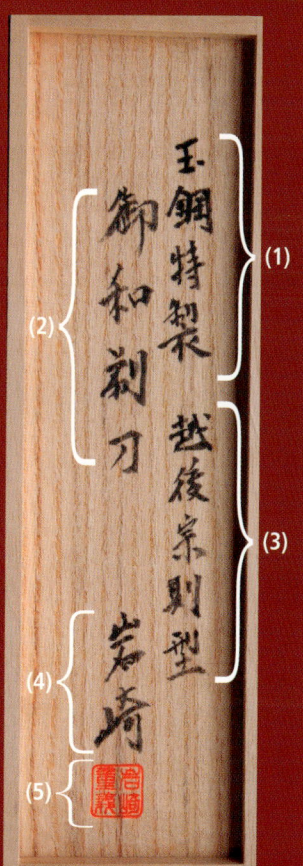

The inscriptions on the wooden box mean:
(1) *tamahagane tokusei*, a special *tamahagane* steel;
(2) *on wa kamisori*, the true Japanese razor;
(3) *echigo munenori gata*, in the munenori style, made in Echigo;
(4) Iwasaki's signature; and
(5) seal "Iwasaki Shigeyoshi."

FEATURES

Features of the Japanese razor on the *omote* side (the side which faces the shaver's face). The reverse side is called the *ura*.

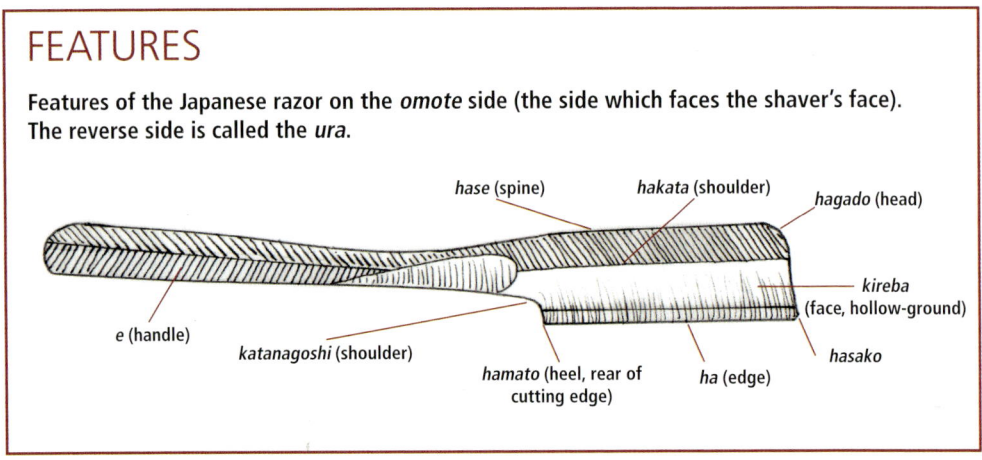

hase (spine)   hakata (shoulder)   hagado (head)

kireba (face, hollow-ground)

e (handle)

katanagoshi (shoulder)

hamato (heel, rear of cutting edge)   ha (edge)   hasako

CROSS-SECTION

Compared to the thick-walled *shigane* base body, the *kawagane* plating is very thin.

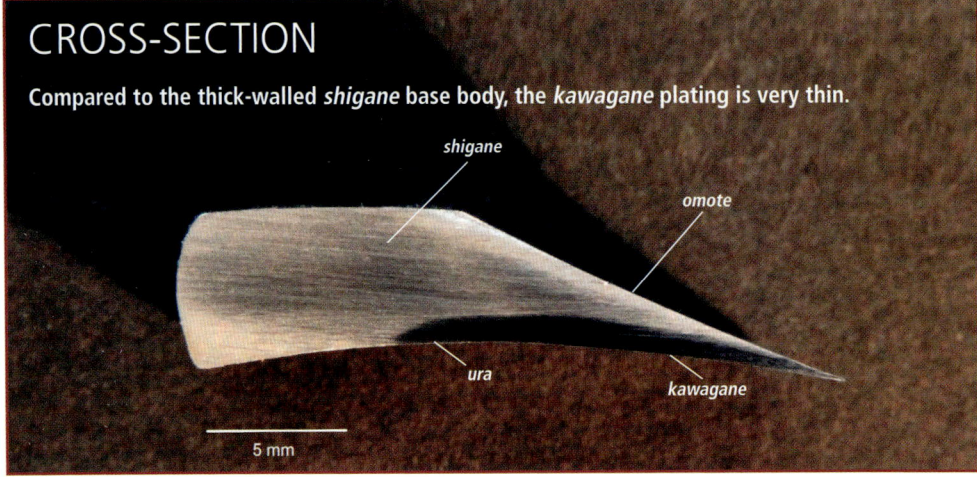

shigane

omote

ura

kawagane

5 mm

Due to the shortage of this material, however, production is now largely limited to a Swedish steel version. Here, too, Mizuochi falls back on old stocks. Sandvik steel with a high carbon content of 1.3% to 1.5%, smelted with charcoal, is still used for the plating. Old iron, mostly from quarries, with a carbon content of about 0.1% is used to make the body of the razor. This material is not only easy to forge and weld but is also particularly advantageous when sharpening on the stone. Both materials must be well forged before welding.

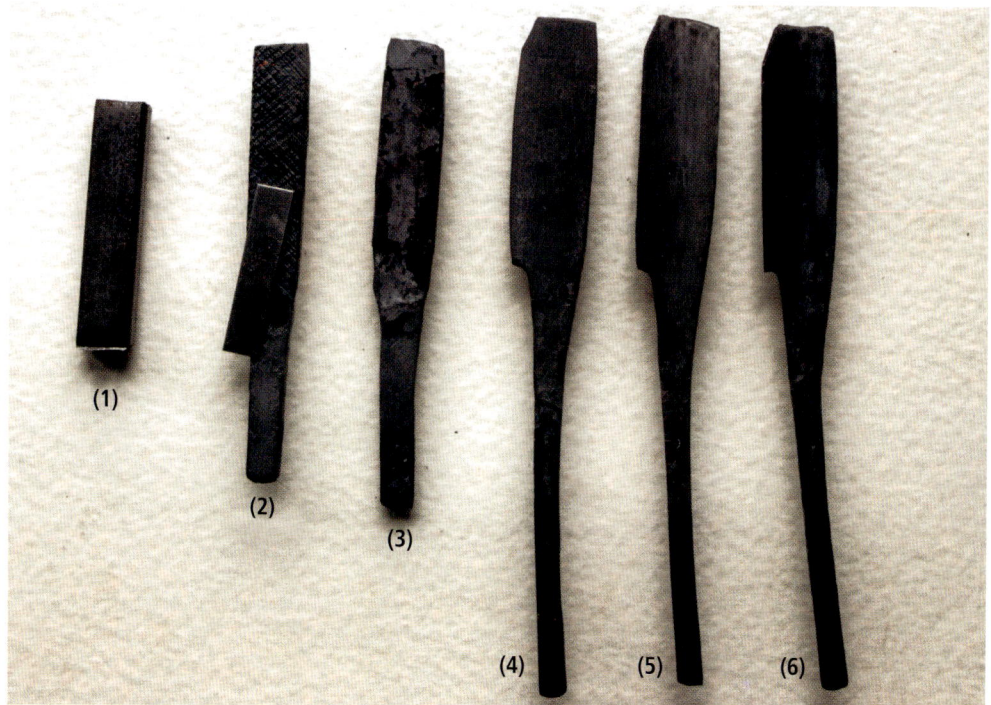

Steps in forging a Japanese razor:

(1) Iron base body.

(2) Roughly forged base body with knurled structure *(gushi)* and plating steel.

(3) Forge-welded blank.

(4) Sized blade.

(5) Completed hollow *(ura)*.

(6) Ground and hardened *kamisori,* condition prior to fine grinding.

Formally, Mizuochi is based on a classic model that was typical of the Echigo Prefecture (the old name for Niigata). This is an all-steel version with about a 180 mm (7.08 in.) total length, 60 mm (2.36 in.) blade length, and 23 mm (0.9 in.) width. The basic body is forged on the spring hammer to a thickness of about 10 mm (0.39 in.) and a width of 16 mm (0.63 in.) in the blade area, and 70 mm (2.75 in.) in length. In the process, the tang is also preformed and bent upward slightly for better gripping.

In preparation for the forge welding, riffling, called *gushi*, is applied to the contact surface with a fluted hammer. This prevents the thin *kawagane* plate from floating away on the flux layer and also improves the weld bond, thanks to the enlarged surface area. The plate, 60 mm long and 10 mm wide (2.36 × 0.39 in.), should not be thicker than 1.2 mm (0.05 in.), and it is slightly beveled along the upper edges.

The base body is preheated in a gas furnace to about 600°C (1,112°F), then a generous amount of flux is applied to the contact surface and the plate is placed so that it protrudes slightly on the long edge and is set back by 1 cm (0.39 in.) on the narrow side. The flux, called *hōsan*, consists of a mixture of boron and iron powder; however, its exact composition is a trade secret.

To compensate for the different rates of heating of the thin platelet and the solid base body, a steel plate about 10 mm (0.39 in.) thick is placed underneath them in the gas furnace. The boiling of the flux and a slight sparking of the *kawagane* indicates that the welding temperature of about 1,200°C (2,192°F) has been reached. When handling the composite, the smith takes great care to prevent the plate from slipping. The hand hammer is used to fix the platelet in the center with gentle blows during the first weld. Mizuochi adds more flux to the gap, then completes the weld in a second pass.

The rough shaping is now done on the spring hammer with a simple die. The handle and the *omote* side of the blade (front side) are forged with a primary bevel of 20°. Through the slightly rounded path of the hammer, the hollow on the *ura* side (backside) is preformed at the same time.

During fine forging with the hand hammer, the hollow *(ura)*, in particular, is formed in several passes with decreasing temperature. This ensures that the thin plating layer remains uniformly strong and is not broken through during grinding. Throughout the forging process, the workpiece is repeatedly brushed with a tuft of damp rice straw to ensure that the scale flakes off and is not driven into the thin-walled workpiece.

Then the nonlaminated overhang on the head side of the blade, about 1 cm (0.39 in.) in length, is cut off with shears, and the edge is also trimmed along the cutting edge. Now the outer contour and the concave surfaces on both sides of the blade are ground to nominal dimensions on the grinding wheel. To relieve the residual stress created during forging and to produce a uniform structure, the blade is recrystallizing annealed at approximately 780°C (1,436°F, cherry red heat), with a holding time of thirty minutes.

Before the blade is hardened, Mizuochi coats it with a clay paste containing charcoal powder. Its purpose is to prevent edge decarburization and scaling during annealing, and to improve wetting during quenching. After the coating dries, the blade is heated in the charcoal embers to the hardening temperature of about 800°C (1,472°F).

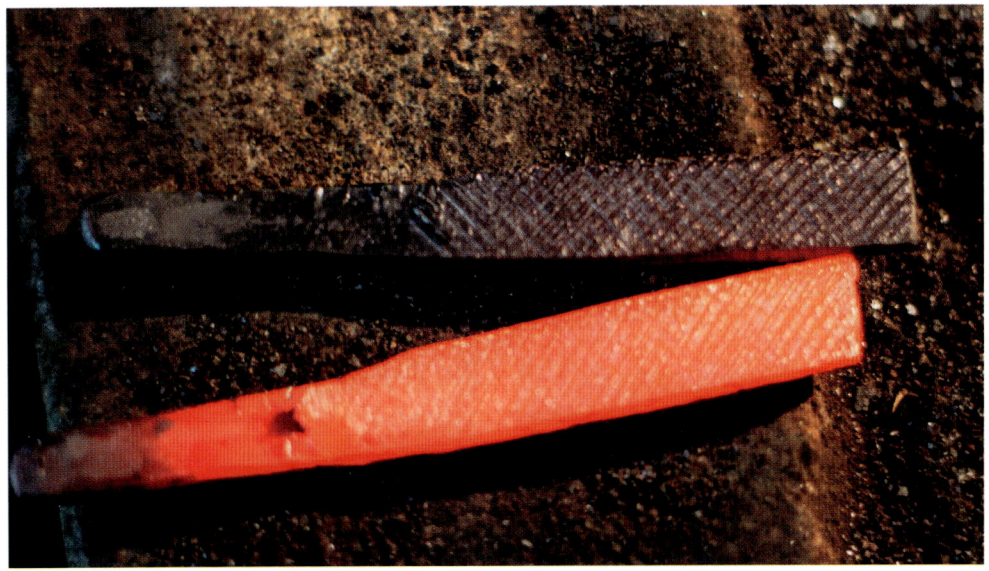

To give the flux and the thin plating steel more grip, the iron blanks are given a surface structure prior to welding.

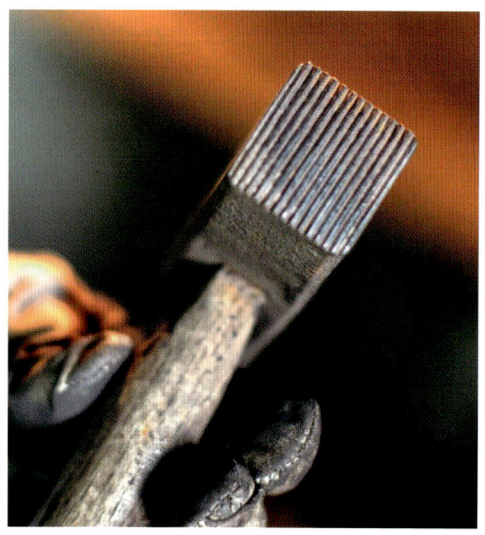

The surface structure is applied with a setting hammer with grooved face.

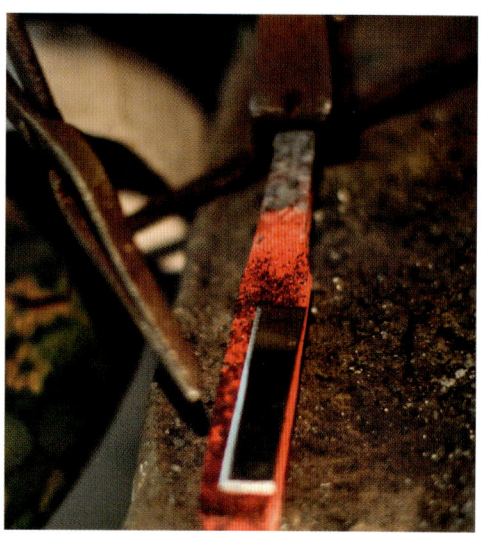

The small plate is placed on the base body about 1 cm (0.39 in.) from the tip.

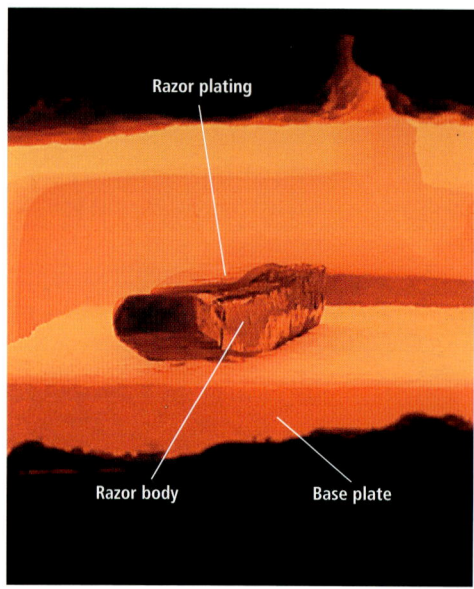

Razor plating

Razor body

Base plate

The composite is heated to forging temperature in the gas oven. The thick steel plate beneath it is used to ensure uniform heating of the plating and base body.

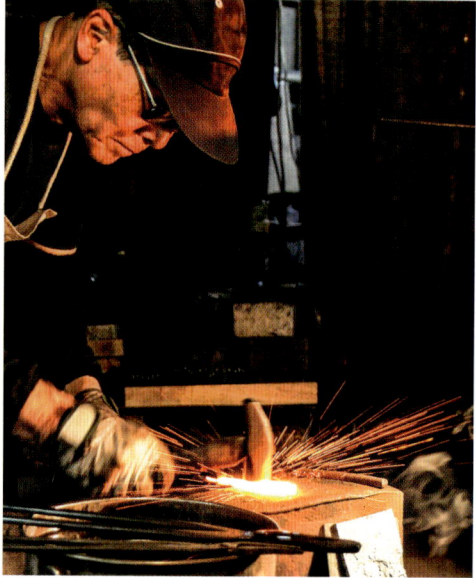

The cutting-edge steel plate is welded with gentle blows.

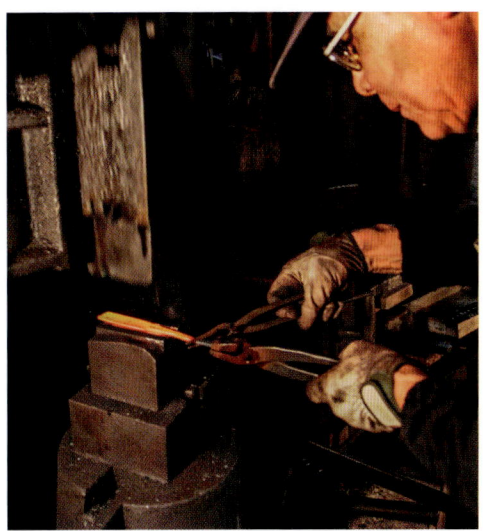

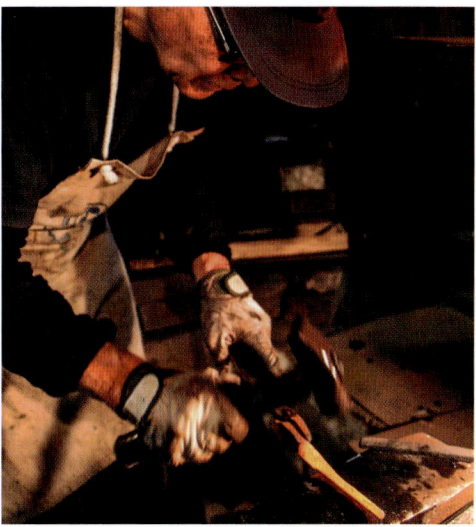

The coarse shaping of the razor and creation of the handle is accomplished in a die, using the spring hammer.

The shape of the tang is crucial for the wielding and balance of the *kamisori*.

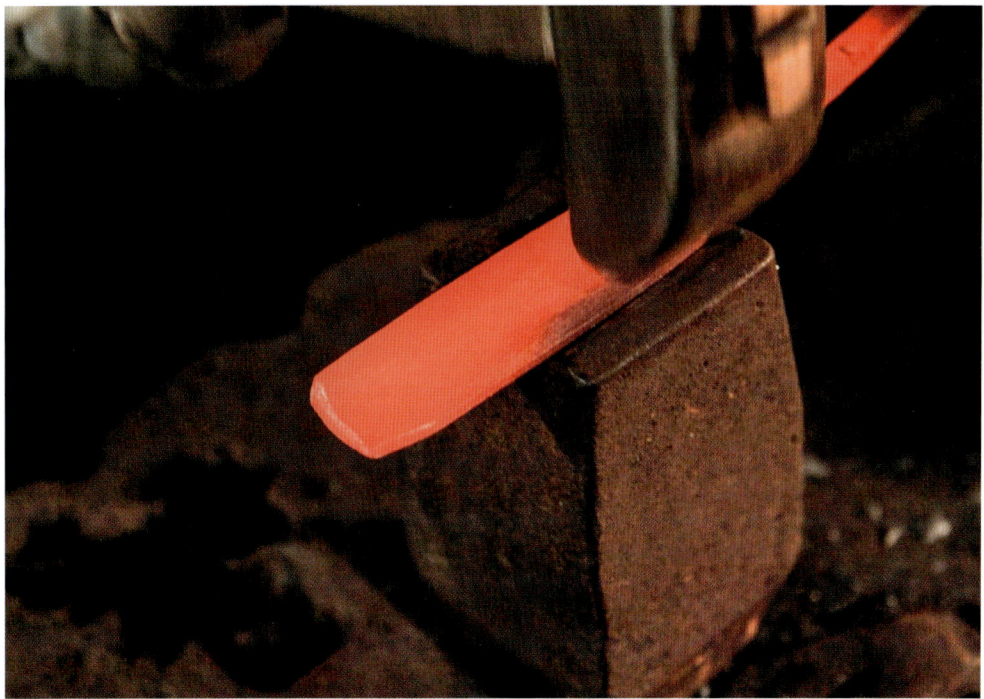

A convex-shaped driving hammer is used to work out the concave face of the razor.

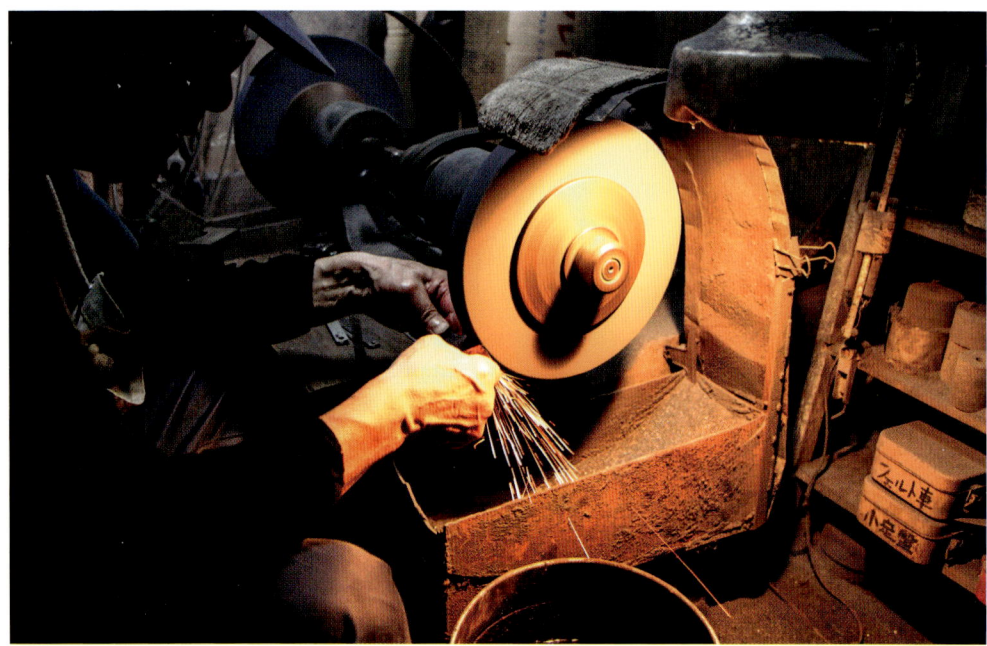

The outer contour, bevel, and concave face are ground on increasingly finer grit wheels before hardening.

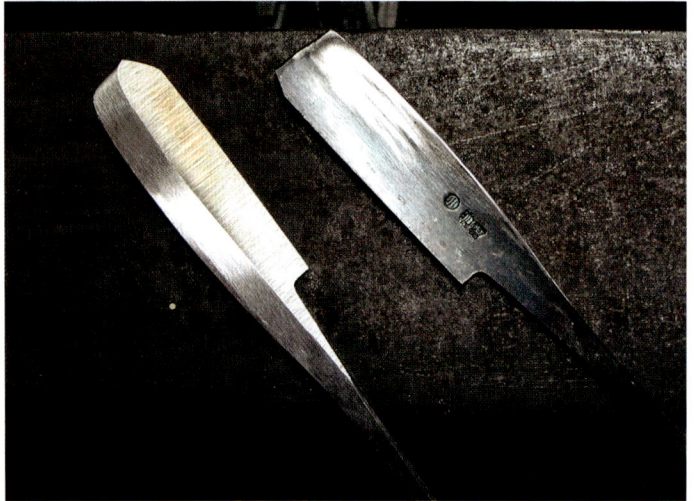

The finely ground and stamped blanks are ready for hardening.

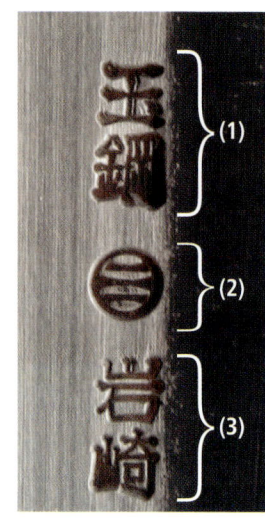

Blade markings:
(1) *tamahagane*
(2) *marusan* (trademark)
(3) Iwasaki

For this purpose, Mizuochi feeds the hearth with finely chopped charcoal obtained from Japanese red pine *(akamatsu)*. It is free of impurities such as sulfur or phosphorus and ensures uniform heating during this crucial process. After quenching in water, the brittle martensite structure is relaxed (tempered) at 160°C (320°F) for about ten minutes, resulting in a final hardness of about 65 Rockwell C. The final hardness is determined by the temperature at which the material is tempered.

By carefully tapping the soft *omote* side, Mizuochi eliminates the inevitable distortions caused by the heat treatment and ensures that the cutting edge is completely flat. Fine grinding of the hollow and the *kireba* face is done on Japanese waterstones of increasingly fine grit. The intersection of these two concave surfaces ultimately results in an extremely flat microbevel of about 8°, which is partly responsible for the blade's excellent sharpness. Only after a strict quality control inspection is the blade finally signed with the name and trademark on the *omote* side.

After the surface is burnished, the *kamisori* is finally sharpened and honed on the finest natural Japanese waterstones. Ryuichi Mizuochi performs the final polishing at his home in the country to avoid the fine dust that is unavoidable in the workshop environment. For resharpening, the expert recommends the exclusive use of natural stones, preferably from the Honyama quarry near Kyoto. After all, in the opinion of his teacher, "steel and whetstone should go together like man and woman."

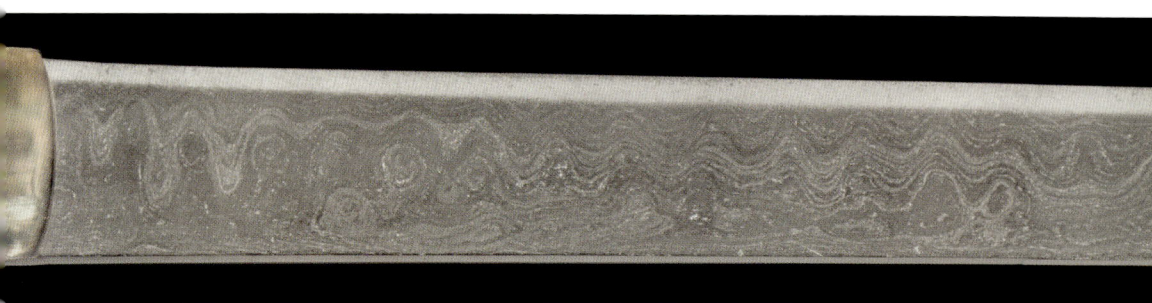

The Japanese Sword (Katana)

The *katana* was given by the sun goddess Amaterasu to the tenno (emperor), her earthly governor. Since then, it forms one of the three crown treasures of the Japanese emperor, who is also the head of the of the state religion, Shintoism. It is therefore not surprising that the *katana* has always had an importance in Japanese culture that goes far beyond its function as a weapon.

Although steel as a raw material reached the Japanese archipelago relatively late, around the sixth century CE, the art of bladesmithing was able to reach its highest bloom within a relatively short period of time, not least because of its mythological significance. During the Kamakura period, in the twelfth century, even emperors took up the bladesmith's hammer. The best sword makers produced blades that were said to be "sharp enough to cut a maple leaf floating down the stream by the force of the current alone."

Although the sword (*katana* is the long sword, *wakizashi* the short sword, and *nihonto* the umbrella term for Japanese swords) lost meaning as a weapon and status symbol in the middle of the nineteenth century with the Meiji Restoration and the resulting disempowerment of the samurai, the few remaining swordsmiths *(katana-kaji)* and polishers *(togishi)* still enjoy high social esteem today.

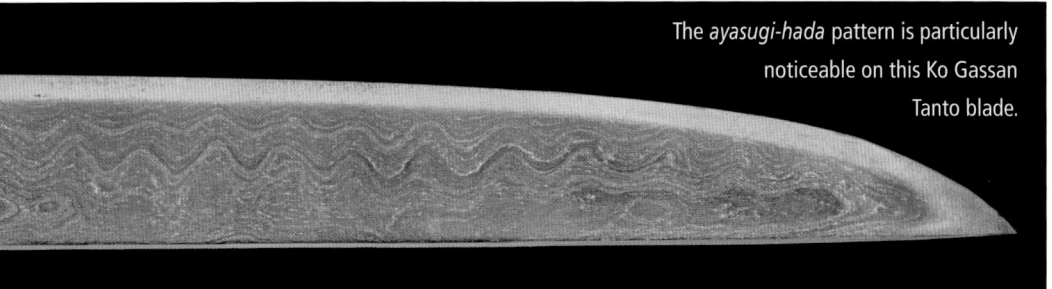

The *ayasugi-hada* pattern is particularly noticeable on this Ko Gassan Tanto blade.

I was able to visit one of their outstanding representatives, Gassan Sadatoshi, at his place of work in Sakurai-Shi in Nara Prefecture in June 2015.

Named after a mountain in Yamagata Prefecture, the Gassan school originated in the Kamakura period and is one of the oldest swordsmithing dynasties in Japan. An unmistakable characteristic of their blades was and is the so-called *ayasugi-hada*, a wavy steel grain structure that tapers toward the tip—figuratively comparable to waves breaking on the beach. The traces of this so-called "Ko Gassan" school disappeared at the end of the 16th century. It was not until the end of the Shogun period, in the early nineteenth century, that it experienced a renaissance under Gassan Sadayoshi. He not only rediscovered the technique for making *ayasugi-hada* but also created blades of extraordinary stylistic clarity with a straight temper line *(suguha)* based on the historical Hosho model. The fine engravings which adorn many Gassan swords to this day can also be traced back to him.

One of his descendants, Gassan Sadaichi (1907–1995), achieved such a degree of mastery that he was named a "living national treasure" *(ningen kokuhō)* by the Japanese government. Today his son, Gassan Sadatoshi, continues the so-called Osaka-Gassan line in the fifth generation. It is the only swordsmith dynasty in Japan to have survived the upheaval of the Meiji Restoration without interruption.

TERMS

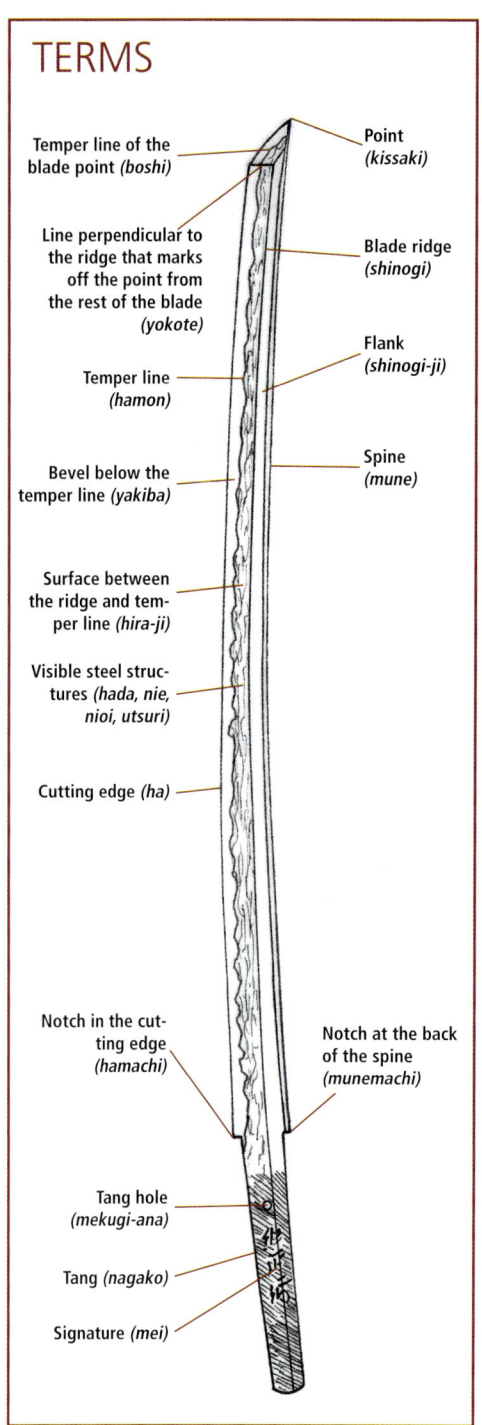

Temper line of the blade point *(boshi)*

Line perpendicular to the ridge that marks off the point from the rest of the blade *(yokote)*

Temper line *(hamon)*

Bevel below the temper line *(yakiba)*

Surface between the ridge and temper line *(hira-ji)*

Visible steel structures *(hada, nie, nioi, utsuri)*

Cutting edge *(ha)*

Notch in the cutting edge *(hamachi)*

Tang hole *(mekugi-ana)*

Tang *(nagako)*

Signature *(mei)*

Point *(kissaki)*

Blade ridge *(shinogi)*

Flank *(shinogi-ji)*

Spine *(mune)*

Notch at the back of the spine *(munemachi)*

BLADE CROSS SECTIONS

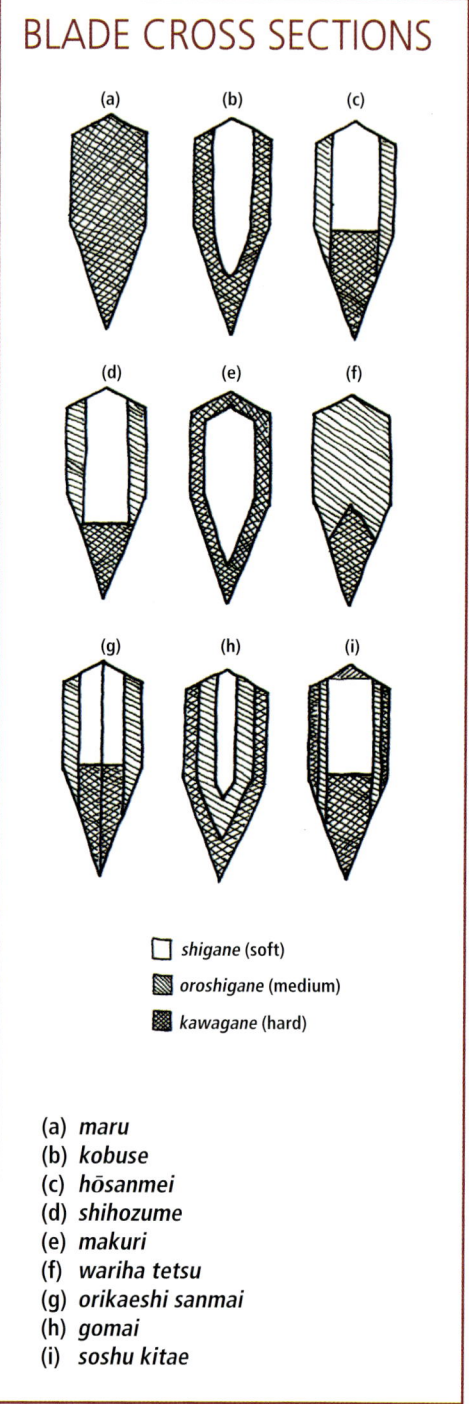

☐ *shigane* (soft)

▨ *oroshigane* (medium)

▦ *kawagane* (hard)

(a) *maru*
(b) *kobuse*
(c) *hōsanmei*
(d) *shihozume*
(e) *makuri*
(f) *wariha tetsu*
(g) *orikaeshi sanmai*
(h) *gomai*
(i) *soshu kitae*

In terms of blade construction, there are countless cross-sectional variations in Japanese swords. They all pursue the same goal; namely, to combine great sharpness and wear resistance with high breaking strength. In the most common *kobuse* design, a layer of hard *kawagane* steel is folded over a core of tough *shigane* material. In the *gomai* technique preferred by Gassan Sadatoshi, the *shigane* is covered with two layers of different composition and hardness *(oroshigane* and *kawagane)*, resulting in a five-layer structure in cross section (*go* = five).

As will be described in the chapter on steel, the *tamahagane* material obtained through the use of a *tatara* smelting furnace is by no means homogeneous. Depending on the carbon content, a distinction is made between at least three grades. Only *tamahagane* of quality grade I, which is very fine grained and has a carbon content of approximately 1.0% to 1.2%, is suitable for the surface steel of a *katana*.

A special feature of the Gassan forging technique is that this material *(tamahagane)* is combined with vintage iron, also created using the *tatara* process. For this purpose, *furutestsu* (nails or fittings at least a hundred years old) is remelted into *oroshigane* crude steel in a special furnace and then forged out in plate form. Only through forge welding of the *oroshigane* plates with the *tamahagane*, which is also forged in the form of plates, and subsequent folding, is the *kawagane* material—which is suitable for use as jacket steel—created.

This elaborate technique is probably also largely responsible for the formation of the characteristic *ayasugi-hada* texture. Through the combination of materials and decarburization during the forging process, the aim is to achieve an optimum final state for hardening of 0.7% to 0.9% C with the formation of a martensitic microstructure.

Gassan Sadatoshi also has an old stock of raw steel produced in-house *(jikaseikō)*, which he also uses in combination with the *tamahagane*. In the remelting furnace, which is comparable to a smelting furnace, he has the option of carburizing or decarburizing the respective material. For decarburization, the steel is placed close to the air inlet nozzles, while for carburizing, it is placed in the upper part of the furnace.

For the *shigane* core steel, a low-carbon, pearlitic microstructure with high toughness is desired. This material is obtained in a similar way, with the difference that predominantly *tamahagane* of grades II to III with a somewhat lower carbon content is used.

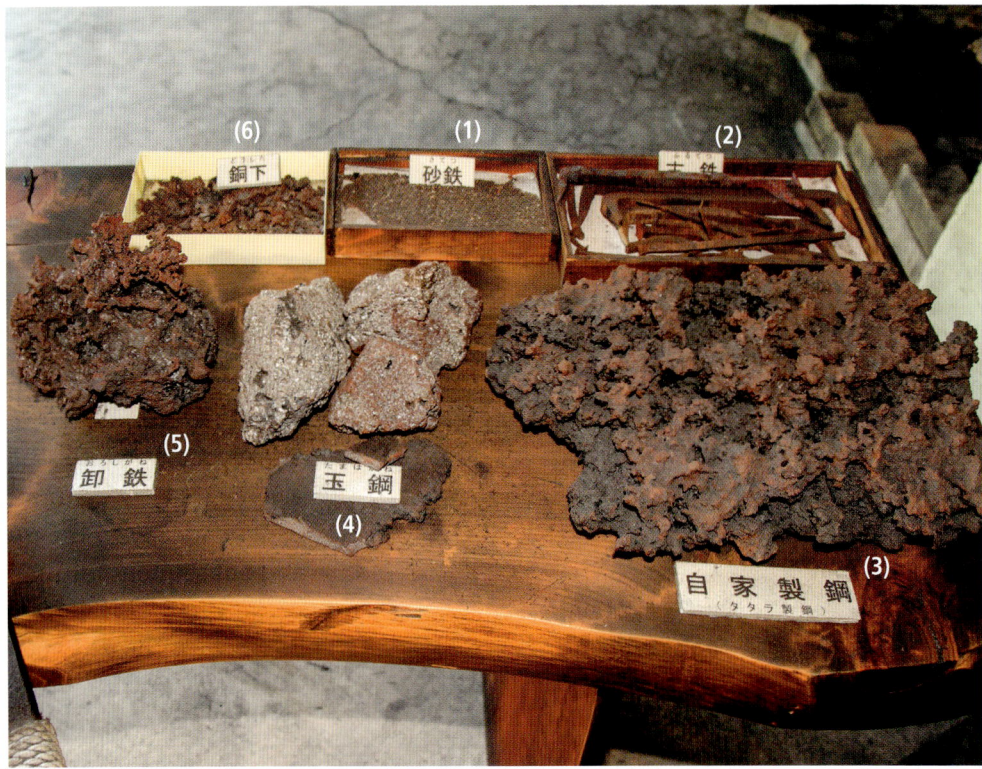

Materials for forging swords:

(1) *satetsu*: iron sand.

(2) *furutestsu*: vintage iron (temple nails, fittings, chain links, etc.).

(3) *jikaseikō*: raw steel produced in one's own *tatara* oven.

(4) Grade I *tamahagane*: in raw state *(above)* and after being forged into a plate by using the *mitzuheshi* process *(below)*.

(5) *oroshigane*: raw steel made from *furutestsu*, *jikaseikō*, and *tamahagane* with medium carbon content.

(6) *doushita*: small pieces of *tamahagane* created by the *mitzuheshi* process.

Jacket Steel

For the production of *kawagane* steel, lumps of Grade I *tamahagane* are first plate-forged to a thickness of about 7 mm (0.27 in.) and quenched in water (*mitzuheshi* process). The resulting brittle material is broken on the anvil with a hammer into pieces 3–5 mm (1.18–2 in.) in size. On the basis of the fracture pattern—a smooth, silvery break is considered an indicator of a high carbon content—the smith selects the pieces suitable for further processing.

A somewhat larger, rectangular *tamahagane* plate is then attached to a rod that is used for handling *(tekogane)*. Selected, fine-grained *tamahagane* pieces are stacked on this carrier plate in as dense an arrangement as possible to form a compact package. In estimating the required quantity, a burn-off loss of about 50% during forging must be anticipated, corresponding to a gross weight of 0.8–1.5 kg (1.76–3.3 lbs.) of *tamahagane*, depending on the blade size.

The pile is then wrapped in wet Japanese paper *(washi)*, sprinkled with rice straw ash, and doused with a special clay slurry *(hajiru)*. Both the ash and the slurry, which contains quartz, serve as fluxing agents. In addition, this dressing stabilizes the package and protects it from contamination and decarburization in the fire, while the ash covering contributes to uniform heating.

Then comes the actual forging process, the first stage of which is called *shita-kitae*. For this purpose, the forge *(hodo)*—as in all processes relevant to the making of the blade—is fired exclusively with charcoal of uniform grade. Even the splitting of the charcoal *(sumi-wari)* into 2–3 cm (0.78–1.18 in.) pieces is no trivial matter, since it is one of the main tasks of apprentices during their first years of training. A single sword requires 12–15 kg (26.45–33 lbs.) of charcoal.

Heated to a uniform white heat (about 1,200°C, or 2,192°F), the composite is first welded with gentle blows and, in the subsequent steps, compacted into a solid ingot *(tsumi-wakashi)* with the help of two beaters. Wielding a small hammer, the master sets the pace and the striking point, which the assistants take turns striking with their long-handled hammers weighing about 1.5 kilos (3.3 lbs.). Despite their relatively low head weight, these hammers generate a high forming force due to their slim design and compact swing path.

Welding with as few shrinkage cavities as possible is indispensable for production of a flawless blade. Larger voids or welding defects cannot be corrected later, even by intensive forging. Then begins the stretching and folding of the block, called *orikaeshi*, which makes the structure finer and distributes the carbon more evenly. During this process, inclusions, impurities (phosphorus, sulfur, titanium, etc.), and micro cavities are largely expelled.

The material is folded alternately lengthwise and crosswise. The block is stretched to twice its width or length. It is then notched with the shot chisel, and the respective half is folded backward. Somewhat smaller hammers are used for the transverse folds than for the longitudinal folds. Before each bonding, clay slurry and rice straw ash are again applied. A wet bundle of rice straw, which the master repeatedly inserts between the hammer and the forging during the working process, is used for descaling.

The material for the surface steel is folded about fifteen times, and the *kawagane* acquires up to 32,000 layers. The complex folding technique, which understandably is not disclosed in every detail, is the secret for the formation of the characteristic *ayasugi-hada*.

Intermediate Layer

In the *gomai* blade structure, the intermediate layer reduces the jump in hardness between the *kawagane* and *shigane*, making the blade even more resilient. For this, Gassan Sadatoshi uses a steel melted in his own furnace, which he calls *oroshigane*. The ingredients are old iron *(furutetsu)* obtained through the *tatara* process, pig iron, and homemade *tamahagane (jikaseik)*. The exact composition, however, is kept as a trade secret.

Due to the nonmetallic silicates and oxides introduced with the scrap iron, the steel melted from it has good damping properties and excellent forgeability and weldability. Similar to the process just described, the amorphous material is compacted in the *tsumiwakashi* process and folded about seven times on the *tekogane*, and its dimensions are set to match those of the cut *tamahagane* block (approx. 12 × 3 × 1 cm, or 4.72 × 1.18 × 0.39 in.).

The *tamahagane* is then welded to the *oroshigane* still attached to the handle, in the so-called *kawaren* process. As with all forge welding, the prerequisites for a good result here are the most exact possible fit of the contact surfaces, effective protection against decarburization (wrapping with paper and clay slurry), and not keeping the material in the embers for too long. The bimetallic block created in this way can now be used to enclose the *shigane* core steel.

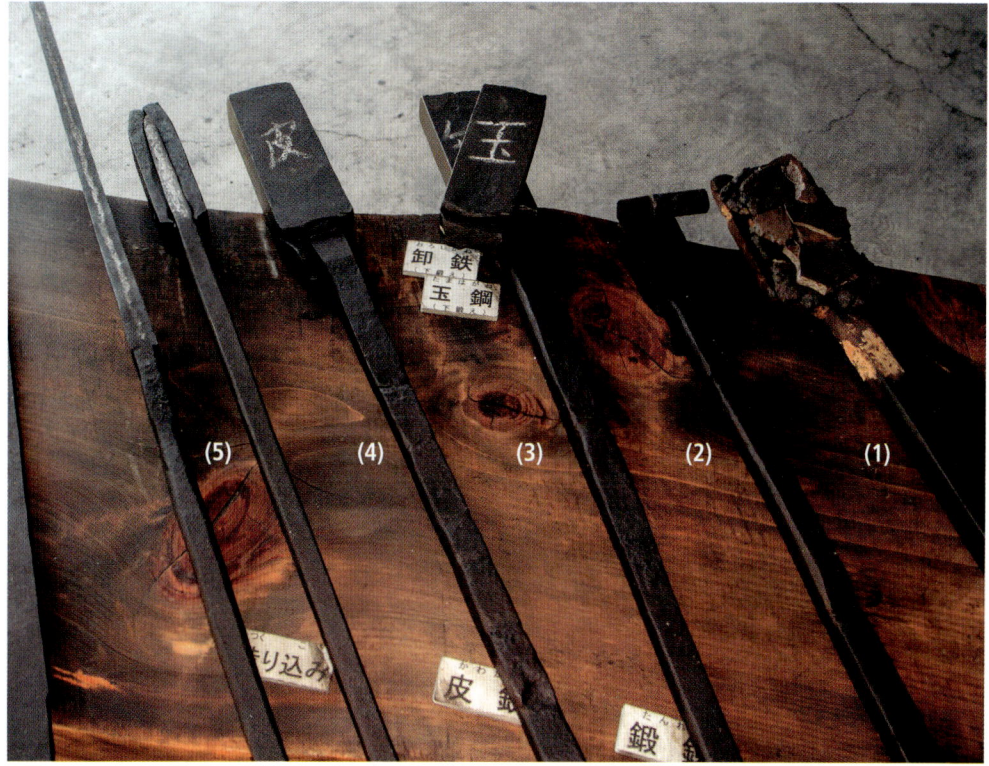

Production steps in sword forging (steps 1 to 5):

(1) *tsumi-wakashi*: Stacking of the fragments made from the *tamahagane* slabs on a flat steel scoop *(tekogane).* S*hita-kitae*: Welding and compacting of the composite to produce the steel ingot for the jacket steel *(kawagane).*

(2) *orikaeshi*: Repeated folding (transversely and longitudinally, up to 15 times) of the steel block.

(3) *tanren*: Making the *oroshigane* steel block as an intermediate layer, similar in size to the *kawagane*.

(4) *kawaren*: Welding of *oroshigane* and *kawagane*.

(5) *tsukurikomi*: Sheathing of the *shigane* with *oroshigane/kawagane* and stretching.

Core Steel

To produce the *shigane*, the master selects lumps of grade II to III *tamahagane*, which have a relatively low carbon content (0.5% to 0.7%, corresponding to about 0.3% to 0.5% after forging). This ensures that the material forms a pearlitic structure during hardening, which makes it particularly tough and fracture resistant. The material is again processed in the same way as the case-hardened steel by being forged into plates, crushed, and compacted into a block on the *tekogane*.

Since the front part of the *tekogane* later forms the tang of the sword, the holding rod must be made of the same material. For the *shigane*, there must also be a homogeneous microstructure over the entire ingot, above all to avoid major distortions during hardening. For this purpose, the ingot is folded about five to eight times. Finally, the core steel is forged on the *tekogane* to a thickness of around 12 mm (0.47 in.), tapering slightly toward the tip.

Sheathing

The "marriage" of the core and jacket steel takes place in a process called *tsukurikomi*. The *kawagane/oroshigane* plate, approximately 8 mm (0.31 in.) thick and well descaled, is placed in a U shape around the *shigane*. The tip is completely enclosed, but the back remains free. A tight fit is a prerequisite for flawless welding. With the addition of ample welding flux powder and a coat of clay slurry, the composite is evenly heated to white heat in a bed of embers and then forge-welded with rapid blows.

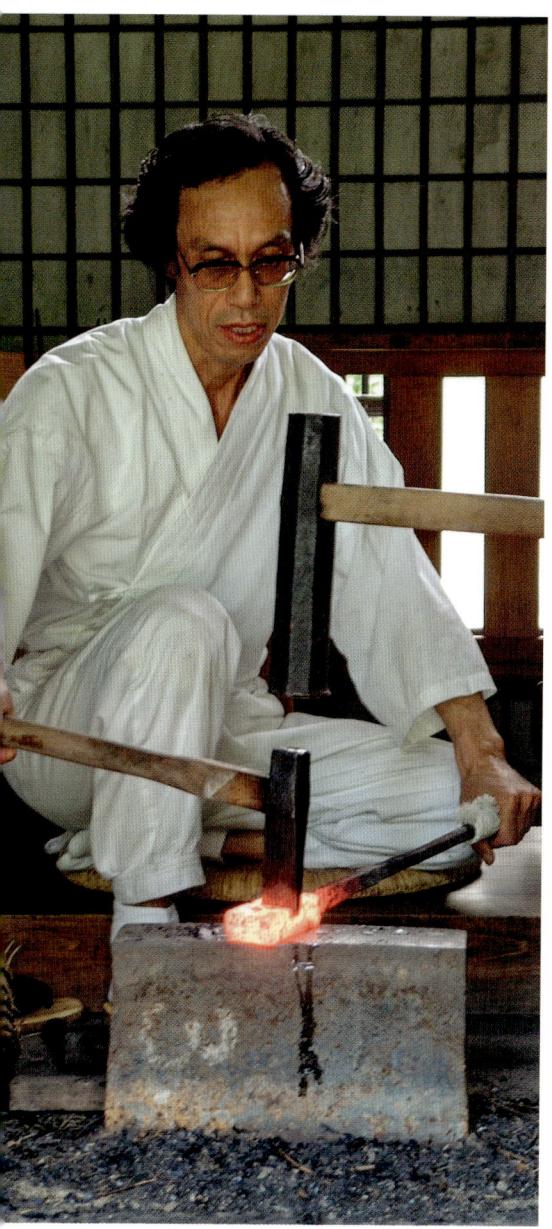

The block for the jacket steel is notched with the chop hammer for the next of a total of fifteen folds.

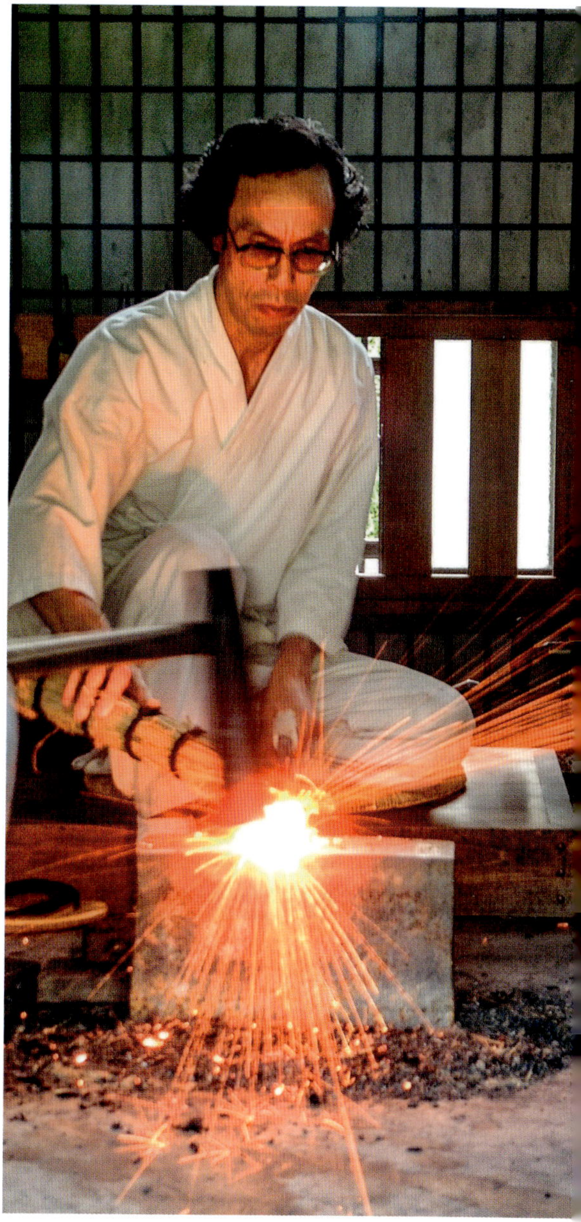

Speed coupled with precision is the key to successful welds: two beaters work the block while the master guides the block and descales it with the moistened bundle of rice straw.

Forging

Next, the shape of the sword blade is formed in the *hizukuri* process. With the help of the hammerers and their long-handled hammers, the workpiece is heated and hammered flat and upright and stretched in the process. With the small hammer, Sadatoshi creates the *shinogi* line and the taper. He devotes special attention to the stepped tip *(kissaki)*. In the *kissakihizukuri* process, it is important that, on the one hand, no *shigane* comes to the surface and that the *kawagane* is not too thick. Finally, the tang is formed in the *nakago-hizukuri* process. This completes the essential forging work, resulting in a finished sword blank *(sunobe)*.

Scraping

In the arami process, various scraping tools *(sen)* are used to smooth the back and flanks, and files are used to file the *hamachi* and *munemachi* at the end of the blade. This completes the shaping *(suguta)* of the sword.

Hardening

The heating-quenching process *(yakiire)* is considered the most demanding operation in sword making. A clay slurry is first applied to the thoroughly cleaned surface. It contains clay (the exact composition is a closely guarded trade secret), charcoal powder, and the dust of fine natural abrasive stones *(omura)*. The thickness of the application determines the cooling rate when the blade is quenched in water.

The clay provides good adhesion and improves surface wetting with water. A thin layer of clay therefore increases the cooling rate. Above a certain layer thickness, however, the insulating effect of the clay predominates. In addition, the clay represents an oxidation barrier, which prevents surface decarburization during heating.

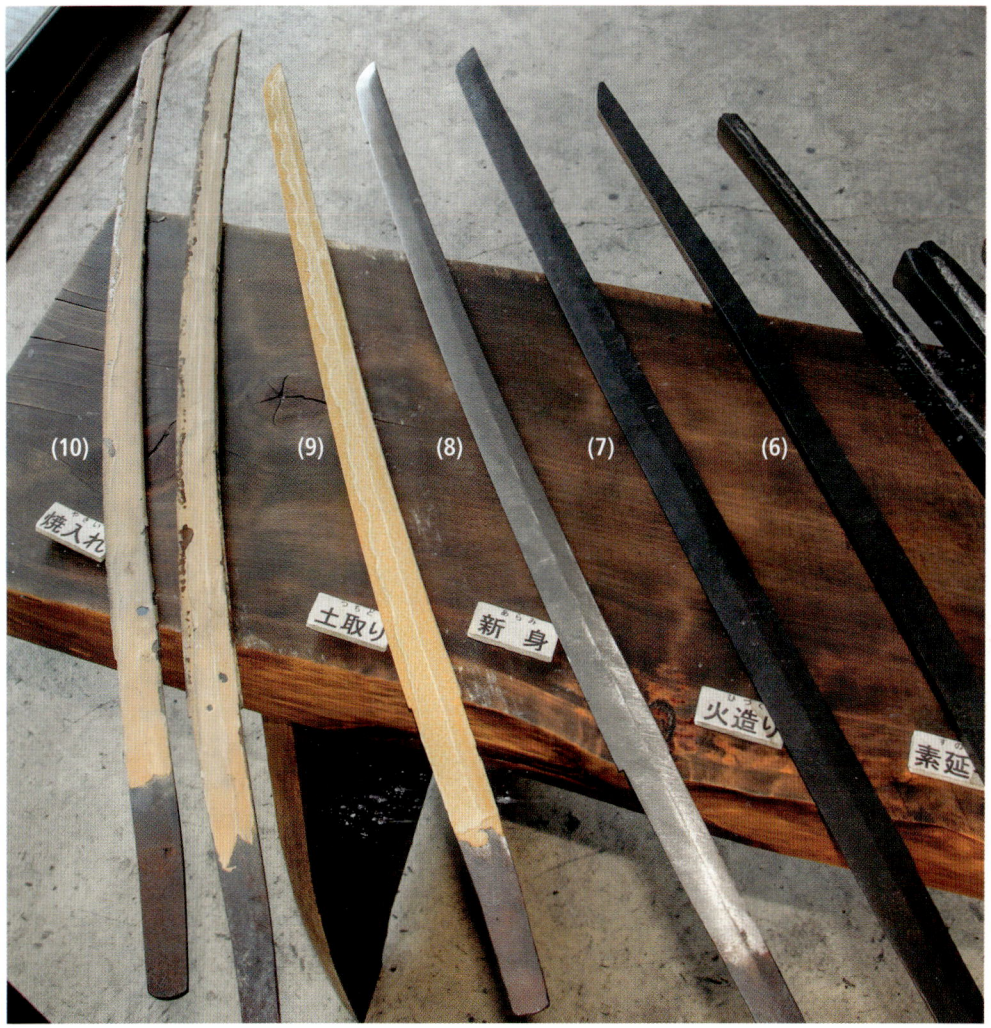

Production steps in sword forging (steps 6 to 10):

(6) *sunobe-hizukuri*: Forging of the sword blank, rough shaping.

(7) *kissaki-hizukuri*: Forging of the point *(kissaki)*, the blade ridge *(shinogi)*, and the tang *(nakago)*.

(8) *arami (shiage)*: Smoothing and shaping with the scraper *(sen)* and file.

(9) *tsuchi-tori*: Preparation for hardening: application of a clay slurry in various layer thicknesses. Composition, thickness, and the patterns carved in the application influence the microstructures and the temper line, which become visible later.

(10) *yakiire*: Hardening of the roughly 780°C (1,436°F) hot blade in the water bath. Subsequent tempering to improve toughness *(yaki-modoshi)*.

The grinding stone powder is to prevent cracks in the clay. The charcoal dust burns during heating, leaving a microperforation in the layer. When quenched, this creates fine water vapor bubbles, which presumably also influence the expression of the superficial microstructures *(hada)*.

The application and processing of the clay layer are done with thin bamboo spatulas and brushes. The beveled edge surface *(yakiba)* is coated relatively thinly *(yakiba-tsuchi)*, while the side flanks and the back receive a layer up to 6 mm (0.23 in.) thick, applied with a trowel. The spatula coating can be used to create certain patterns, which find expression in the microstructure after hardening. For example, small transverse waves created with the spatula generate so-called *ashi*, toothed perlite bulges, in the *yakiba* area.

The layer is then partially removed again with a scraper around the planned temper line *(hamon)*, and patterns can also be carved into the layer. These operations, which are essential for the formation of the *hamon*, a trademark of every swordsmith, are called *tsuchi-tori*. Gassan Sadatoshi devotes special care to the tip *(kissaki)*, whose pattern of hardness lines *(boshi)* is of decisive importance for the evaluation of the sword. After the thorough drying of the clay application, the blade is ready for hardening.

Only finely chopped charcoal, sorted according to size and quality, is used for heating to the hardening temperature of 780°C (1,435°F), so as not to damage the clay layer and to produce a temperature that is as uniform as possible. The blade must not remain static in the embers; rather, it is slowly moved back and forth with the edge pointing upward.

Hardening takes place in the open workshop in total darkness (i.e., at night with a new moon), in order to better assess the slightly distorted annealing color of the steel. Only an eye with decades of training is able to recognize the right moment to remove the red-hot blade from the fire and immediately plunge it into the water basin standing next to it.

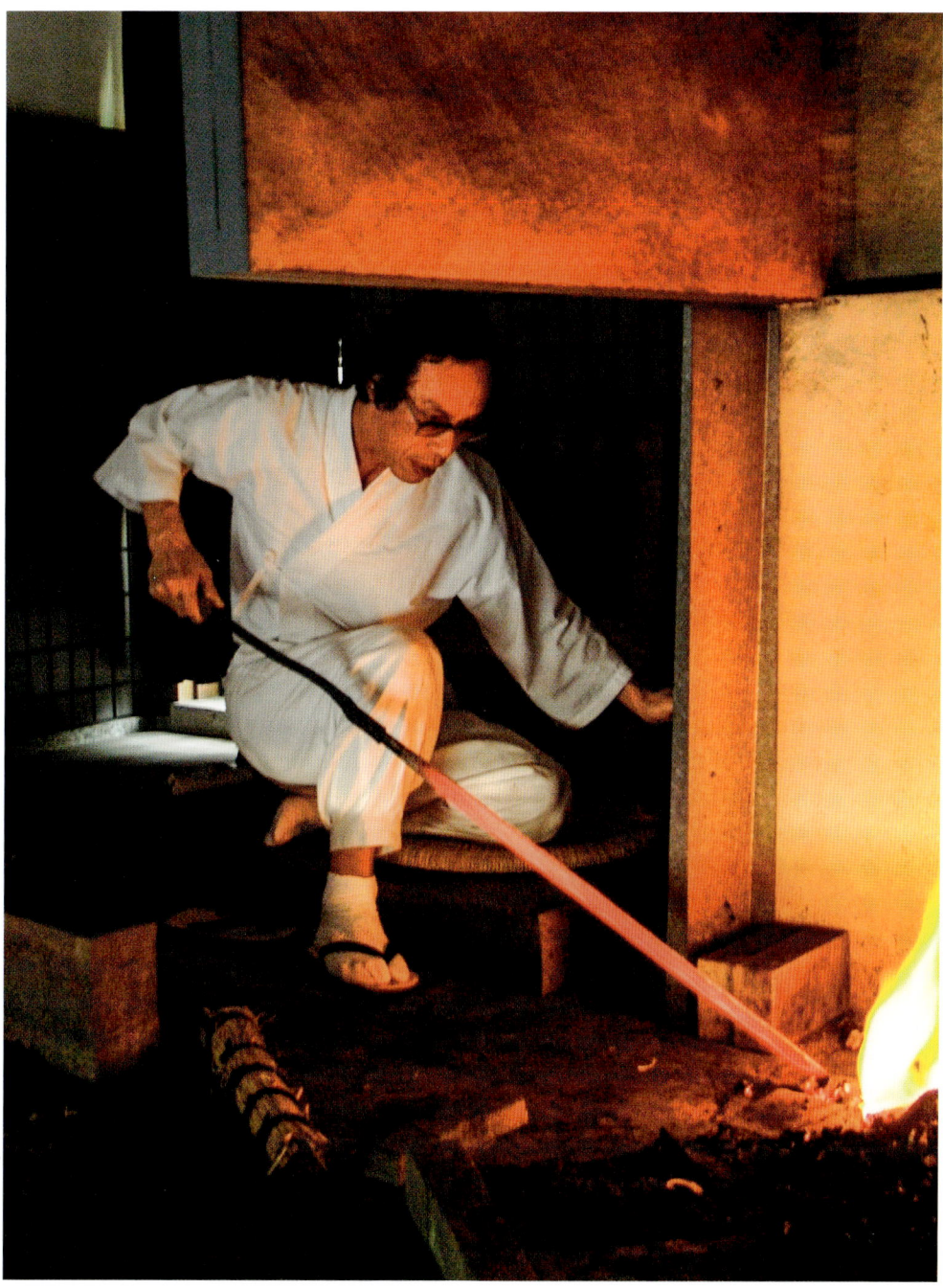

The decisive moment in the hardening process: the blade must have an absolutely uniform bright red glow (about 780°C, or 1,436°F) over the entire length.

The quenching water should be well stagnated so that it no longer contains any oxygen, which would reduce the quenching effect. The position of the blade during immersion, its movement, and the time spent in the water also have an influence on the result, as does its temperature.

That this was one of the best-kept trade secrets, at least in earlier times, can be gathered from a gruesome anecdote: a blacksmith received a visit from a colleague. When he accidentally let his finger slide through the quenching water basin, the bladesmith cut off the man's finger with a sword.

During hardening and the associated formation of martensite along the cutting edge, the blade undergoes a warpage of 1–2 cm (0.39–0.78 in.) in addition to the curvature already created during forging. This is due to the 4-percent increase in volume of the martensite in comparison to the austenite and pearlite in the remaining cross section. High stresses build up in the blade, which in extreme cases can lead to hairline cracks. This danger exists, above all, if the hardening temperature is too high.

To check the result, the blacksmith removes the baked clay layer with the grindstone immediately after hardening. Not only are any cracks then visible, but also the path of the temper line. For a better assessment, the surface can be slightly etched with diluted sulfuric acid.

To reduce the stresses, the *katana-kaji* usually undergoes a tempering treatment *(yaki-modoshi)* after hardening. For this purpose, the blade is heated in a charcoal fire to about 160°C to 180°C (320°F to 356°F) to reach an annealing color of ocher yellow and then is cooled in a water bath. If the smith is not satisfied with the path of the temper line, the hardening process could be repeated, after previous soft annealing. However, due to the associated carbon diffusion, any further annealing treatment changes the crystalline structure of the blade and thus its quality.

Straightening

Finally, the blacksmith can straighten and adjust the curvature *(sori)* of the now-hardened blade. During this *sori-naoshi* process, the curvature of the blade can be adjusted by stretching the material over the *shinogi* line to reduce the overall curvature or to correct it locally by partial heating of the spine.

Basic Sharpening

Before the smith hands the blade to the polisher *(togishi)*, he does the basic sharpening *(kaji-togi)* himself, first on the grinding wheel and then on water-block stones of coarse to medium grit. The *shinogi* line and the shape of the tip and the back are worked out and emphasized. At the same time, this process serves as a precise check for possible microstructural defects, superficial cavities, or hairline cracks. No blade that is not completely flawless would ever leave Sadatoshi's workshop.

Tang

Finally, the tang is processed with the file in diagonal strokes. The file pattern *(yasurime)* created in the process is one of the distinguishing marks of each swordsmith. To drill the mortise, about 7–8 cm (2.75–3.15 in.) behind the *hamachi*, a machine is used for the first and only time during the entire manufacturing process. In earlier times, the hole was punched. Gassan Sadatoshi applies his signature *(mei-kiri)* only after the polisher has done his work.

Engraving

Among the characteristic features of many Gassan blades are the often very elaborate engravings *(horimono)*. Contrary to common practice, Sadatoshi Gassan engraves the ornamental motifs taken from Japanese mythology into the less hard side flanks of the blade itself. For this purpose, he has more than a hundred self-forged gravers and chisels.

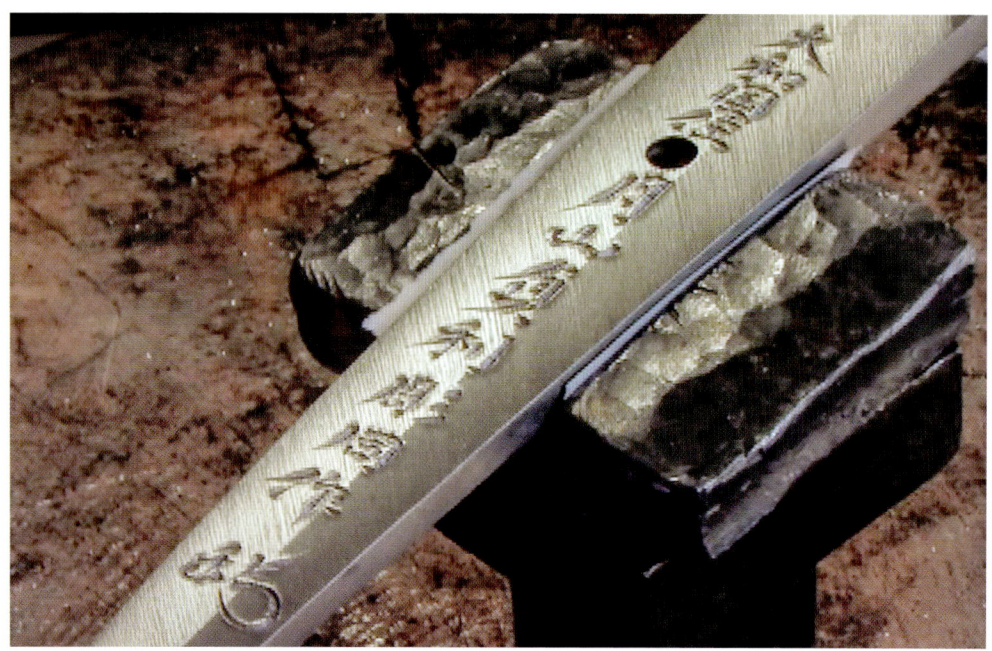

The tang signature *(mei-kiri)*: the tang is signed with the calligraphic symbol *(kaō)*, the full name of the swordsmith (Gassan Sadatoshi Horidōsaku), and the place of origin (Yamato = old name for Japan).

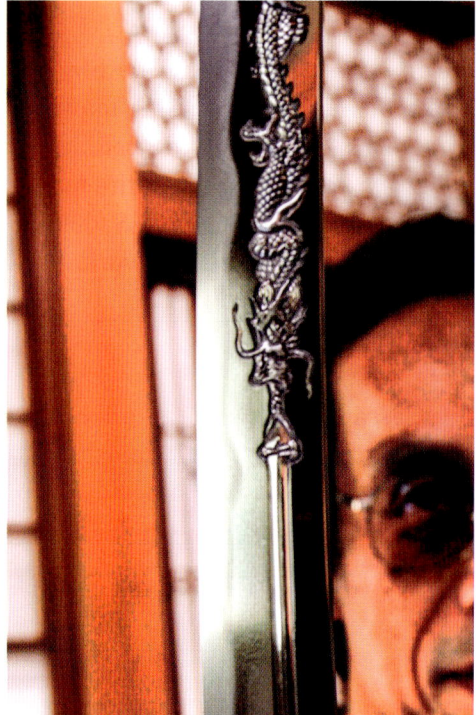

Artful engravings—here, a dragon motif—are among the characteristics of Gassan blades.

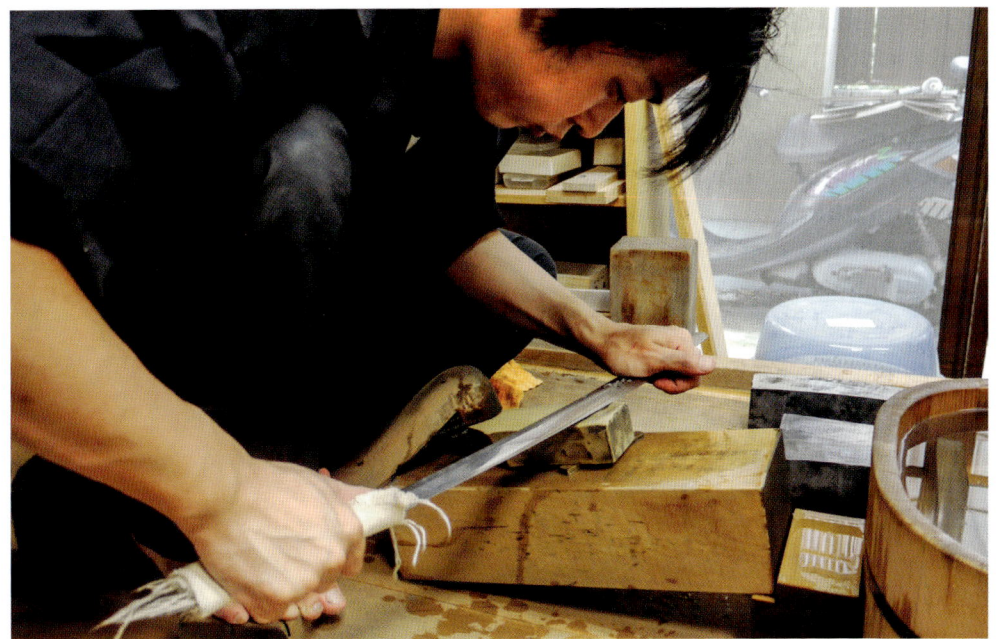

The polisher brings out the true beauty of the blade.

Polishing

Through polishing, the inner workings of a blade are revealed. Gassan entrusts this crucial final step to Nara-based polisher *(togishi)* Katsuyuki Sekiyama. The process is basically divided into shaping—in which rather coarse natural and artificial stones are used to elaborate the shape given by the swordsmith—and the actual polishing—in which only natural stones are used to smooth the surface, sharpen the blade, and highlight the steel structure. Of course, a good *togishi* follows the stylistic guidelines of the blacksmith, but at the same time, he strives to perfect the character of each blade. In doing so, it is imperative not to remove more than the most necessary material.

First, the surface is smoothed on *kaisai* and *chu-nagura* natural stones. The marks left by the coarse stones are ground out with short, rocking movements perpendicular to the longitudinal axis of the stone. Then follows the fine processing on the *uchigumori* block stone. Here, the blade is held diagonally to the stone and pushed or pulled in the longitudinal direction of the cutting edge with little pressure, whereby the steel structure and the temper line stand out. The purpose of the further polishing steps is to make the surface clearer and to highlight the course of the temper line, the texture of the structure, and the folded steel layers. In this process, the blade is no longer passed over the horizontal stone but is worked by means of small pieces of *hazuya* and *jizuya* placed on the tip of the thumb.

To polish the tip, the master uses a thin *uchigumori* plate that rests on a springy lamellar wood block. To increase the contrasts and highlight the *hamon,* the surface is then subjected to *nugui* polishing. The polish required for this is obtained by finely grinding forging scale with the addition of oil and is applied by means of a cotton swab, darkening the *shinogi* surface and spine.

During the final *migaki* process, a mixture of wax and horn powder is applied with an *ibota* cotton cloth dispenser as a polishing and lubricating agent, and the surface is polished to a mirror finish. Katsuyuki is not satisfied with his task until the structure of the blade he has been entrusted with is as clear as its lines.

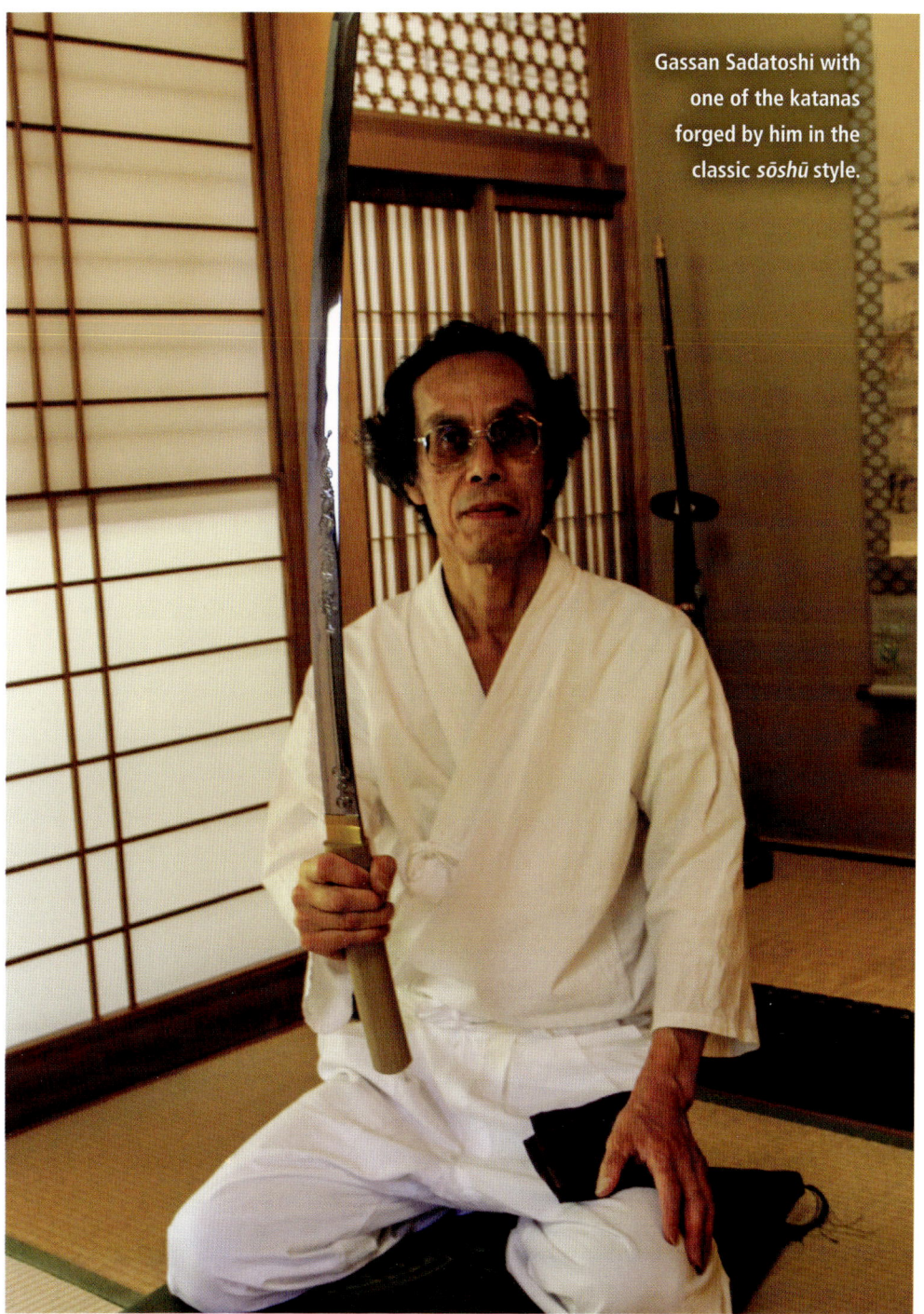

Gassan Sadatoshi with
one of the katanas
forged by him in the
classic *sōshū* style.

The Steel

For over 3,000 years, the element iron and its hardenable variant, steel, have formed an important basis of our human existence. The blades of almost all cutting tools were and are made of this metal.

Steel is a so-called wrought alloy (i.e., an iron alloy that can be shaped by forging or rolling and can be hardened by its content of 0.2% to 1.7% carbon). As with all metals, steel is a crystalline material. Its matrix, also referred to as microstructure, consists of areas of homogeneous crystallites, also known as grains.

The properties of steel are essentially determined by its average grain size. Small grains result in a homogeneous microstructure with good mechanical strength values (fracture strength, notched bar impact strength, possible sharpness, and service life for cutting steels). Grain refinement can be achieved by adding certain alloying elements as well as by normalizing, hardening, and for certain steels, also low-temperature treatment.

The forming technique has a significant influence on the mechanical properties of steel. Careful forging at correct temperatures makes the structure more homogeneous, and a so-called "texture" can also be produced. In this process, the lattice is aligned according to the stress, comparable to the fibers in wood. This is why the term "fiber structure" is also used—though not quite correctly in technical terms. A quality-conscious smith will, for example, shape an axe head in such a way that the lattice is stretched in the longitudinal direction in the body of the blade in order to achieve high bending and breaking strength. At the cutting edge, however, he will allow the "fibers" to run transversely in favor of good cutting-edge stability.

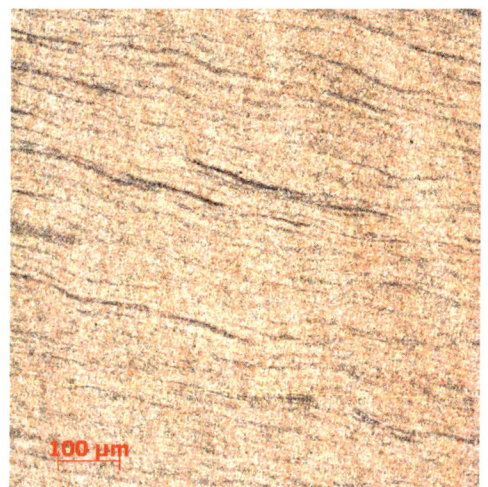

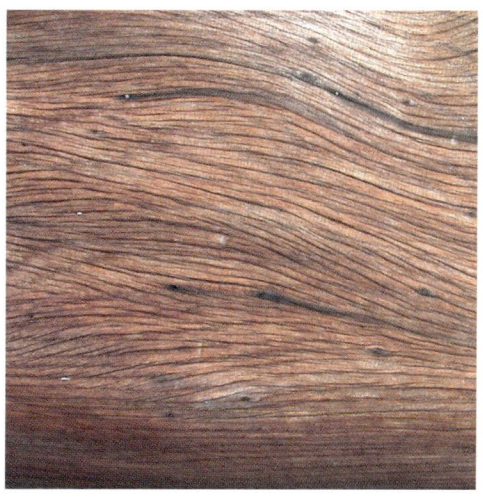

Forging aligns the lattice to meet stress requirements: a micrograph of forged and hardened low-alloy tool steel (Cr 1.3%, Mn 0.3%, Si
0.6%), 100x magnification.

Example from nature: the fiber structure of
cypress wood.

The manufacturing processes commonly used in the mass production of
cutting tools, such as rolling, punching, or pressing, can hardly achieve this
stress-related optimization, which also continues in the material structure.
In this respect, there is no substitute for the sensitive hand of an experienced
toolmaker. He performs the tightrope walk between maximum deformation
and minimum permissible temperature which leads to outstanding results.

A further increase in quality can be achieved with thin blades by cold
working and the resulting strain hardening. Today, this processing step is
practiced only by very experienced smiths due to the associated risk of
brittle fracture.

Types of Steel

Carbon Steel

A steel that contains only carbon (0.2%–1.7%) and is little alloyed is called carbon steel. This classic steel for cutting tools is not stainless. During hardening, it forms a so-called martensite structure, which enables a high level of sharpness. Martensite is a fine-grained, needlelike lattice formation of the steel, which is formed by rapid quenching during hardening. Up to a C content of 0.8%, the so-called eutectic, the carbon atoms are completely incorporated into the atomic lattice. At higher carbon contents (hypereutectic steel), part of the carbon is used to form carbides (Fe_3C), which do not integrate into the lattice. However, they can have a positive effect on cutting-edge retention.

Pure carbon steels achieve the highest sharpness but are relatively brittle, especially at hardness levels above 60 Rockwell C. In Japanese blades, they are often joined to form a laminate with a tougher steel or pure iron, with the carbon steel always forming the cutting edge. It should be noted that pure martensite has a specific volume 4.4% higher than other steel modifications (pearlite, austenite). For this reason, high internal stresses and, in extreme cases, even cracks can occur during the hardening of laminate steels.

Alloyed Tool Steel

To influence the properties of steel, metallic alloying elements such as chromium, molybdenum, cobalt, vanadium, or tungsten are added to most cutting-edge steels for hand tools, in addition to the carbon necessary for hardening. Many of these "steel refiners" form carbides with the carbon—very hard particles that are embedded in the crystalline matrix like foreign bodies. When the carbide particles are finely distributed in the matrix, they can significantly improve the service life of a cutting edge because they act like wear-protective microserrations on the cutting edge. Their configuration depends on the composition of the steel, the heat treatment, and the forming process.

HSS

High-alloy tool steels also include high-speed steel, usually called "HSS" (High Speed Steel). It contains up to 2 percent carbon and a total of up to 30 percent by weight of alloying elements (Cr, W, Mo, V, Co, Ti), which are precipitated by special heat treatment as so-called special carbides. They make HSS highly resistant to wear.

PM Steel

Powder metallurgy (PM) is a relatively new discipline in alloying technology. In this process, molten steel is transformed into powder by spraying and then hot-isostatically pressed (sintered) into semifinished products at high pressure. The advantage is that the composition is freer than in the case of alloying in the liquid state, since the usual segregation processes do not occur due to the special cooling technique. High degrees of hardness (up to 70 HRC) are achieved with good toughness and high-temperature strength. However, despite continual further development, the crystalline structure of PM steels is still relatively coarse grained and heterogeneous.

Damascus Steel

The vividly patterned Damascus steel, also known as "Damascus," is particularly popular with cutlers. Occasionally it is also used for other cutting tools such as scissors, hatchets, or chisels.

The name is derived from the city of Damascus, the ancient trading center for metals of all kinds. The coveted blade steel was usually smelted in Asia Minor, from where it was transported as semifinished products to the Syrian trading metropolis for marketing. In contrast to the welding method commonly used today, the patterns in historical Damascus are due to segregation processes during the cooling of the raw steel in the crucible. In this process, zones with different carbon concentrations and consequently different microstructures (pearlite, austenite, martensite) are formed in the cross section of the hollow.

Alloying Elements

Chromium (Cr): The formation of chromium carbides increases edge retention and wear resistance and improves the hardenability. Up to 11% by weight, chromium is "consumed" to form chromium carbides; above this, it serves as corrosion protection by forming a chromium oxide layer on the surface. Hardenable steels with a chromium content of about 13% or more are considered "stainless" (it would be more accurate to refer to them as "rust resistant"). They are therefore preferred for cooking and outdoor knives, cutlery, scissors, and medical instruments. Since the corrosion resistance and ductility of chromium steels deteriorate rapidly with increasing hardness, they cannot be hardened to very high levels.

Manganese (Mn): Reduces the negative effect of sulfur and improves hardenability (depth of hardness), tensile strength, forgeability, and weldability.

Molybdenum (Mo): Improves the building of fine grain and reduces brittleness in alloy steels. Strong carbide creator; increases wear resistance and toughness; in stainless steels it improves corrosion resistance.

Vanadium (V): Strong carbide creator; increases tempering temperature and thus the high-temperature strength. Contributes to grain refinement and improved weldability in higher alloy, hardenable steels.

Nickel (Ni): Improves toughness and corrosion resistance. From 7% Ni together with at least 13% Cr, pure austenitic, acid-resistant, and nonmagnetic steels are produced. Since nickel counteracts the formation of martensite and fine grains, it is not used in cutting-edge steels.

Cobalt (Co): Used to refine grain and increase high-temperature strength, preferred for HSS steels. Does not form carbides.

Tungsten (W): Forms very hard carbides and increases high-temperature strength, preferred for HSS steels.

Impurities: Unfortunately, undesirable elements also occur in the steel structure. The main impurities are aluminum (Al), sulfur (S), and phosphorus (P), which have a strong affinity for iron and are therefore difficult to remove from the melt. Even the smallest amounts lead to embrittlement due to precipitation at the grain boundaries. A high metallurgical purity (P + S $\leq$ 0.03%) is therefore considered a decisive quality criterion for cutting-edge steels.

Through repeated forging and folding of this raw material, also known as "wootz," the various steel structures emerge to the surface, where they appear as wavy or arabesque patterns. Soft and hard structural components also alternate on the cutting edge.

In the case of welded Damascus, on the other hand, steels of different compositions are forge-welded in the forge, and then ornamental patterns are deliberately produced by folding, torsion, or indentation. In Japanese multilayer steels *(suminagashi)*, on the other hand, a hard monosteel layer is always embedded as the cutting layer in a blade base body that has a structure comparable to that of Damascus steel.

Hardening and Tempering

What happens during hardening? To harden steel, it is heated to a certain temperature (so-called transformation temperature, 750°C–1,050°C or 1,382°F–1,922°F, depending on the type of steel) and then quenched in a medium (oil, water, or air). In the process, the modification (lattice structure) typical of the elevated temperature is "frozen," as it were. Residual stresses are generated in the lattice, which increase deformation resistance and thus the hardness of the steel. At the same time, quenching also produces a fine microstructure, since the rapid cooling gives the individual crystals little time to grow.

It should be noted, however, that the toughness of the steel (ductility) decreases with increasing hardness. Immediately after quenching, it is therefore usually too brittle to be useful as a tool or knife blade. For this reason, the workpiece is then heated again, but under precisely controlled conditions (160°C–300°C or 320°F–572°F), and held there for a defined period of time. During this process, called tempering, the desired hardness value, which is usually a compromise between tool life and toughness, can be precisely adjusted.

In the case of high-alloy steels (HSS), the precipitation of special carbides and thus so-called secondary hardening can be brought about by special heat-treatment measures.

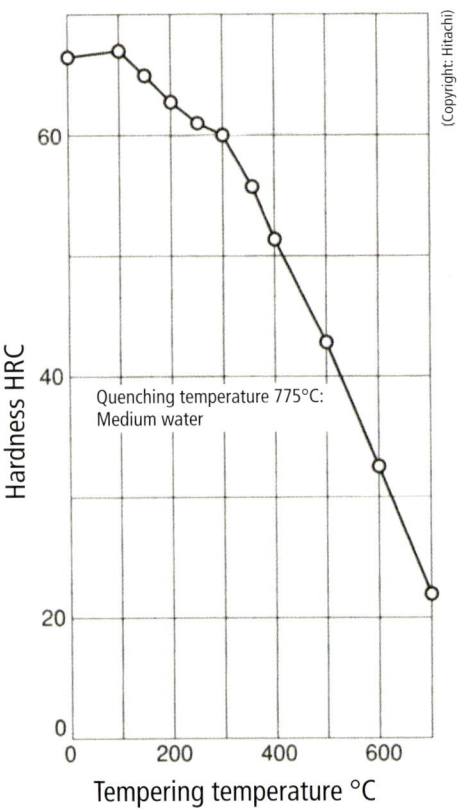

Quenching temperature 775°C:
Medium water

Hardness HRC

Tempering temperature °C

(Copyright: Hitachi)

The diagram shows the decrease in hardness as tempering temperature increases for *shirogami* 2, a Japanese carbon steel.

The Hardness Test

For cutting tools, hardness is usually indicated by the Rockwell C scale hardness value (HRC), which is determined by measuring the indentation depth of a diamond cone loaded with 10 kp (22 lbf). Common values are 56 to 60 HRC for carbon monosteels and low-alloy tool steels, 61 to 63 HRC for laminated (Japanese) carbon steels, 63 to 65 HRC for HSS steels, and 66 to over 70 HRC for PM steels and hard metals (sintered materials).

In this hardness test, however, only the hardness of the matrix is measured, not the hardness of the embedded carbides. The Rockwell hardness test requires a plane-parallel surface and sufficient material thickness and is therefore usually not feasible in the cutting-edge area of tools or knives. Here, the hardness can be determined only by a relatively complex micro-hardness test, or an approximate value can be obtained with a hardness-testing file.

Japanese Tool Steels

Japanese tool steels are generally classified according to the Japanese JIS standard. This is comparable to the German DIN or the American ANSI standard for the standard grades. For example, a carbon steel with 0.45% C is designated as:

- Japan (JIS): S 45C
- Germany (DIN): C45
- USA (ANSI): 1045

However, regarding homogeneity and metallurgical purity, these standards define only a minimum standard, which is usually not sufficient for demanding applications in the cutting-tool sector. There is, therefore, a higher quality class of carbon tool steels in the Japanese JIS standard, designated SK. In addition, Japanese steel producers have developed high-quality alloyed and unalloyed steels specifically for the cutting-tool industry and blade forges, some of which significantly exceed the minimum standards and are marketed under proprietary designations. A selection is shown in the table on page 130.

The most important producers of high-quality Japanese tool steels are Takefu Special Steel, Kobe Steel (Kobelco), and the market leader, Hitachi Heavy Metals Company, based in Yasuki. Following the example of the traditional *tatara* process (see page 137), Hitachi now uses industrial methods to produce high-purity cut steels named after the production site (YSS, Yasuki Special Steels).

As in the historical process, only iron sand from Shimane Prefecture is used, which is characterized by a high ore content and minimal impurities. As a classic carbon steel, it is sold under the brand name *shirogami* (white paper steel) or in a low-alloy version as *aogami* (blue paper steel), both named for the color of the packaging paper.

The metallurgist Dr. Kōsuke Iwasaki, who was introduced in the chapter on razors, played a major role in the development of these steels, as well as in their naming. Both grades have a high carbon content and harden purely martensitically. Their high metallurgical purity enables the best service life, even with very thinly ground cutting edges. Finely distributed iron carbides (Fe_3C) further enhance cutting-edge durability. In *aogami* steel, the precipitation of tungsten carbides further improves tool life.

Comparable carbon steels are offered by Takefu Steel under the brand names V1, V2, or Shiro 2.

Both Hitachi and Takefu produce high chromium alloyed, stainless tool steels, which are mainly used in the production of chef's knives and scissors. Examples are the silver paper steel listed in the table (Gin 3 and Gin 1, respectively) or the VG-10 (C 1.0%, Cr 15%, Mo 1%, V 0.2%, Co 1.5%) offered by Take–fu.

Standard Japanese Tool Steels (Cold-Worked Steels)

Designation	C	Mn	Mo	W	Cr	V	P	S
Sk 7 (JIS)	0.60 - 0.70	0.15 - 0.50	–	–	–	–	< 0.03	< 0.035
Sk 6 (JIS)	0.70 - 0.80	0.15 - 0.50	–	–	–	–	< 0.03	< 0.035
Sk 5 (JIS)	0.80 - 0.90	0.15 - 0.50	–	–	–	–	< 0.03	< 0.035
Sk 4 (JIS)	0.90 - 1.00	0.10 - 0.50	–	–	–	–	< 0.03	< 0.035
Sk 3 (JIS)	1.00 - 1.10	0.15 - 0.50	–	–	–	–	< 0.03	< 0.035
Sk 2 (JIS)	1.15 - 1.30	0.15 - 0.50	–	–	–	–	< 0.03	< 0.035
Yellow Paper Steel 3 (YSS Kigami 3)	0.90	0.20 - 0.30	–	–	–	–	< 0.03	< 0.006
Yellow Paper Steel 2 (YSS Kigami 2)	1.05 - 1.15	0.20 - 0.30	–	–	–	–	< 0.03	< 0.006
White Paper Steel 3 (YSS Shirogami 3)	0.80 - 0.90	0.20 - 0.30	–	–	–	–	< 0.025	< 0.004
White Paper Steel 2 (YSS Shirogami 2)	1.05 - 1.15	0.20 - 0.30	–	–	–	–	< 0.025	< 0.004
White Paper Steel 1 (YSS Shirogami 1)	1.25 - 1.35	0.20 - 0.30	–	–	–	–	< 0.025	< 0.004
Blue Paper Steel 2 (YSS Aogami 2)	1.05 - 1.15	0.20 - 0.30	–	1.00 - 1.50	0.20 - 0.50	–	< 0.025	< 0.004
Blue Paper Steel 1 (YSS Aogami 1)	1.25 - 1.35	0.20 - 0.30	–	1.50 - 2.00	0.30 - 0.50	–	< 0.025	< 0.004
Blue Paper Steel Super (YSS Aogami Super)	1.40 - 1.50	0.20 - 0.30	–	2.00 - 2.50	0.30 - 0.50	0.30 - 0.50	< 0.025	< 0.004
Silver Paper Steel 3 (YSS Gin 3)	0.95 - 1.10	0.60 - 1.00	–	–	13.00 - 14.50	–	< 0.03	0.02
Silver Paper Steel 1 (YSS Gin 1)	0.80 - 0.90	0.45 - 0.75	0.30 -0.50	–	15.00 - 17.00	–	< 0.03	< 0.02

Data in % by weight. The final hardness indicated depends not only on the tempering temperature but also on the tempering time.
Sources: www.hitachi-metals.co.jp, www.tokkin.com

Even higher alloy contents can be achieved using powder metallurgical processes. However, PM steels still have development potential in terms of fine grain size.

Due to their high chromium content, stainless tool steels and PM steels precipitate chromium carbides at elevated temperatures, which preclude hot-dip welding under normal conditions. For this reason, the high-chromium steels are offered mainly as laminated sheets produced under inert gas or by the diffusion process (see page 134).

Remarks, Heat Treatment
Standard carbon steel for hammers, axes, simple knives, etc. Hardening temperature 790-850° C (1,454-1,562° F) (oil, recommended), 760-820° C (1,400-1,508° F) (water), annealing 200-250° C (392-482° F), hardness > 58 HRC.
Standard carbon steel for hammers, axes, simple knives etc. Hardening temperature 790-850° C (1,454-1,562° F) (oil, recommended), 760-820° C (1,400-1,508° F) (water), annealing 200-250° C (392-482° F), hardness > 59 HRC
Standard carbon steel for hammers, axes, simple knives etc. Hardening temperature 790-850° C (1,454-1,562° F) (oil, recommended), 760-820° C (1,400-1,508° F) (water), annealing 200-240° C (392-464° F), hardness > 59 HRC
Standard carbon steel for hammers, axes, simple knives etc. hardening temperature 790-840° C (1,454-1,544° F) (oil,recommended), 760-810° C (1,400-1,490° F) (water), annealing 190-230° C (374-446° F), hardness > 58 HRC
Standard carbon steel for hammers, axes, simple knives etc. Hardening temperature 790-830° C (1,454-1,526° F), (oil, recommended) 760-810° C (1,400-1,490° F) (water), annealing 180-230° C (356-446° F), hardness > 60 HRC.
Standard carbon steel for hammers, axes, simple knives etc. Hardening temperature 790 - 830° C (1,454-1,526° F) (oil, recommended), 760-810° C (1,400-`1,490° F) (water), annealing 180-230° C (356-446° F), hardness > 61 HRC.
Higher grade carbon steel for cutting tools. Hardening temperature 760-800° C (1,400-1,472° F) (medium water), annealing 180-220° C (356-428° F), hardness 58-60 HRC.
Higher-grade carbon steel for cutting tools. Hardening temperature 760-800° C (1,400-1,472° F) (medium water), annealing 180-220° C (356-428° F), hardness > 60 HRC
Highest purity carbon steel, medium hardness, chisels, axes, knives, saws. Hardening temperature 760-800° C (1,400-1,472° F) (medium water), 780-820° C (1,436-1,508° F) (oil), annealing 180-220° C (356-428° F), hardness > 58 HRC (water quenched) or > 52 HRC (oil quench)
Highest purity carbon steel, high hardness, cooking knives, chisels, plane irons etc. (laminated blades only). Hardening temperature 780-830° C (1,436-1,526° F), medium water, annealing 160-230° C (320-446° F), hardness > 60 HRC.
Highest purity carbon steel, highest hardness, chef's knives, chiisels, plane irons, razors, etc. (laminated blades). Hardening temperature 760-800° C (1,400-1,472° F), medium water, annealing 180-200° C (356-392° F), hardness > 62 HRC.
Alloy steel with good wear and heat treatment properties, high quality cutting tools, razors.Hardening temperature 780-830° C (1,436-1,526° F), medium water or oil, annealing 160-230° C (320-446° F), hardness > 59 HRC.
Alloy steel with very good wear and heat treatment properties, high quality cutting tools, razors. Hardening temperature 780-830° C (1,436-1,526° F), medium water or oil, annealing 160-230° C (320-446° F), hardness > 60 HRC
Alloy steel with very good wear and heat treatment properties, high quality cutting tools, razors. Hardening temperature 780-830° C (1,436-1,526° F), medium water or oil, annealing 160-230° C (320-446° F), hardness > 60 HRC.
Stainless steel for kitchen knives, scissors, razors, etc. Hardening temperature 1,000-1,050° C (1,832-1,922° F), medium air or oil, annealing 100-150° C (212-302° F), hardness 59+ HRC. Not forge-weldable.
Highly alloyed steel for increased corrosion resistance, kitchen knives, scissors etc. hardening temperature 1,040-1,090° C (1,904-1,994° F), medium air or oil, annealing 100-150° C (212-302° F), hardness 57+ HRC. Not forge-weldable.

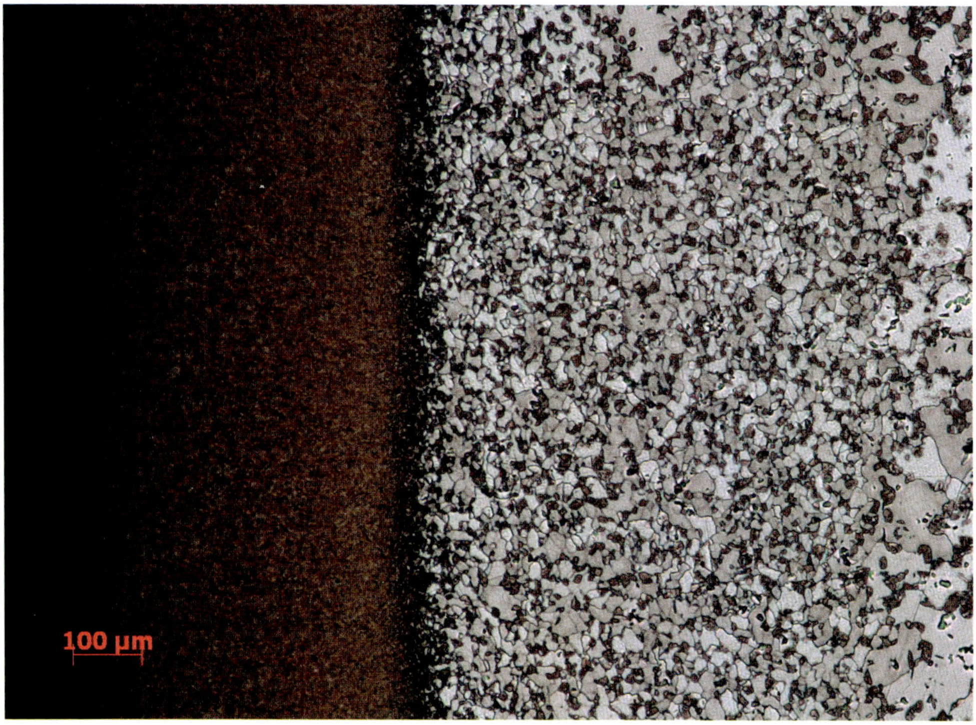

Significant differences in grain size become apparent in this cross section of a two-ply blade (100× magnification). At left is Hitachi *shirogami* 2, hardened to 62 HRC; at right, unalloyed iron.

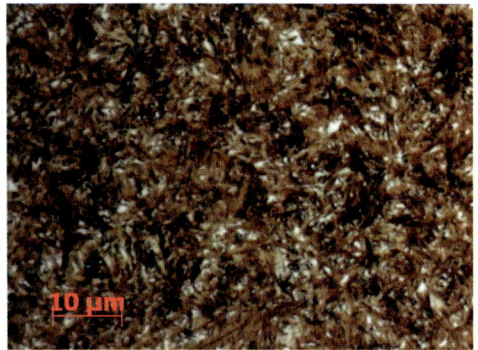

A prerequisite for a closed cutting edge with maximum possible stability: under 1,000× magnification, the fine, acicular martensitic structure of *shirogami* 2 steel.

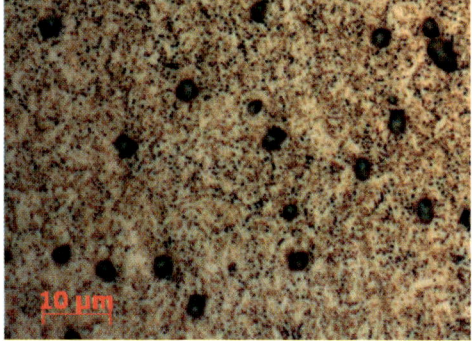

Advantageous: finely distributed tungsten carbides of uniform size in a martensitic matrix in *aogami* 2, a low-alloy tool steel made by Hitachi, hardened and tempered. 1,000× magnification.

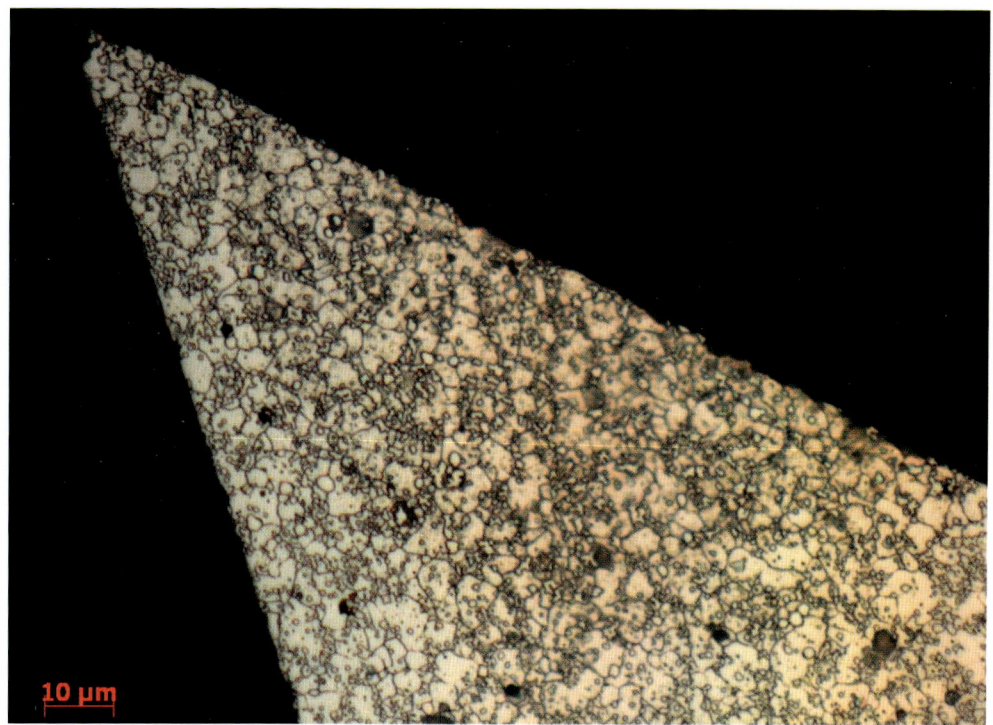

Cut through a knife tip, Japanese PM steel SG 2 (C 1.25%–1.45 %, Cr 14.0%–16.0%, Mo 2.3%–3.3%, V 1.8%–2.2%, Mn 0.4%): the relatively coarse-grained, heterogeneous microstructure resulted in an intergranular outcrop at the tip (800× magnification).

The Tatara Process (Steel Smelting)

Forging is similar to cooking: the end product can only be as good as the ingredients. Thus, the outstanding properties of samurai swords are based not only on the virtuoso skill of the bladesmiths, but also on the exquisite quality of the starting material, the so-called *tamahagane*. This steel with its spongelike structure has been produced in Japan since the early seventh century CE, using the so-called *tatara* process, a smelting process comparable to the European bloomery process.

Roll Welding (Industrial Laminate Technology)

For reasons of rationalization, industrial methods were developed as early as the second half of the twentieth century to produce double- and multilayer semifinished products as starting products for cutting tools. In addition to pressing processes, hot rolling has proved particularly effective for welding sheets and slabs of various dimensions. The aim here, just as in the case of manual forge welding, is to combine a tough and fracture-resistant material for the blade body with a hard, stable steel for the cutting edge.

One of these plants has already been operated for over three decades in Niigata Province by the Yamamura company. The rolling mill operates in reversing mode, in which the direction of rotation of the rollers is reversed after each pass. Then, after the rollers have been reset, the rolled stock passes through the stand again.

During the author's visit in June 2015, the plant was producing two-ply laminated sheets consisting of unalloyed iron (C 0.05%) and Sk 5 carbon steel (C 0.8%). In their initial state, the sheets were about 0.6 m long and 12 mm (0.47 in.) (iron) or 6 mm (0.24 in.) (steel) thick. For preparation, they are ground on the contact surfaces before being placed on top of each other in pairs and electrically welded all around on the narrow sides. To allow the trapped air to escape, the weld seam is not completely closed on the end faces.

The plates are then heated in the continuous induction furnace to the specified welding temperature, in this case 1,150°C (2,102°F), and fed to the roll stand. The first pass is used only for welding the two sheets and therefore has only a small reduction. Immediately after leaving the roll gap, the sheet is cooled to about 950°C (1,742°F) by spraying it with water. The required final hot-rolled thickness, in this case 10 mm, is then produced in one or more reversing passes. Before further processing by cold rolling, stamping, and closed-die forging or pressing, the material must be homogenized by normalizing annealing and descaled by sandblasting or a chemical pickling treatment.

Today, roll lamination is used to produce most of the semifinished products for multilayer knife blanks in the lower and medium price segments. Semifinished products for scissor blades, plane irons, or, as in the current case, chisel blades can also be produced quickly and relatively inexpensively in this way. Due to the precise annealing and the speed of the process, only a low level of edge decarburization is to be expected, since the carbon has only little time to diffuse. Roll-welded blades are therefore not necessarily of lower quality than traditionally manufactured ones, especially if they are shaped according to the projected stress by subsequent forging.

Roll lamination must be distinguished from diffusion welding. In the latter, metals that are otherwise difficult or impossible to weld can be joined under high pressure and at elevated temperatures, but well below the melting temperature. Using the diffusion process, Takefu Steel Co. in the city of the same name, for example, produces stainless two-to-sixty-nine-layer blanks from high-alloy, partly stainless steel sheets. Combinations of nonferrous metals such as titanium, copper, or aluminum with steel are also possible.

After diffusion welding, the bundles are usually brought to their final thickness by rolling. They are used by professional knifemakers and amateur blacksmiths as a starting material for production of damascened knife blades in the *suminagashi* style. Semifinished products produced by diffusion welding are also sold under the designation "clad metal" or "Mokume." The latter material, usually consisting of different colored precious metals, is used primarily in the jewelry sector.

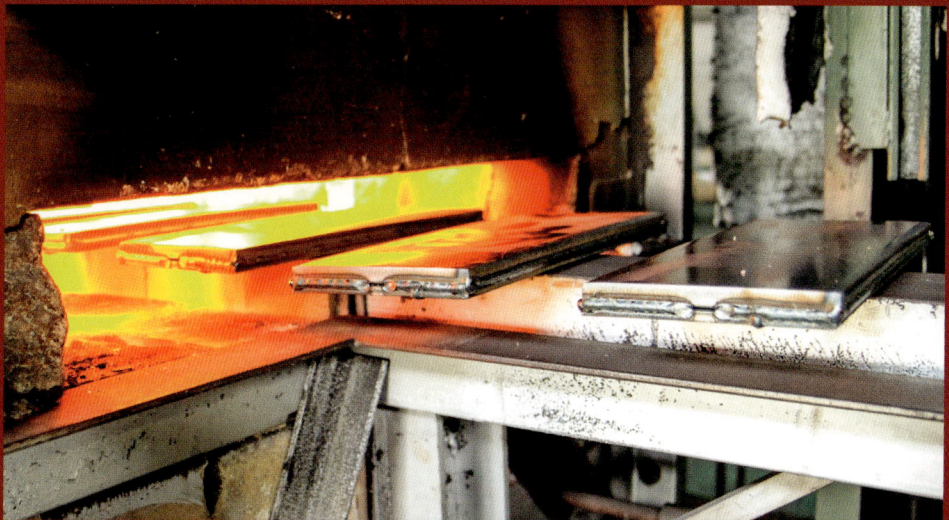

The narrow-side welded plates are heated to 1,150°C (2,102°F) in a through-type furnace.

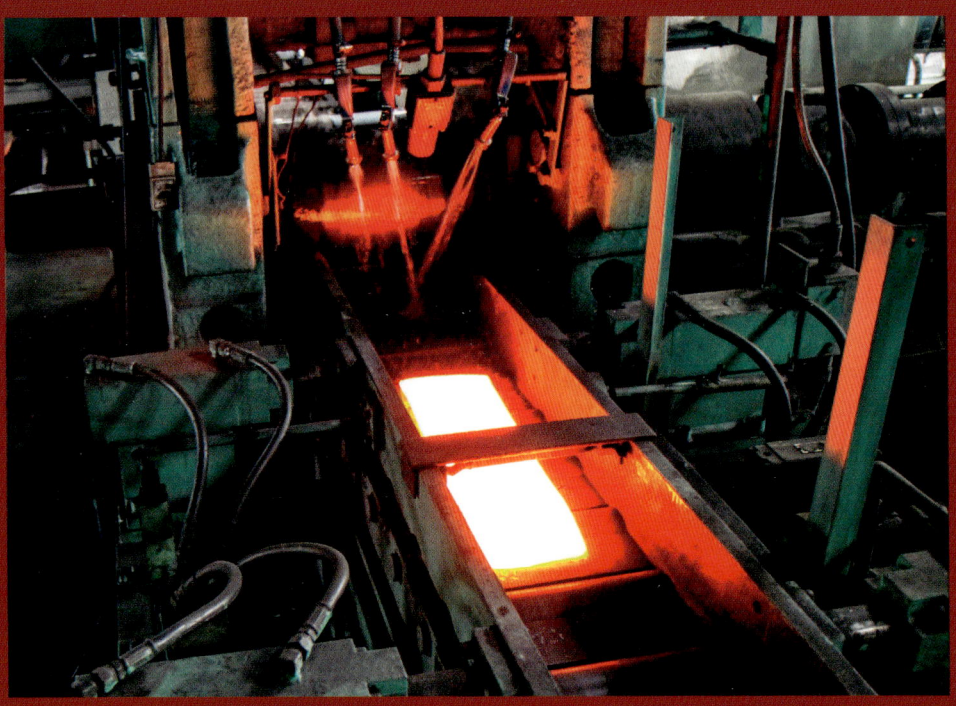

In the reversing mill, the plates are welded together in the first pass and stretched by about 50% in the following reverse pass.

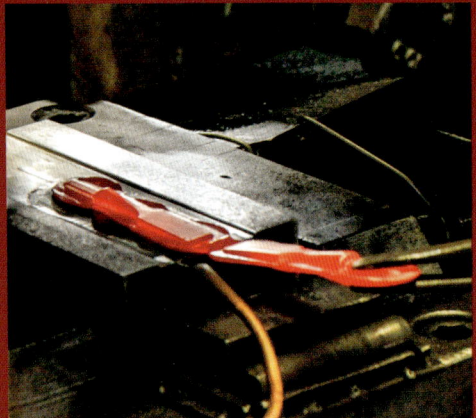

The two-layer steel sheet is converted into chisel blanks in the die press in just one work step.

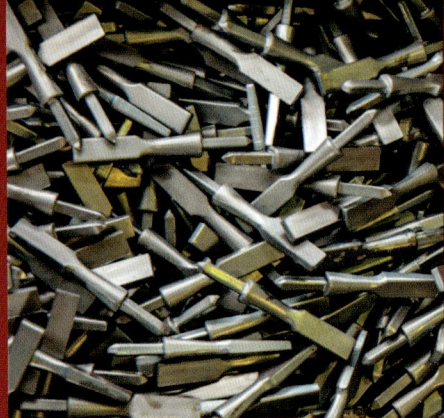

The die-cut *nomi* (chisel) blanks are ready for grinding and hardening.

It differs from the latter not only in the rectangular (instead of round) shape of the furnace, but also in the special care taken in the selection of ingredients and process control. For example, only charcoal of the same size and grade, obtained from slow-growing mountain pine trees, is used as fuel. However, the decisive factor for the quality of the steel is the iron ore that is used.

The preferred raw material is iron sand of high chemical purity, mined high in the Chugoku Mountains. This so-called *masa satetsu* is concentrated by magnetic sorting to an iron content of 60% in order to produce as little slag as possible. This raw material is characterized not only by its high concentration of iron, but also by its exceptionally low content of impurities such as phosphorus and sulfur. Even on an industrial scale, *masa satetsu* is still the preferred starting material to produce high-quality cutting-edge steels; for example, for the "white paper steel" *(shirogami)* produced by Hitachi.

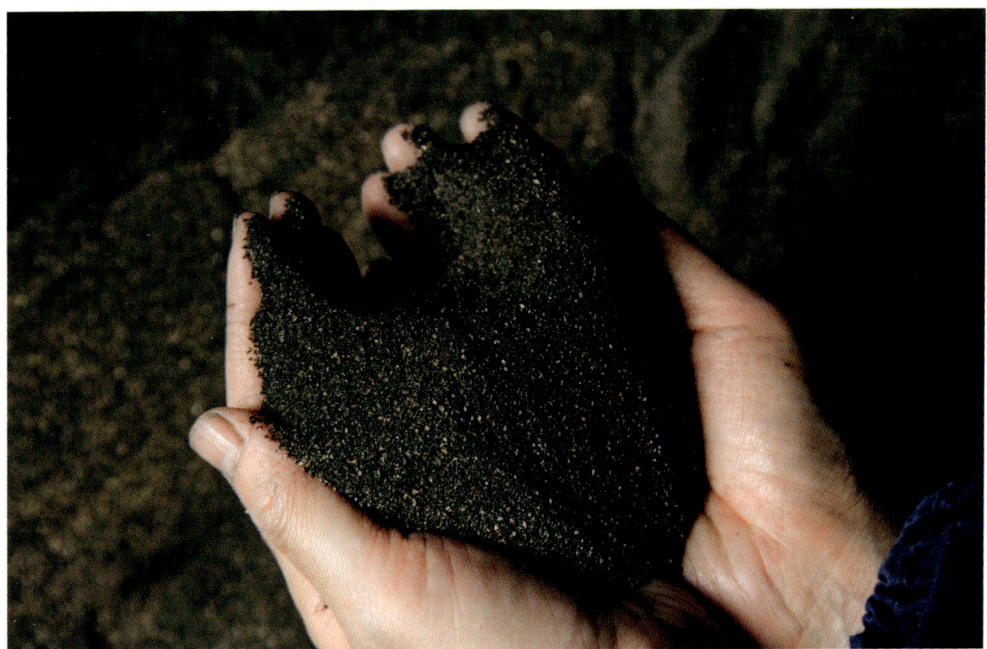

The *masa satetsu* (iron sand) is characterized by a high concentration of iron and an extremely low content of impurities (P ≤ 0.03%, S ≤ 0.002%).

The Process Principle

Although iron is the fourth most abundant element in the earth's crust, accounting for 6 percent of its total mass, it very rarely occurs in nature in pure (elemental) form, such as in iron meteorites or special basalts. Iron ores containing the highest possible content of iron oxides, preferably magnetite (Fe_2O_4), are used to produce iron and steel.

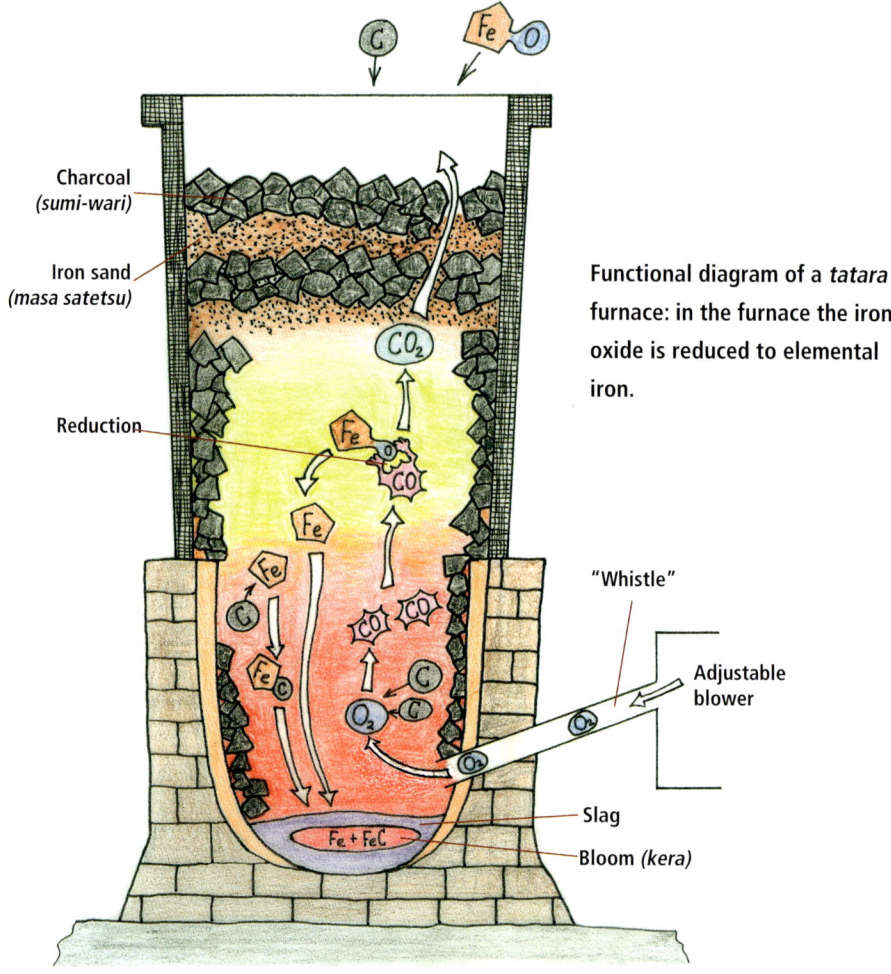

Charcoal
(*sumi-wari*)

Iron sand
(*masa satetsu*)

Reduction

"Whistle"

Adjustable
blower

Slag

Bloom (*kera*)

Functional diagram of a *tatara* furnace: in the furnace the iron oxide is reduced to elemental iron.

For this reason, iron smelting is not a pure smelting process, but a reduction process taking place at high temperature (1,200°C to 1,500°C, or 2,192°F to 2,732°F) under controlled conditions. In this process, the oxygen is separated from the iron molecule *(see sketch on the left)*, leaving elemental iron behind. For a reducing atmosphere to prevail in the furnace, the ore must be shielded from the free access of atmospheric oxygen during firing. These relationships, which were not understood by our Bronze Age ancestors for a long time, were the reason why iron did not gain importance as a material until much later in human history than copper or bronze, for example.

But how do you get from iron to steel? At the existing high temperatures, the carbon in the fuel (in this case, charcoal) has a high affinity to the iron, with which it combines to form a so-called solid solution. We call this iron-carbon compound "steel" when the carbon content is between 0.2% and 1.7%. This material is what is aimed for in the *tatara* process.

If the carbon content is higher, the carbon is precipitated as graphite at the grain boundaries. This material, known as pig iron, is very brittle and cannot be forged. It would have to be remelted or "refined" again for further processing into steel. In order to obtain steel of the desired composition in just one process step, the quantity of ore used and the fuel material must be precisely coordinated. Furthermore, not too much and not too little air (oxygen) must be fed through the nozzles, also called "pipes." If there is an excess of air, no reduction will take place, and if there is a lack of oxygen, the required reaction temperatures will not be reached.

From this simplified description of the complex facts, it is clear that the success of the *tatara* process, which is carried out with relatively primitive means, depends not only on the quality of the ingredients, but also decisively on the process control.

The Process Sequence

The traditional *tatara* process is practiced today in just two traditional smelting furnaces. Near the city of Yokota in Shimane Prefecture stands the Nitto-ho Tatara smelter with a kiln about 4.5 m (14.75 ft.) long in which 2.5-to-3-ton blooms *(kera)* are produced three times a year in a three-day firing. The operator is the Japanese sword company NBTHK (Nihon Bijutsu Token Hozon Kyokai), which sells the *tamahagane* obtained exclusively to the three hundred licensed swordsmiths.

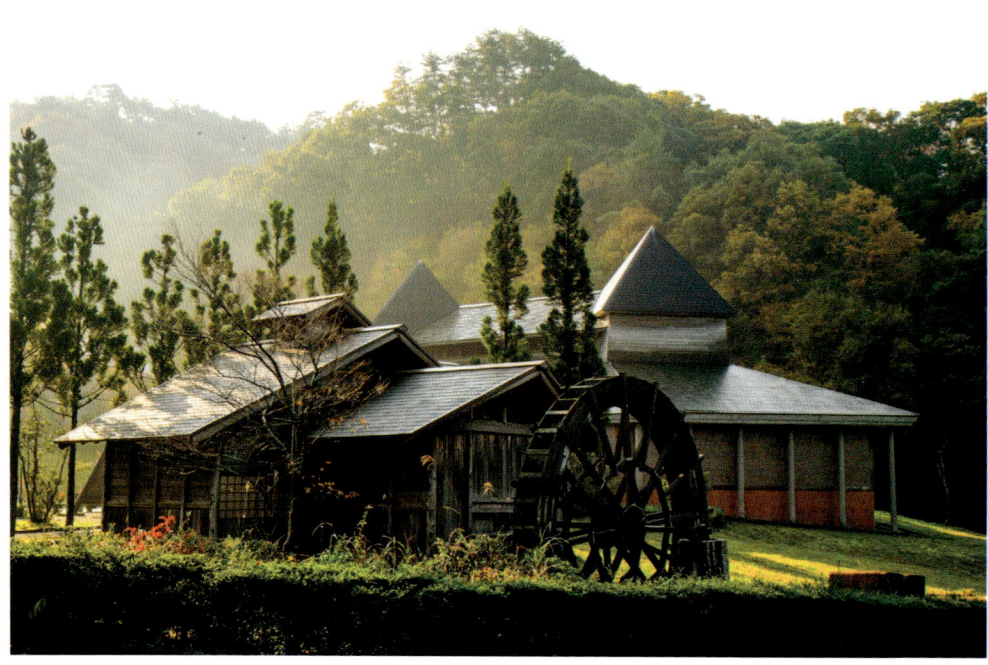

Historic *tatara* hut near Yoshida.

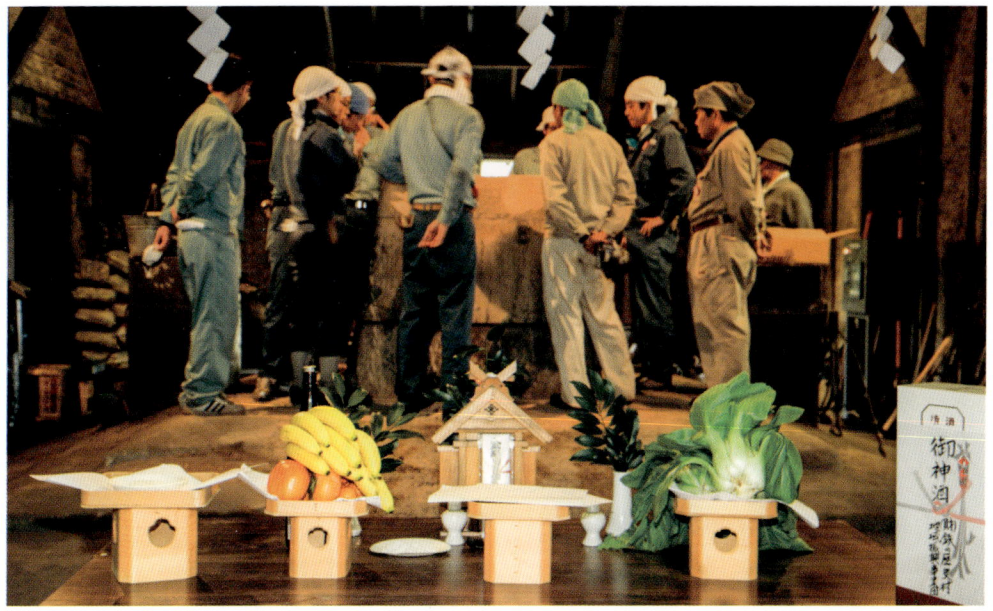

Before the start of the *tatara* process, a sacrifice is made to the Shinto gods for a successful and accident-free work session.

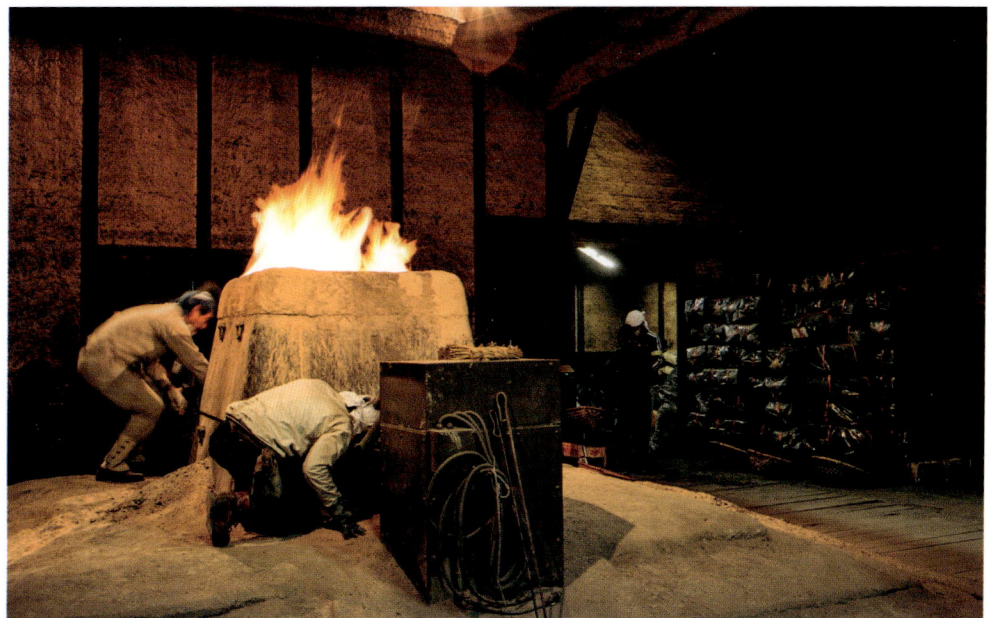

Before it is charged with iron sand, the furnace must be preheated for several hours. The fuel (charcoal) is stacked in the background on the right.

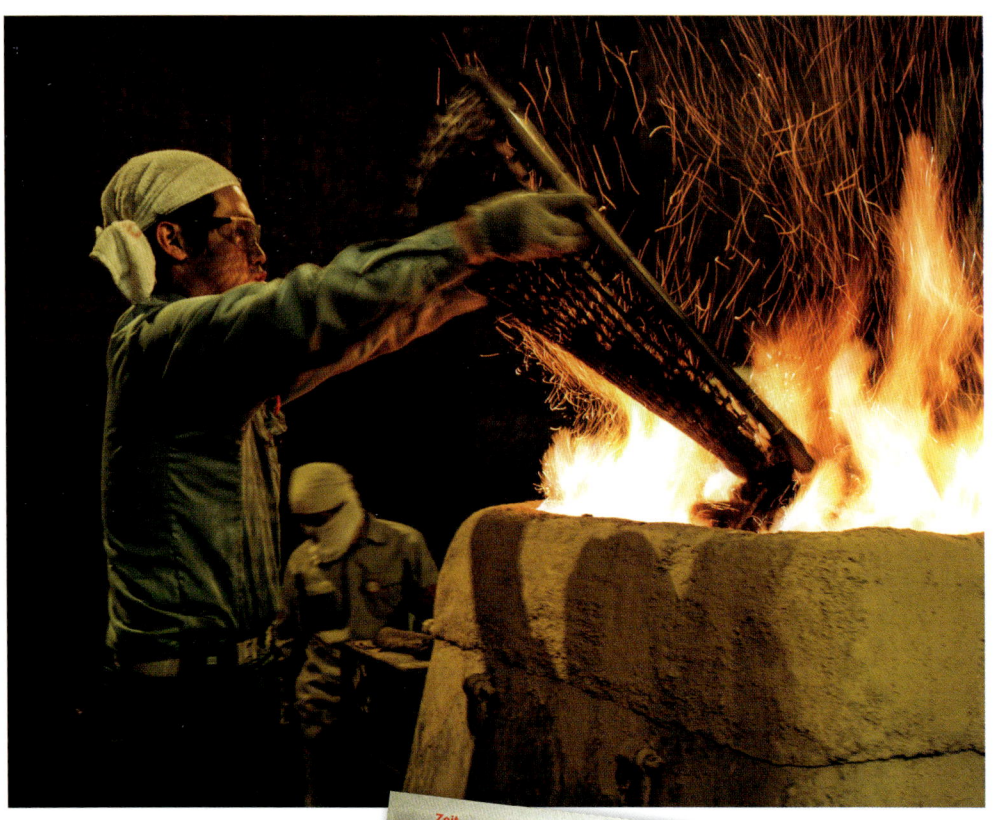

The kiln is charged with charcoal and iron sand over a period of twenty-four hours in the cycle times and quantities specified by the *murage* (the smith in charge of the forge).

The quantities and times are recorded precisely in the session record (excerpt).

Not far away, in the small town of Yoshida, a smaller, twenty-four-hour *tatara* firing is conducted annually in November, with a yield of about 150 to 200 kg (330 to 440 lbs.). The author was allowed to witness this ritual, conducted by the local Society for the Preservation of Historical Smelter Technology (Tetsu no Rekishimura), in November 2006.

Shintoism, the Japanese religion of nature, requires that the protective goddess Kanayogo-kami, who lives in the Chugoku Mountains, be commemorated before smelting begins. Thus, the eighteen helpers gather around the table set with offerings, while the project manager, Rie Yoshida, called the *murage*, asks that the task might proceed smoothly. She then gives instructions for the upcoming tasks to the three alternating shift teams.

Now the charcoal fire can be started, and after a preheating period of several hours, the feeding with iron sand can begin. Over the following twenty-four hours, the kiln is continuously operated in batches of 15 kg of charcoal and 15 to 25 kg (33 to 55 lbs.) of iron sand at intervals of about fifteen to thirty minutes. For this purpose, six helpers are assigned to each of three shifts.

At periodic intervals of about two hours, slag is discharged through an opening near the bottom. Its viscosity and composition are important evaluation criteria for process. On the basis of these and other empirical values such as the color and pattern of the fire and the smoke development, the *murage* determines the feeding times and the respective proportions of iron sand and charcoal. The feeding intervals tend to be longer at the beginning and become shorter toward the middle of the process. In the course of the process, the ratio of iron sand to charcoal decreases from about 1.5 to 1 initially to about 1 to 1.

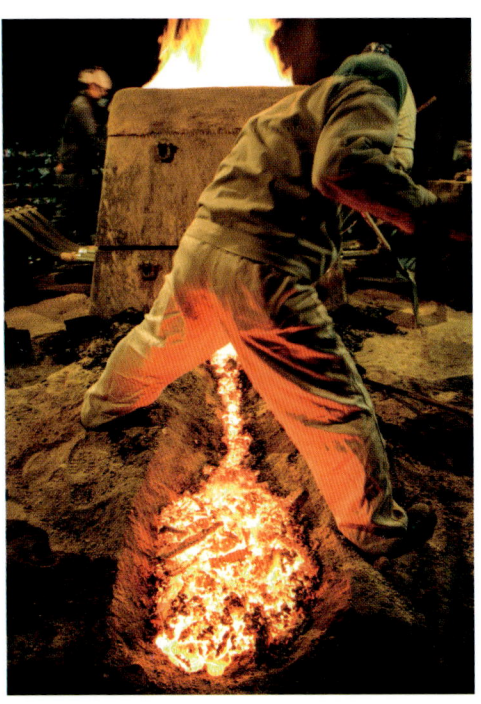

Toward the end of the process, the residual slag is drained off through an opening near the bottom of the furnace.

After one day of firing, the furnace is dismantled with the help of the overhead crane.

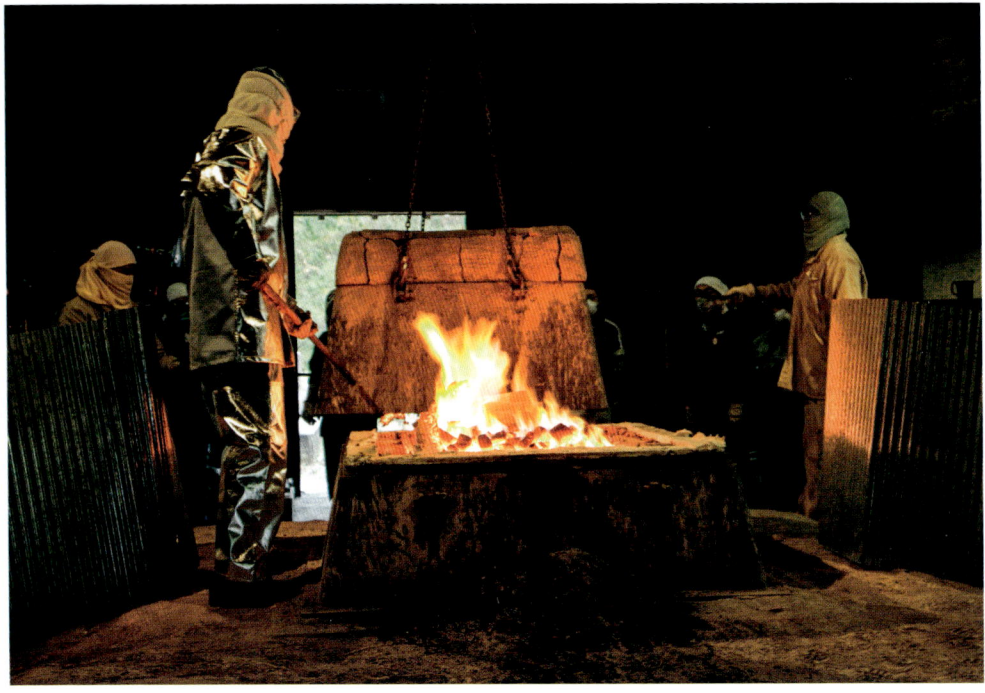

The *murage* is also responsible for controlling the flow of air via the blower and the eight pipes so that a process temperature of 1,200°C to 1,500°C (2,192°F to 2,732°F)—that is, below the melting point of pure iron (1,539°C, or 2,732°F)—is maintained inside the furnace. This must not be achieved with excess air. Rather, a reducing atmosphere must be present inside the furnace, in which the carbon monoxide formed in the lower furnace sector "steals" the oxygen from the iron sand (iron dioxide) in the upper sector. The resulting elemental iron sinks to the bottom of the furnace due to its higher specific gravity, again depositing carbon in the structure. To obtain the desired *tamahagane* steel, the final carbon content must not exceed 1.7%.

After the furnace has been "fed" with a total of about 1.5 tons of iron sand and 1 ton of charcoal, the archaic spectacle ends after one day and one night. First, the residual slag collected in the sump, consisting mainly of silicon and calcium oxide, is drained off. Now that the fire has gone out, the furnace can be dismantled. Whereas the historical clay-built furnaces had to be completely demolished, the "modern" version used here can be dismantled and thus partially reused.

The fireclay-clad steel rings are lifted off with an overhead crane until the steel placenta, the *kera*, is revealed. After a lengthy cooling phase—water must not be used, since this would destroy the insulation underneath—the bloom is pulled out into the open air and, as soon as temperatures permit, subjected to an initial inspection. With a yield of 180 kg (396 lbs.), this time the tatara goddess has rewarded the sweaty work. Helpers and *murage* hold a short ceremony to thank her for the accident-free process.

Not only is the ingot amorphous in appearance, but its metallurgical composition also varies greatly across the cross section. Only a maximum of half consists of *tamahagane* with a carbon content of 0.2% to 1.7%, of which only one third is of the optimum quality of 1.0% to 1.2% C. The carbon content generally decreases toward the center of the block, and values below 0.5% C are referred to as *hōchō-tetsu* ("knife iron"). This tough material is also needed for sword forging (e.g., for the blade core *(shigane)*, although only in relatively small quantities.

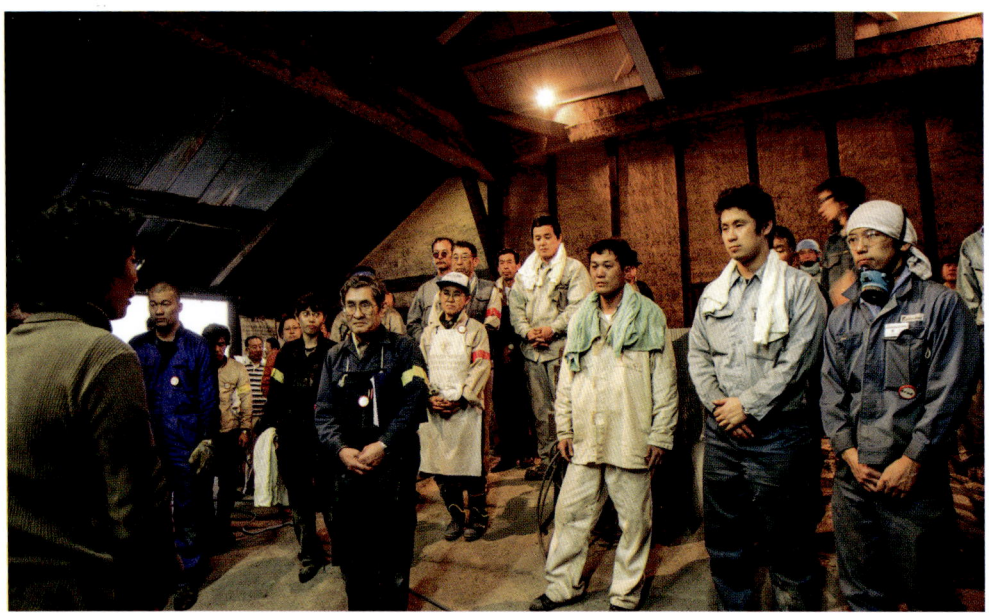

In a brief ceremony, the *murage (left)* thanks the team and the *tatara* goddess for the success of the melting process.

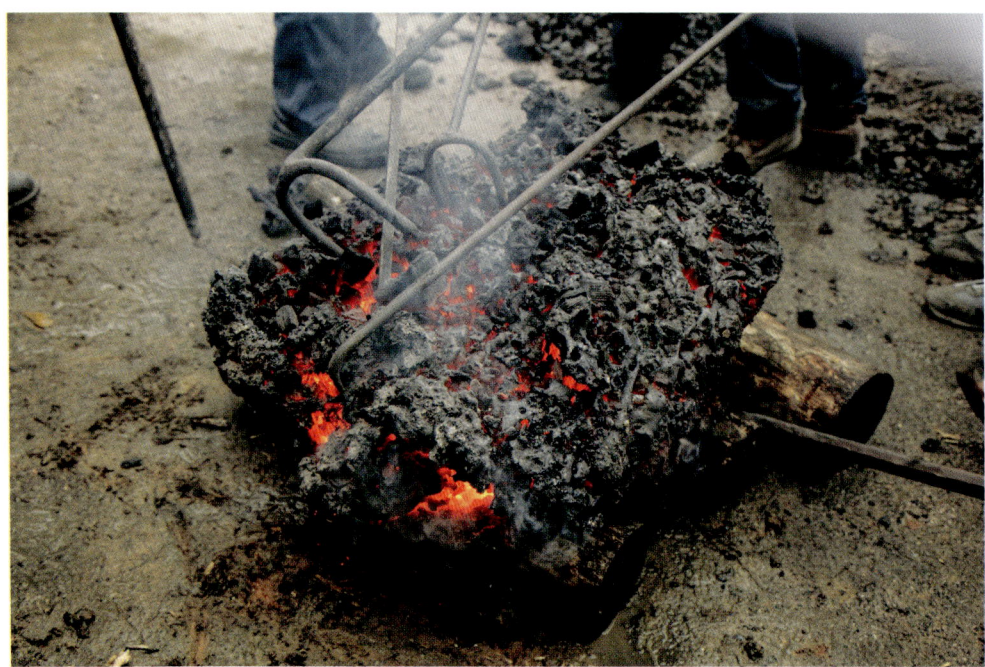

The resulting *tamahagane* bloom weighs about 180 kg (397 lbs.).

For sorting, the cooled block is broken with a drop hammer into individual chunks about the size of a fist. On the basis of the fracture pattern, the color, and the crystal structure, the pieces are qualitatively presorted by experts and then distributed to the swordsmiths. They, too, usually influence the carbon content again through special annealing processes or blending to compose their individual steel. From this initial material, called *oroshigane*, the *katana kaji* finally forms the *katana*, the queen of blades, in a process involving countless folds and welds.

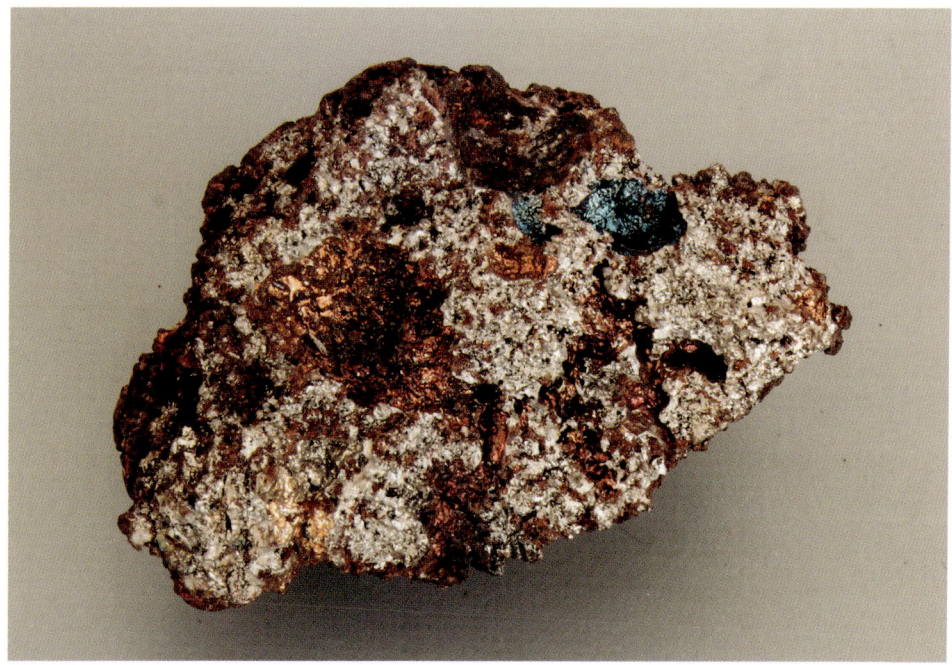

The porous *tamahagane* fragments must be compacted by forging.

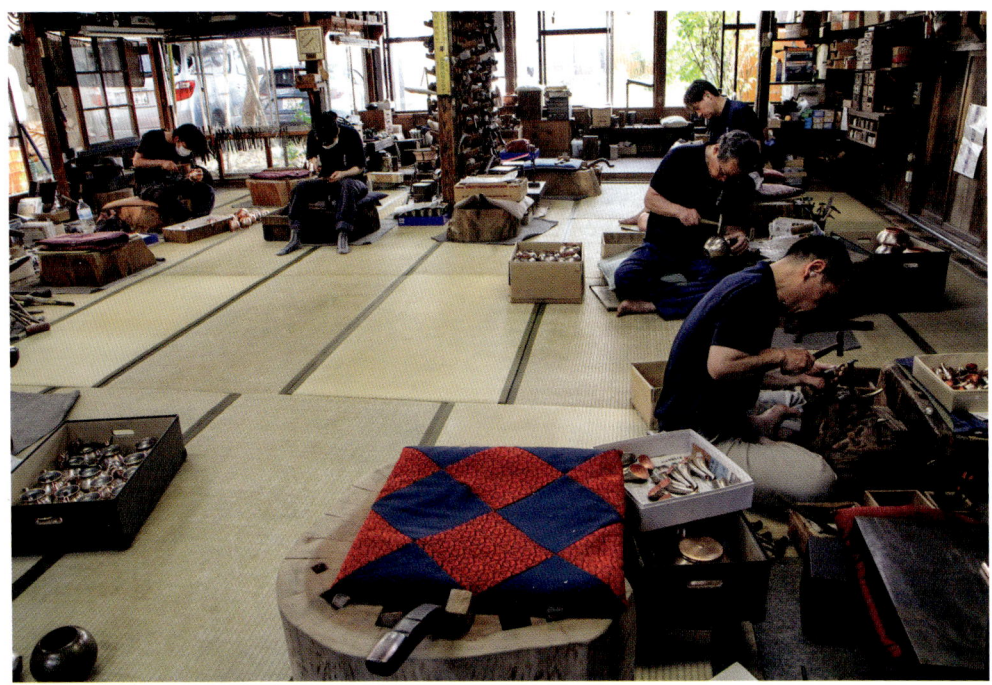

Keeping alive a two-hundred-year-old tradition: coppersmiths in the Gyokusendo workshop, a listed building, laid out with tatami mats.

The Coppersmith

Anyone entering the listed rooms of the Gyokusendo coppersmiths is immediately captivated by an impressive soundscape in the foyer. A veritable percussion concert is heard by the visitor from the historic open-plan workshop, where almost a dozen coppersmiths dance their hammers on multiarmed anvils. One of the unforgettable impressions of this visit to the workshop is that despite the wide variety of work processes, the workers create an overall rhythmic, almost melodious sound.

Gyokusendo is the oldest copper forge in Japan. Tsubame, now a medium-sized industrial city in Niigata Prefecture, developed into a center of metal processing from the beginning of the Edo period due to the nearby copper and silver mines. Here, in 1816, Kakubei Tamagawa founded the Gyokusendo copper forge, which initially produced everyday utensils such as pans, bowls, and buckets. Over the generations, their product range evolved into fine objects such as teapots, tea caddies, bowls, and vases, often decorated with engraved ornaments. However, the basic manufacturing method remained the same throughout these two centuries.

Tsuiki-doki, "beaten copper," is the name given in Japan to the traditional technique of making vessels with a driving hammer. A 1–2 mm thick sheet of copper is first formed into a bulbous round shape with a wooden mallet in a wooden die. This is then further worked on stock anvils, called *toriguchi* ("bird's beak"), of which Gyokusendo has an arsenal of over three hundred different shapes. Depending on the process, one or more *toriguchi* are fixed in a heavy wooden block *(agari ban)*, which also serves as a seat for the smith. The most suitable wood for the seat block is the tough Japanese elm *(erumu)*, which effectively dampens vibrations thanks to its high density.

With the scythe hammer—there are about two hundred variants to choose from—the smith rhythmically strikes the same point on the anvil while slowly rotating the vessel on it. The art is to place the blows exactly next to each other, so that no two blows hit the same spot on the workpiece. Hammering makes the sheet not only thinner, but also harder and more brittle. To prevent it from breaking or cracking, it must be repeatedly softened in the charcoal furnace. Charcoal is the ideal burning material for this because, unlike coke or gas, it does not contain any sulfur, which would make the copper brittle.

The more advanced the manufacturing process, the lighter the blows must be and the more frequently intermediate annealing must be performed. For example, masters of their trade can turn a piece of sheet metal into a complete teapot, including the spout, in two weeks of work, with the aid of several dozen anvils and hammers, interrupted by about thirty annealing processes. The subtle hammer marks that remain on the final product give the surface a lively appearance. It makes each object not only an aesthetic but also a haptic experience.

Finally, the surface is carefully cleaned, degreased and stained, and patinated or colored in chemical baths with substances that are kept secret. Teapots or drinking cups are additionally tin-plated on the inside so that the taste of the beverage is not affected. For flower vases, however, copper is the ideal surface because it preserves the water and prolongs the shelf life of the flowers. A polish with carnauba wax protects the surface and gives it a silky sheen. But only daily use and the associated patina fully brings out the true beauty of these objects.

The Japanese state has declared the *tsuiki doki* craft and the Gyokusendo work-shop itself to be an "inviolable intangible cultural asset" *(mukei bunkaszai)*. One member of the family, Norio Tamagawa, was even named a "Living National Treasure" *(ningen kokuhō)* in 2010 in recognition of his achievements.

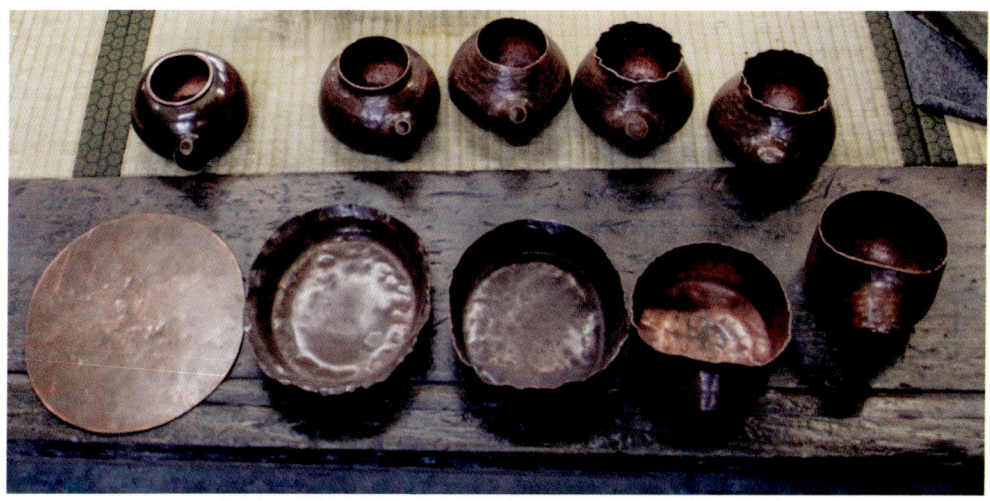

A flat piece of copper sheet *(bottom left)* is transformed into a teapot *(top left)* after two weeks of work with embossing hammers.

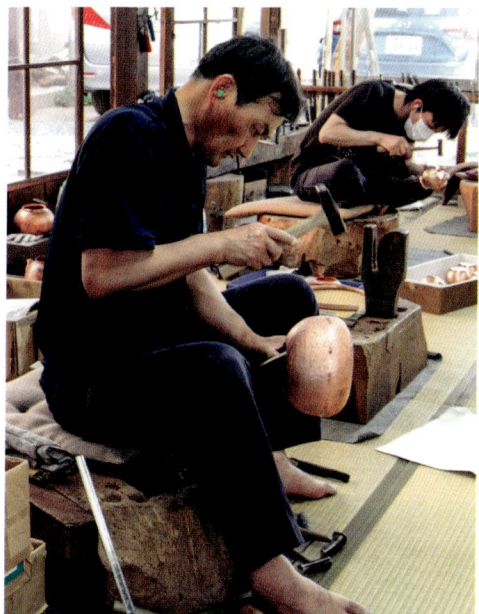

A heavy black of elm holds the anvils and also serves as a seat.

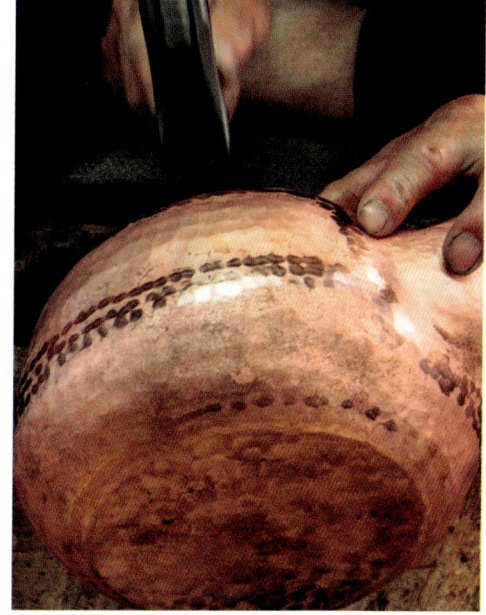

The shaping of such complex objects from just one round blank is the supreme coppersmithing discipline. The hammer blows, not too hard and not too soft, must be placed exactly next to each other.

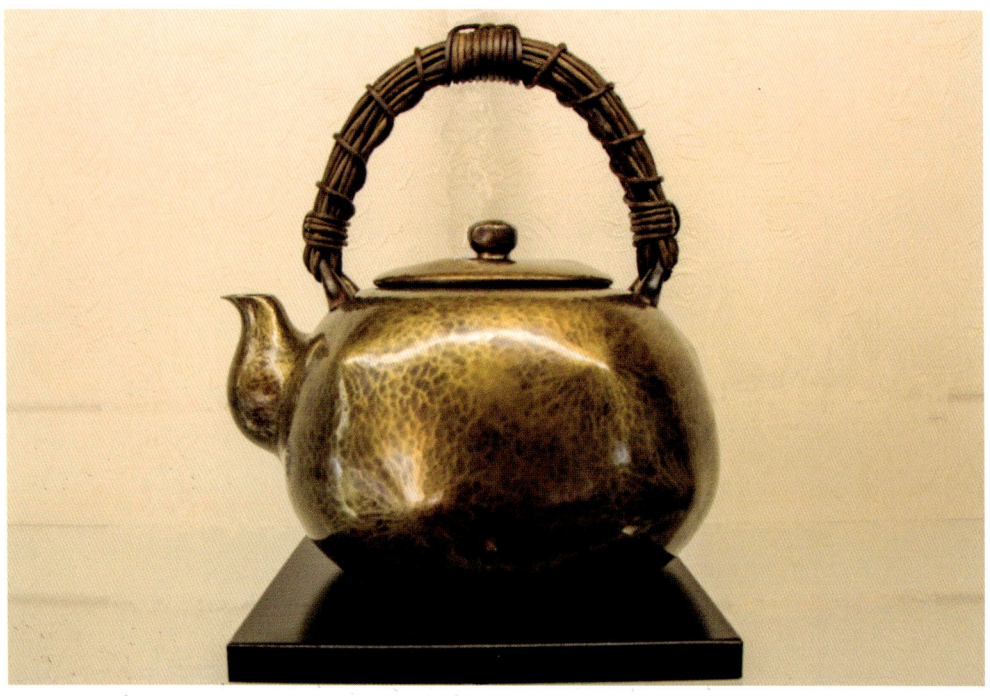

This teapot in so-called "mosaic" finish was made entirely from just one piece of copper sheet. The finely textured surface flatters the eye and the sense of touch.

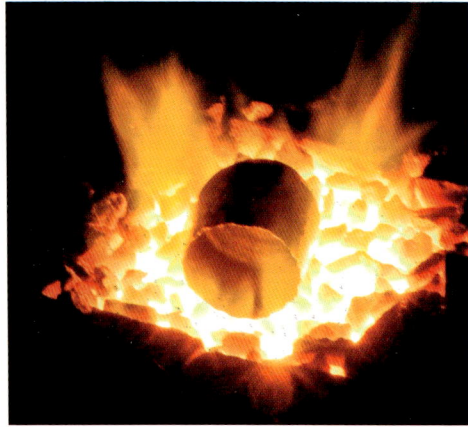

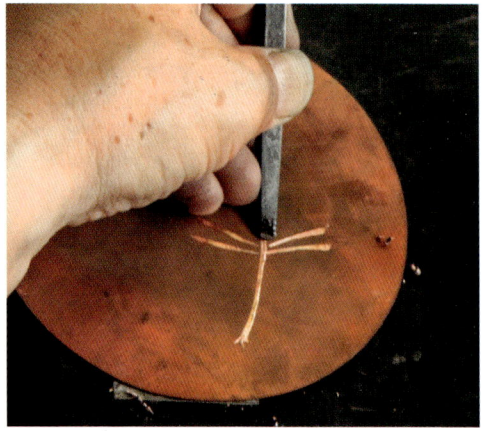

As the copper becomes harder and more brittle during hammering, the workpieces must be repeatedly annealed in order to be able to further process them.

A chisel is used to engrave traditional ornamental patterns or mythological motifs. The dragonfly *(tombo)* symbolizes courage and fertility.

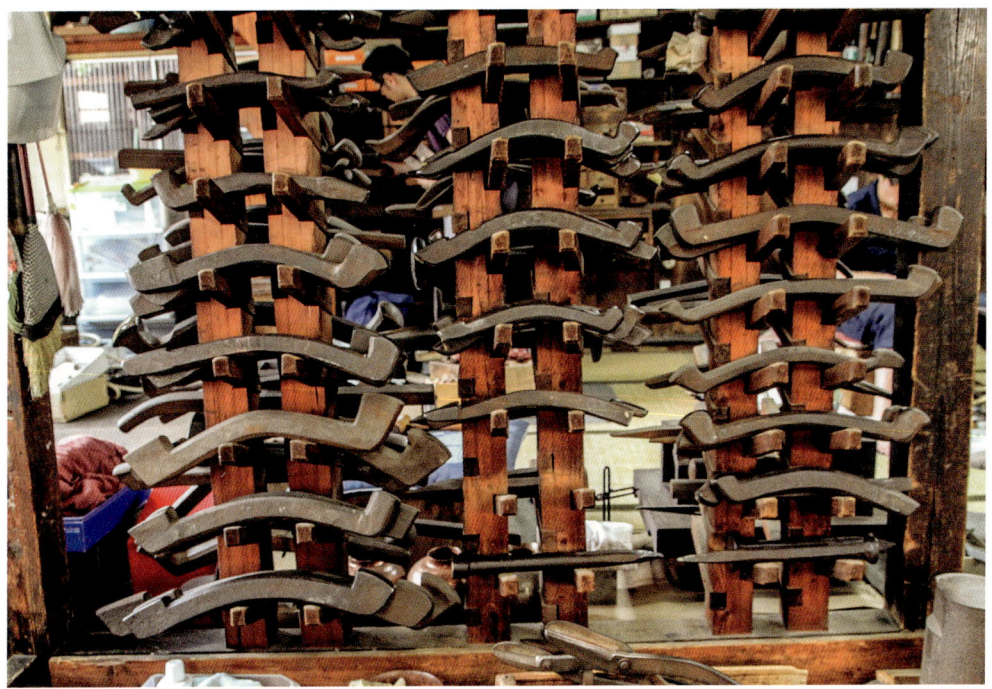

For shaping, there is an arsenal of over three hundred different stock anvils and two hundred types of hammers to choose from.

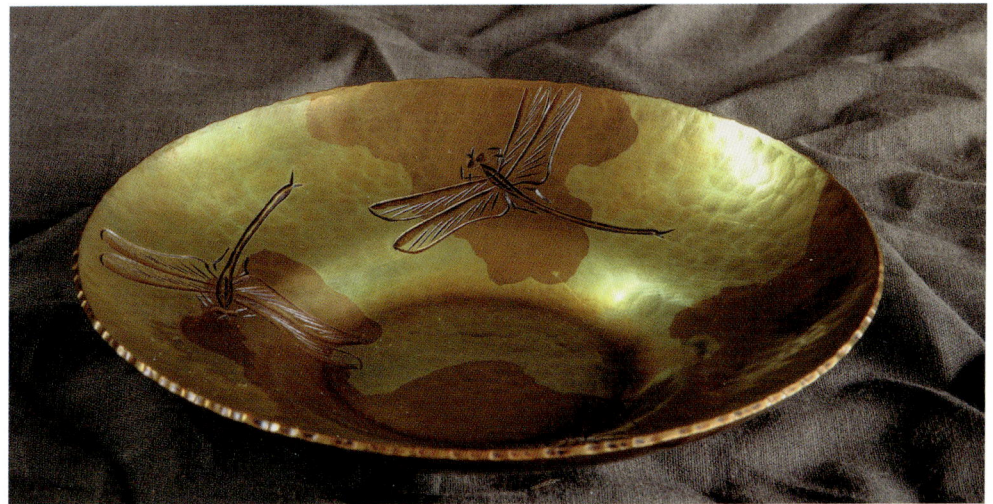

The hammer marks, together with the discreet, two-tone patination, make each piece a unique specimen.

Index

Bibliography

Bergland, Håvard. *Die Kunst des Schmiedens* [The art of forging]. Wieland Verlag, 2008.

Dick, Rudolf. *Japanese Knife Sharpening.* Schiffer Publishing, 2015.

Guggermeier, Kerstin. *Die Perfektion der Klinge* [The perfection of the blade]. LIT Verlag, 2012.

Hocho to Toishi Daizen [All about cooking knives and whetstones]. Seibudo Shinkosa, 2014.

Iwasaki, Kosuke. *Hamano no Mikata* [How to assess a blade].

Landes, Roman. *Messerklingen und Stahl* [Knife blades and steel]. Wieland Verlag, 2002.

Nomi Daizen [All about nomi]. Seibudo Shinkosha, 2013.

Takaiwa, Setsuo, Yoshindo Yoshihara, Leon Kapp, and Hiroko. *The Craft of the Japanese Sword.* Kodansha America, 2012.